D1562969

Advance Praise for *Collision on Tenerife*

"This book tells the story of what my parents went through as they miraculously survived the Pan Am crash. Yet, only those close to my mother would know the impact this crash had on everything she did for the remainder of her life."

—LINDA HOPKINS, one of Caroline and Warren Hopkins' daughters

"*Collision on Tenerife* is compelling and engaging, taking the reader from how it happened to why it happened, and revealing the series of individually inconsequential decisions that perfectly aligned and resulted in disaster. A must read."

—MARK MARTIN, captain, American Airlines (retired)

"As one of 75 initial survivors of the Canary Islands aircraft accident on March 27, 1977, and a contributor to this book, I am interested to read what some of the other survivors have to say about their experience. How could two 747s collide on the ground? They did, and this is our story. Jon Ziomek has compiled a great list of survivor memories."

—DAVID ALEXANDER, Tenerife survivor and author of
Never Wait For The Fire Truck

"Here we have – finally – a harrowing account, impressively researched and thoroughly reported, of the world's worst air disaster. Ziomek offers deep insight into not only the behavioral errors that led up to the disaster but also the psychological aspects of catastrophe and its aftereffects. A story that lingers in the mind long after the reading."

—GILLIAN FLYNN, author of the #1 *New York Times* bestseller
Gone Girl and *Sharp Objects*, soon to be an HBO series

"I can't remember using all of these adjectives to describe a book: dramatic, poignant AND informative. But those are the adjectives I use to describe *Collision on Tenerife*. I left this book enlightened about many things human and factual. It's a great read."

—AL BERNSTEIN, *Showtime* sports broadcaster
and author of *30 Years, 30 Undeniable Truths*

"Jon Ziomek has written a riveting, deeply moving account of the worst aviation disaster in world history. This narrative reads like a novel – but the lessons it imparts could save your life. Everyone who flies regularly for business or pleasure should read this important book."

—KEVIN PERAINO, journalist and author of *A Force So Swift: Mao, Truman, and the Birth of Modern China, 1949* and *Lincoln In The World*

"Ziomek's nail-biting narrative of the horrific crash and aftermath of two jumbo jets – still the worst air crash in history – is impossible to put down. The detailed account of each step leading to the disaster is both frightening and a cautionary tale on how a few missed signals and miscommunications can put a plane on a trajectory to doom. More important, it outlines what has been done to prevent similar crashes in the future – and what still remains to be done."

—ELLEN SHEARER, professor, Medill School of Journalism at Northwestern University; co-editor, *Truth Counts: A Practical Guide for News Consumers*; editor and author of three other books

"A work of exhaustive reporting and riveting storytelling, Ziomek's *Collision on Tenerife* recounts the string of bizarre events that resulted in one of the world's most horrific transportation disasters, and how the deaths of more than 500 people on a remote island airstrip changed the way airlines think about safety in the air and on the ground. Read it – and make sure you know where the exit rows are."

—CRAIG LAMAY, Northwestern University professor and author of *Exporting Press Freedom, Inside the Presidential Debates* (with Newton Minow), and five other books

"Ziomek paints a vivid, moment-by-moment portrait of a tragedy that both occurred 40 years ago and went unrecorded by any video camera. The level of detail is staggering – the emotions raw and real. As the tragedy unfolds before your eyes and the mistakes that could have prevented it are unveiled, I could not put *Collision on Tenerife* down."

—RICH O'MALLEY, author of the upcoming *One Lucky Fan* and former executive editor of the *New York Daily News*

"It has taken four decades, but we finally have a definitive, remarkably comprehensive account of what remains the worst disaster in aviation history. Journalist Jon Ziomek tells the gripping story of the perfect storm of weather and human error that took 583 lives at Tenerife airport on a foggy evening in March, 1977. Not since Piers Paul Read's *Alive* have we had such a meticulous account of a plane crash and all the lives it took, and touched – yet without sentimentalization. *Collision on Tenerife* is many things: a detailed post-mortem of what, exactly, went wrong; an agonizing narrative of how hundreds of people managed to survive the terrible ordeal; and a striking lesson in what to do, and not do, in the event of a disaster. A few of the takeaways: Get out of your seat. Help those around you. And no, the flight attendant isn't coming."

—LAURA KWEREL, journalist and public radio producer

"In a Twitter world, analysis is a fortune cookie hissy fit. To understand how and why things really happen means doing the hard journalistic work that reveals the concentric circles of connectedness before, during and after catastrophes. *Collision on Tenerife* is it."

—JACK HAFFERKAMP, Chicago journalist
and author of *Sepsis* and *Into The Gap*

"Author Jon Ziomek's book about the worst aviation catastrophe in history is far more than just a chronology of what happened. It is a riveting account of the fatal collision of the KLM Royal Dutch Airlines 747 and the Pan American World Airways 747 that reads like a made-for-TV fictional movie script. Forty years after the fiery tragedy that claimed almost 600 lives in the Canary Islands, Ziomek's *Collision on Tenerife* brings readers into the last fateful moments of the victims and the survivors on that fog-shrouded runway. Even though we know the outcome, Ziomek's meticulous research and first-class writing tell a mesmerizing story. Survivors reveal the panic of passengers just moments before they are engulfed in a fiery inferno and the psychological pain that can outlast their physical injuries. Rich in detail, the book discloses conversations between flight crews and control tower, of major and minor mistakes and coincidences, of heroic efforts to save everyone. And it explains what has changed to improve aviation safety. Ziomek has crafted an astounding narrative of historical fact blended with the adrenaline rush of the best fiction. He joins the noted authors who bring history to life in a special art form: narrative non-fiction. We can hope this is not his last offering."

—CHARLES LOEBBAKA, author of five books,
including *Paris Orphan: Escape From Evil*

Collision
on Tenerife

The How and Why of the World's
Worst Aviation Disaster

Jon Ziomek
with Special Material from
Caroline Hopkins

Post Hill Press
New York • Nashville
posthillpress.com

Published in the United States of America

Dedication

To the victims and their families

TABLE OF CONTENTS

INTRODUCTION

Shortly after 5 p.m. on Sunday, March 27, 1977, a KLM Royal Dutch Airlines 747 jet moving at 150 miles an hour smashed into a Pan American World Airways 747 jet taxiing on a foggy runway in the Canary Islands.

The KLM plane had 248 people on board; the Pan Am plane had 394.[1] The KLM jet, which was only seconds from full takeoff, crashed back onto the runway after the impact and burst into flames. Everyone on board was killed. The Pan Am plane, struck at an angle by the KLM jet, also caught fire but did have survivors. More than 100 Pan Am passengers were alive and conscious after the impact, according to survivor estimates. Yet only about 70 were able to make their way out of the Pan Am plane before it, too, was consumed by flames and eventually disintegrated. Ten of the Pan Am passengers who were able to evacuate later died of their injuries.

The collision and fires killed 583 people. This included all 248 people on the KLM plane and 335 of those on the Pan Am plane. At the time, it was – and more than 40 years later, it remains – the worst disaster in the history of aviation.

And it would not have happened if there hadn't been a sickening series of coincidences and mistakes in the hours and minutes and seconds before the collision. Changing any of them could have prevented the disaster.

This book is an examination of those coincidences and mistakes. It introduces some of the passengers on the Pan American plane. It presents

---

[1] Different seat configurations account for the different totals.

the chronology of events that led up to the moment of collision, the aftermath of the accident, and efforts in the decades following to prevent those coincidences from happening again.

A married couple from Northbrook, Illinois, Caroline and Warren Hopkins, started the process that led to the research and writing of this book. Both were passengers on the Pan Am plane. They survived their jet's collision with the KLM jet and were able – with bravery and with difficulty – to escape. They then went through their own personal hell in the following days, months, and years, coping with the long-term effects of their experience.

I met Caroline and Warren Hopkins long after the accident. At the time, I was a journalist and teacher living in Chicago. After extended discussions, all agreed that a book could be written about the Hopkinses' experiences. Caroline started the project by providing her personal diary. After the project was underway, we decided to include the experiences of other Pan Am passengers and to discuss aviation safety. Over the next several years, more than one dozen other Pan Am passengers were interviewed.

Although the chronology of the crash remains compelling, the intention was to increase the book's usefulness by discussing modern themes of crisis behavior and aviation safety, including the difficulties of responding quickly in an emergency, and also to discuss the psychological pain that in many cases can long outlast physical injuries. Aviation and behavioral experts contributed to this discussion.

At the time, only a few studies about the human factors in tragedies had been carried out. One of the most important was by a section of the Federal Aviation Administration known in its early days as the Office of Aerospace Medicine. A 1970 research project by C. C. Snow, J. J. Carroll, and M. A. Allgood, "Survival in emergency escape from passenger aircraft," reached this conclusion:

"Within a few seconds, a passenger must make a perilous journey from seat to sanctuary through fire, smoke and a maze of physical and human barriers…[survival] depends largely upon the number and location of exits, which of these are blocked by flame or impact damage, the human help he receives along the way and the intensity of the fire and smoke within the

Photo courtesy of Linda Hopkins

Caroline and Warren Hopkins, in a photograph taken a few years before their fateful trip.

cabin. But in addition to these extrinsic factors, his chance of survival is also influenced by physical and mental attributes of his own that may enable, or prevent, his effective exploitation of the short time he has remaining."

The Tenerife crash offered dramatic examples of the challenges discussed in that Snow-Carroll-Allgood report. It helped generate enormous interest in the topic. In the decades since the Tenerife crash, much professional work has been done in this area.

Behavioral experts such as psychologist Daniel Johnson and Dr. John Duffy and others broke important new ground with their work as they examined who can best respond in a severe emergency, as well as their studies about the long-term effects of being in a terrible accident. They and others, included in this book, were pioneers in this field and deserve much credit for the attention they've brought to this field.

Which brings us back to Warren and Caroline Hopkins, who were among the first to evacuate the Pan Am plane, thanks mainly to Warren's cool-headedness.

This book would not be possible without the wonderful cooperation of the Hopkins family. The death of Caroline Hopkins a few years after this effort got underway was a severe impediment to the project's momentum. In the intervening years, most of the survivors have also passed away. (Nevertheless, pseudonyms have often been used in place of some passengers' real names because of the circumstances of their deaths in this crash. Real names were used for the survivors who I interviewed later, or for those victims who received extensive media coverage.)

But a renewed vigor by the Hopkins family and me to reach closure has resulted in the completion of this book, which may help bring some sense of completion to the victims' families.

It's commonly assumed that everyone in a jet crash will be killed, but that's not true. U.S. government statistics[2] show that far more than half of all the passengers in plane crashes of the last several decades have survived. Who can best respond in such a crisis? There are obvious categories of passengers, such as soldiers, private pilots and crew members, who've been trained to respond in difficult situations.

But this book will also make the emphatic point that those Pan Am passengers who had taken a minute or two after they boarded in order to understand the safety instructions given in the cabin had a significantly better chance of survival than those who paid no attention. This simple act – *paying attention to the flight attendants and learning what to do if something bad happens* – is an important tool for survival, as discussed in this book by several aviation safety officials. It's just as true today as it was in 1977.

The FAA's Civil Aerospace Medical Institute (the department's current name), has studied, and continues to study, crash survivability, including passenger evacuation patterns, crew training, and air traffic controller language.

---

[2] The National Transportation Safety Board is the source for these and other related statistics used in this book.

The efforts to understand this complex, important area began in earnest not long after the Canary Islands crash. As a CAMI official said in 2015:

> Survivors of the Tenerife accident have provided aviation cabin safety researchers with a wonderful insight into how people behave in airplane emergencies. The passenger successes and failures from this one event remain relevant and are illustrative of the potential benefits of continuing the efforts to improve passenger safety awareness in the face of marked public apathy.

That was Cynthia L. McLean, a CAMI senior human factors research specialist in the FAA's Protection and Survival Research Laboratory in Oklahoma City. She made these observations in an email to the author.

The field of passenger safety has received increased attention from the industry and from federal agencies ever since the Canary Islands crash. But now, more than 40 years after one of the most horrible disasters imaginable, complacency may be setting in. Many airline passengers continue to ignore airline safety procedures, either out of indifference or sublimated fear. A 2007 presentation by FAA human factors specialists Cynthia McLean and G. A. "Mac" McLean was titled "Passenger Safety Awareness Reprise 2007: Still Ignorant After All These Years." Much can be read into that title.

But it's not all on the passengers. A 2005 *Time* magazine article on emergency behavior said this about G. A. McLean: "He is convinced that if passengers had a mental plan for getting out of a plane, they would move much more quickly in a crisis. But, like others who study disaster behavior, he is perpetually frustrated that not more is done to encourage self-reliance. 'The airlines and the flight attendants underestimate the fact that passengers can be good survivors, [McLean said.] They think passengers are goats.'" More detailed safety briefings could save lives, McLean believes, but airline representatives have repeatedly told him they don't want to scare passengers.[3]

As for the long-term effects of being a survivor, decades of work with victims has shown the value of helping survivors work through their sadness. This field received almost no attention in the late 1970s. The now-commonly used phrase "post-traumatic stress" was a rarely used part of our

---

[3] Amanda Ripley, "How to Get Out Alive," *Time*, April 25, 2005.

vocabulary then, and usually referred only to men with lingering psychological pain because of wartime combat service. ("Combat fatigue" was a common term for that condition, too.)

In the last few years, this term and this concept been applied to civilians who've experienced a major trauma such as a flood, tornado, earthquake, fire, air crash, or other disaster – perhaps most notably including the Sept. 11, 2001, attacks, 2005's Hurricane Katrina in New Orleans, and the 2017 hurricanes in Texas and Puerto Rico.

Jon Ziomek

CHAPTER 1

It was cold and rainy on the night of Saturday, March 26, 1977, as a Yellow Cab pulled in front of the Pan American World Airways terminal at JFK International Airport in Flushing, Long Island, New York. A well-dressed man and woman climbed out of the taxi's rear seat and the driver unloaded their luggage onto the sidewalk.

It was just after midnight, when even one of the world's busiest airports slows down. The whining and rumbling of big jets diminishes considerably on the late-night shift, much to the relief of nearby residents. There had been efforts in the 1970s to have JFK shut down completely between midnight and 8 a.m. in order to allow locals to get some uninterrupted sleep, but those efforts had been unsuccessful. Planes bound for overseas destinations and cargo flights coming in from various points around the United States often use the late-night hours for their arrivals and departures.

Still, it was quieter than daytime, at least. Barely 100 flights used the entire overnight shift in early 1977, a stark comparison to the 85 arrivals and departures every hour during the peak afternoon rush period.

One of the few commercial jets that would be leaving JFK on the night of March 27 in that midnight-to-dawn period was Pan American World Airways 1736, a 747 jumbo jet chartered by San Francisco-based Royal Cruise Lines. With the flight's New York departure, every seat on the jet would be occupied – even the seats at a permanent card table in the first-class section and the seats in the second-level lounge in back of the cockpit.

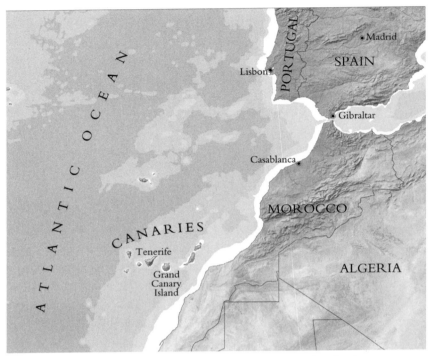

Pan Am 1736 and KLM 4805 were charter flights scheduled to fly their passengers to Las Palmas on Grand Canary Island in the Canary Islands chain near Africa.

The travelers were on their way to the Canary Islands, off the northwest coast of Africa, and a port called Las Palmas. A cruise ship called the *Golden Odyssey* was already docked and waiting to take everyone on a 12-day cruise through the Mediterranean, with exotic ports of call including Funchal, Casablanca, Messina, and Athens. "Mediterranean Highlights," the cruise was called.

The cruise had been sold mainly to travelers from California, especially Southern California, including Los Angeles, San Diego, and several nearby communities. But there were also other states and one other country represented among the passengers: Texas, Arizona, Oregon, Washington, Hawaii, Minnesota, and British Columbia, Canada.

And there was one couple from Illinois.

2

"Let's see if we can find a skycap," Warren Hopkins said to his wife, Caroline, as they entered the Pan Am terminal. Loaded down with two large garment bags, two overseas bags, and two designer carry-on bags — one set for each of them — they looked around as their cab pulled away into the chilly March evening.

The terminal was almost deserted. Carrying their bags two at a time, the Hopkinses managed to get their luggage inside the door. Then Mrs. Hopkins stood guard over the bags while her husband searched for a porter or a cart. While she waited, Caroline stood patiently. Blonde and trim at age 48, she was dressed well, in high heels, a tan suede matching skirt and top, and a multi-colored silk blouse. Despite her calm exterior, she was excitedly looking forward to the upcoming trip. Although experienced travelers, she and her husband had never been to the Mediterranean. Caroline hoped the weather would be good.

Her rising excitement was understandable. They'd flown to New York from their home near Chicago two days earlier so that her husband could make some business contacts for his meat brokerage before they left on vacation. He'd been quite busy both days while she spent leisurely hours wandering through midtown Manhattan, looking in the fancy shop windows. They'd marked their last evening in New York City by splurging on a fancy dinner at the 21 Club restaurant. Both had been amused by the toy trucks that hung from the restaurant's ceiling. Warren, an easy conversationalist, had an extended chat with the men's room attendant, who was especially pleasant, offering good wishes and a life full of faith to Warren. The attendant's kind words would take on a special meaning for Warren barely one day later — and stay with him for years.

It would be a long evening — their flight wasn't scheduled to leave until 1:45 a.m. — so the Hopkinses had lingered over dinner. Mistakenly, they hadn't gotten any Broadway show tickets. So they strolled back to their hotel for some last-minute packing and a leisurely scan of the early Sunday edition of the *New York Times*, purchased on the street a few hours earlier.

They had dawdled as much as possible. After several efforts, Warren and Caroline had managed to reach both their daughters on the telephone: Linda, 19, a student at the University of Oregon now on spring break in

Florida with Mrs. Hopkins' parents; and Diana, 20, at Southern Methodist University in Dallas, who was spending her Saturday evening studying for an upcoming final exam.

While they were exchanging goodbyes, Caroline suddenly, on impulse, gave each young woman her travelers' cheque numbers and the location of some jewelry at home. "Why are you telling me this?" one of the daughters asked. "Just a precaution," Caroline answered, but in fact she wasn't sure herself. She hadn't done that on past trips when they were away from their daughters.

She'd had a curiously strong urge to do some other important paper-work, too. Back in their Chicago suburb, Caroline had seen their attorney at a recent neighborhood bridge game. They'd gotten to talking about wills, and Caroline became obsessed with the desire to complete her will before she and Warren left on this trip. She'd worked hastily on the papers and barely finished them in time, mailing them from Chicago's O'Hare Airport when they had left for New York.

Again, she wasn't sure of the reason for her urgency. She was, after all, planning on coming back, she thought to herself.

The strolling, newspaper reading and telephone calls had been suc-cessful in passing the time for the Hopkinses. They arrived at JFK at 12:30 a.m. Allowing for a few minutes of check-in time in this pre-security era of the 1970s, that made them just a bit early for the plane's scheduled departure.

Warren Hopkins returned with a luggage cart commandeered from among several he'd found parked nearby. He loaded the couple's baggage, and they moved to the Pan Am ticket counter near the front door, but it was deserted. They headed for the loading gate after checking the announce-ments board for arrivals and departures. Hopkins wheeled the cart in front of him, his wife's heels clicking on the airport tiles as they walked.

Hopkins, 50, was dressed in a three-piece navy blue pinstripe suit and Borsalino hat, with a tie and cuff links. He walked with a smooth, athletic gait. As was customary in the 1970s, both he and Caroline were dressed well for travel. They looked good, and they would be sitting in the first-class section when the plane arrived – which, they found out when they got to the gate, would not be for quite a while yet. The flight had originated at Los Angeles International Airport, known by its airport code of LAX, and had left an hour late.

When the Hopkinses arrived at the gate, they found about two dozen people waiting for the plane, a number that grew by a few more by the time the plane arrived. Only 14 people would be getting on as passengers, though. Another 14 would be boarding as crew members because the cockpit crew and the flight attendants were changing here.

After waiting in silence on a bench for a few minutes, Caroline Hopkins began strolling around the waiting area. She caught sight of a well-dressed woman of about 60 sitting by herself and holding a can of beer from a nearby refreshment stand.

"Hello," Mrs. Hopkins said. "Are you waiting for the flight also?"

"Yes, and I'm hungry," the woman laughed. She'd just flown from Minneapolis to make the connection, and there'd been no dinner served on the plane, she explained.

The woman introduced herself as Clara Johns of St. Paul.

Actually, Mrs. Johns went on, it was her son's fault that she was hungry. He was supposed to pick her up early enough to have dinner with her before her flight, but he had been late, and they'd had to go straight to the airport.

"You know how young people are," Mrs. Johns said. "They're always late."

"Honestly," Mrs. Hopkins tsk-tsked sympathetically.[1]

So here she was, Mrs. Johns said, sitting in an airport terminal at nearly one in the morning with an empty stomach, and all she could get at the refreshment counter was a beer – which she continued to sip as they talked.

Mrs. Hopkins invited Mrs. Johns over to meet Warren Hopkins. Meanwhile, Warren had struck up his own conversation with a small, meticulously dressed man named Miguel Torrech. Torrech was a steward on the upcoming flight. From him, the Hopkinses and Mrs. Church found out that most passengers on the cruise were from California.

---

[1] This conversation, and related conversations, are from the diary of Caroline Hopkins and the recollections of Caroline and Warren Hopkins.

They continued to chat. Mrs. Johns explained that her late husband had been a doctor. He'd left her with some retirement money, but she was on a fixed income and really didn't think she should be going on this trip because it was expensive. But a friend from California had wanted company, so Mrs. Johns had agreed to go.

As they chatted, a Pan Am counter attendant arrived to begin checking in the passengers and confirm seat assignments. She announced that the plane would arrive about 45 minutes late, which was greeted with a collective groan. Arrival had been scheduled for 12:30 a.m., with a 1:45 a.m. departure, but the plane would not pull up to the gate until close to 1:30 a.m., she said. She did, however, check everyone's baggage and got the tickets in order.

When the jet arrived at the gate, everyone lined up and waited until the jetway tunnel was opened.[2] Warren Hopkins helped Mrs. Johns with her hand luggage. A few of the passengers from Los Angeles decided to stretch their legs by deplaning for a few minutes.

Hopkins, a soft-spoken man who chose his words carefully, could not resist making an observation to his wife as they prepared to board. "My God, aren't there any young people on board this cruise?" he asked dryly.

Mrs. Hopkins reminded her husband that cruises are a popular form of travel for older people. But she had noticed it, too.

Among the passengers was a contingent of residents from Leisure World, a retirement community near La Mesa, California, which restricted its residents to 52 years of age or older. Thirty of the community's residents were coming along for the cruise, escorted by Jean Brown, herself 58 years old. She and her husband, Gordon, ran a travel agency in Leisure World called Good Time To Travel, through which the Leisure Worlders had booked their passages.

The waiting New York passengers watched further as more passengers came through the jetway into the waiting area, wandering off toward bathrooms or vending machines, or standing around and smoking, which was permitted in that era of air travel. Mrs. Johns's friend got off the plane,

---

[2] The late arrival of Pan Am 1736 was the first of the coincidences that contributed to the inevitability of the disaster.

both of them waving and smiling at each other, then exchanging hugs. Mrs. Johns brought her friend over to the Hopkinses, eager to introduce them.

Her friend, Ginger Grimes, was from Long Beach, she said. They chatted while others from the plane drifted over and joined in the conversation. Mrs. Grimes – who appeared to be in her late fifties, wearing a pink and white slacks and suit top – said she hadn't really wanted to go on the trip, thereby refuting what Clara Johns had told them only minutes before. "To tell the truth," Mrs. Grimes said, "I really wasn't that interested in going myself. But I thought Clara needed a vacation, seeing the rough winter she'd had, and I thought I'd go along to keep her company."[3]

The Hopkinses were amused by the discrepancy, but as Midwesterners, they knew what Mrs. Grimes meant about the weather. It had indeed been a miserable winter, one of the worst in years. In fact, Warren Hopkins had wanted to go someplace warm like the Caribbean.

"But we've been to the Caribbean, and this would be different," Caroline had assured him, so he had agreed. Neither of them had ever been to most of the ports of call the ship would be visiting – thus there was an excitement at trying something new.

But there had been a last-minute hesitation by Warren. Shortly before they left, a bill had come in the mail from American Express for the cost of the entire trip. Unsure about the trip to begin with, Hopkins had been dismayed.

"Gee, we haven't even gone on the trip yet," he had commented to Caroline, waving the bill in the air, in a final effort to change her mind. He reminded his wife that the wind chill factor in Northbrook had reached 60 degrees below zero several times just two months previously. And the Chicago area had marked the 10th anniversary of a famous 1967 blizzard by having another blizzard – almost as severe. Expressways jammed up, Chicago's elevated train tracks froze in several spots, and in general it was another miserable Midwest winter. So how warm would it be in the Mediterranean in March? Warm enough to forget about Chicago's weather? He was skeptical.

---

[3] Clara Johns and Ginger Grimes are pseudonyms, as explained in the Introduction. Neither survived the crash. Their names were changed as a courtesy to surviving relatives.

Warren had even called the American Express travel office to see if the space they'd reserved could be sold, but it was too close to the travel date, an agent told him. So he decided the hassle of changing their plans wasn't worth it. It still didn't seem right to pay the bill before they'd even gone on the trip, though. What if the ship had a fire or something? But he didn't want, as he later put it, "anyone with their hand on our shoulders while we're trying to walk up the gangplank," so he paid the bill.

"I'd rather be back in Pacific Palisades myself," said an elderly gentleman, breaking into the Hopkinses' airport conversation with their new friends. His name was Ed, the man said, as he shook everyone's hand. Warren guessed his age at about 75, but Ed was acting as lively as a 20-year-old. "Got a beautiful garden in Palisades," Ed said. "Spend a lot of time in it."

"But you see that young lady over there?" he gestured behind him at a woman who was perhaps 70 years old. "This gal in the pink pajamas?" The remark brought a smile from everyone because the woman wasn't really wearing pajamas but a pants suit.

"That's my girlfriend," Ed said. "Her husband died, and my wife died. She wanted to go on this thing, not me. So that's the reason we're going. Me, I'd rather be back in my garden."

It was peculiar to find so many who didn't seem to want to be on this trip. The plane had been completely booked, with every seat taken, yet a number of those people apparently would rather have been back home, or at least taking another route to the Canary Islands.

Like Walter Moore, for example. A retired Navy admiral, now 70, he didn't want to ride on a Boeing 747. He'd never liked big planes, he'd reminded his wife, Beth, back at their San Francisco home.

"That's the one thing that bothers me about this cruise," he'd told her, as they considered taking the trip. "We have to go on a big jet to get to the ship."[4]

The idea of a cruise itself was pleasant to him, though – his Navy career had included plenty of sea duty. He'd served on a cruiser, the U.S.S. *Juneau*, during difficult combat near Guadalcanal in the early days of World War II,

---

[4] Mrs. Moore was interviewed by Jon Ziomek several years after the crash.

and like many old salts, never forgot the roll of the deck under his feet. His wife later recalled that he'd enjoyed his tour of duty on board the *Juneau* so much that when his tour was up, he ignored his orders to return to Washington. The Navy command almost had to chase him off the ship by sending his replacement out to the South Pacific and then having both men switch ships using a ship-to-ship transfer via a bosun's chair.

Shortly after his transfer, Moore received word that the *Juneau* had been attacked by the Japanese navy and sunk, with only 10 survivors out of the crew of about 700.[5]

Moore left sea duty after a few years and held important desk jobs for the Navy. He was on the U.S. negotiating team at Panmunjum during the Korean War and later was assigned to Portugal as an official adviser to Portugal's navy. He felt a deep affinity with the ocean.

But flying was different. The 747s were too big. They made Moore uncomfortable, and he reminded his wife of that on several occasions when they were making plans for the cruise. He'd be fine once he got on board the *Golden Odyssey*, of course.

When Moore boarded Pan Am 1736 in Los Angeles, he made one gesture of defiance to the plane, just so there would be no misunderstanding between him and that monstrous piece of machinery. Bending his tall frame to get in the door, he paused just inside the cabin. "I may have to fly on you," he announced to the jet, "but I don't have to like you." And that was that.

When the plane stopped in New York to pick up the remaining passengers, Moore was one of those who got off the plane for a leg stretch. A tall, distinguished man wearing a bright red sweater, he was noticeable in the crowd and was easily picked out by the Hopkinses and others as they watched the plane's passengers debarking.

There were others on the cruise list who had decided they didn't want to fly overseas and back on a specific date, as dictated by this particular

---

[5] The ship's sinking became famous for a uniquely sad reason: included in the terrible loss of life were all five brothers of the Sullivan family of Waterloo, Iowa. The Sullivan family story was made into a movie, *The Fighting Sullivans*. After this, President Franklin Roosevelt's administration banned members of one family from serving in the same combat unit.

cruise and flight package. Several couples had decided to fly to the Canary Islands several days before the cruise departure, thus giving themselves the luxury of a freer schedule to look around the Canary Islands beforehand.

A total of 75 passengers chose a means of getting to Las Palmas other than flying on Pan Am 1736, according to later media reports. Some, such as Fred and Ingrid McCay of San Marco, California, did so by choice. Others, like Dr. and Mrs. Richard Stoughten of Rancho Santa Fe, California, were unable to get onto the charter flight because it was full by the time they signed up for the cruise. They were put on a waiting list by Royal Cruise Lines, but as the departure date grew near and no seats opened up, they had no choice but to fly by scheduled commercial airliner to Madrid and then to Las Palmas.

Marjorie Hanson of San Diego had also been put on the charter flight's waiting list. A manager of a travel agency in Escondido, she hadn't put her own name in soon enough to have a seat held for her on the plane. But a number of her customers had. In fact, 21 area residents had made their reservations for the cruise through her agency.

The result of these improvised arrangements was that 75 people who'd made their own way to the Canary Islands were on board the *Golden Odyssey* by Sunday afternoon, March 27, and were waiting for the arrival of Pan Am 1736 so the cruise could get going.

They'd been willing to make that extra effort to get to the ship because this particular cruise was a popular one, with the promise of an exotic 12 days. The plane was scheduled to arrive at Las Palmas at 1:15 p.m. Sunday afternoon, in plenty of time for a bus tour of Grand Canary Island before boarding the *Golden Odyssey*, "the newest and most luxurious cruise ship to sail the Mediterranean Sea," the brochure trumpeted. "The *Golden Odyssey* is so much more than just a beautiful ship; she is a gracious lady whose officers and crew know the true meaning of service."

After pulling away from Las Palmas at 5 p.m., the partying would start immediately with a Captain's Welcome. The ports of call for the cruise were, first, Funchal in the Madeira Islands, then Casablanca, Tangier, Gibraltar, the islands of Palma de Mallorca and Malta, Heraklion on the island of Crete, the island of Santorini and then Athens. Those flying on the chartered Pan Am flight would return from Athens, leaving at 8:30 p.m. local time on April 8, arriving at JFK International at 3:30 a.m. the next morning, and then departing an hour later to get into Los Angeles at 7 a.m. local time April 9.

Of course, it all sounded marvelous. Yet there were those who had made arrangements to take the cruise but had to cancel for various reasons.[6] Edwin Mayall, his wife, Angeli, and their 15-year-old daughter, Patricia, all of Stockton, California, had signed up. After talking with Mrs. Mayall's aunt and uncle, the relatives had decided to go along, too. Emily and Cliff Morris of Burbank, Mrs. Mayall's aunt and uncle, were to fly with their niece, along with two family friends who also got interested in the cruise: Charlotte Waltz of Reno, Nevada, a former Stockton resident, and a friend of Mrs. Waltz, Eleanor Crosby of Oroville, California.

But five weeks before the departure date, in mid-February, Mr. Mayall, an attorney, realized that he had too much work to do on a lawsuit. So the Mayalls had to cancel, much to their distress. Instead, they traveled to Lake Tahoe, where Mayall could take depositions for the case, while their friends and family were flying to the Canary Islands.

However, they did spend Friday evening, March 25, dining with Mrs. Waltz and Mrs. Crosby in Stockton, telling them how lucky they were to be going on the cruise, and wishing them a good voyage.

Others were forced to cancel, too. Margi Poulos, the manager of E & J Travel Service in Sacramento, had to turn down an invitation to go on the cruise because of business obligations.

Margaret Langhorn of Littleton, Colorado, had figured she would probably go with her daughter, Nancy, and Nancy's friend, Rene Roberson, both of whom lived with her. Both were 40 and had become friends while serving in the U.S. Air Force. They were excited about the trip and had been planning it since before Christmas.

But as the time for the cruise drew near, Mrs. Langhorn decided it wasn't worth the energy. She'd rather stay home with their pet schnauzer and dachsund than go through the hassle of arranging to have a neighbor

---

[6] Much of the information in this section is from later media reports.

watch them or putting the animals in a kennel. So she decided to stay home and let the young women have fun on their own.

Perhaps the most unusual cancellation was a situation that came to light in later media reports. Ben and Sylvia Weinberg had been booked on the cruise but canceled because of a doctor's appointment. As reported later, Weinberg, an art dealer, had gotten ill and gone to his doctor several weeks before the trip. The doctor told Weinberg to come back in two weeks, but Weinberg told his doctor that he and his wife were scheduled to be away. The doctor told Weinberg to come in after the trip, but at that suggestion Weinberg got reluctant. No, he told his physician, perhaps it would be better to cancel the cruise, just to be safe, even if it meant losing the $400 deposit.

Weinberg did return to his doctor several days before the charter flight and was given permission to travel, but this time, Mrs. Weinberg said no. "We won't go now," she said. Perhaps it was superstitition, perhaps it was intuition, but she was sure that once they had canceled, they should just let it go at that. So they remained in Los Angeles when Pan Am 1736 lifted off from Los Angeles International Airport. All of this, of course, didn't come out until after-the-crash reports in the media.

When the New York passengers finally got on board the flight, fears and reluctance had been pushed aside and replaced by anticipation. Only one small incident marred the Hopkinses' boarding.

"Where are you sitting?" Ginger Grimes asked Caroline Hopkins as they moved down the jetway.

"Row 5," Mrs. Hopkins answered.

Mrs. Grimes made a long face, and Clara Johns looked disappointed. "Oh, that's too bad," Clara said. "We're way back in Row 46."

Mrs. Hopkins was disappointed, too – they'd been fun to chat with. "I guess we won't see you until we get on board the ship," she replied. "But we'll get together then." They both nodded, and as everyone entered the plane, the Hopkinses turned left, into the first class section, and Clara Johns and Mrs. Grimes turned right into the economy section.

The Hopkinses never saw the two women again.

CHAPTER 2

Few of us who have flown on a Boeing 747 have seen one up close from the outside because we usually board and disembark planes through airport jetway tunnels. But even from an airport waiting area window, 747s jets are so much larger than "normal" planes like Boeing 737s or Airbus 320s that they have a paternal appearance, almost like a parent next to a child. This was especially true in the years just after their introduction.

A standard 747 (there are several models) is 231 feet, 10 inches long, meaning that it's almost twice as long as the entire first flight by Orville Wright at Kitty Hawk, North Carolina, in 1903.[1] If you plunked a 747 on a football field with the tip of the tail over one goal line, the fuselage would reach all the way past midfield, with the nose above the opposing 23-yard line. The wingspan is 211 feet. The captain and crew sit nearly 30 feet above the ground – almost the height of a three-story building – and the tail reaches another three stories (63 feet).

Although the 747 has declined in usage because it isn't as fuel-efficient as newer big jets like Boeing's 777 and 787, jumbo jets remain a major part of the fleet of all large airlines in the 21st century. Older travelers can still recall the excitement when big jets were introduced in the 1970s. The 747 started its existence during the Lyndon Johnson administration, when then-Secretary of Defense Robert MacNamara announced a design competition among airline manufacturers for a wide-bodied military transport plane.

---

[1] Orville flew 120 feet.

When all the bids were in, Lockheed, with a design for a plane eventually designated the C-5A, was given the contract. Boeing's 747 was an also-ran.

But Boeing decided to turn its rejected design into a commercial passenger aircraft. Pan American World Airways was the airline that made this possible when it placed a $525 million order for 25 of Boeing's new jumbo planes in 1966.[2]

The first 747s were finished at Boeing's Everett, Washington, assembly line in 1970, and they were a quick success with the traveling public.[3] Travelers liked the spaciousness of a cabin with two aisles, a higher ceiling and the fact that the planes had a second floor – originally used as lounges, they added something of a party atmosphere to flying, an image which was an important part of airlines' marketing in the first decades of jet travel. For those who are too young to remember, take a look at old airline television commercials on YouTube. Steak dinners, the latest movies, cute flight attendants (they were usually called stewardesses then), and fun and relaxation in the air were parts of the experience – and the marketing – of flying.

Other aircraft manufacturers' wide-bodied jets – the Lockheed L-1011 and the McDonnell Douglas DC-10 – followed shortly after the Boeing 747. All became an important part of the airline industry's fleets as more Americans flew for business and pleasure. The number of air passengers jumped from around 200 million a year in 1975 to nearly 350 million by 1980.[4] After a temporary dip in the slower economy of the early 1980s, U.S. air traffic has climbed steadily ever since, with nearly 750 million domestic passengers in 2017 (more than four billion worldwide).[5]

---

[2] A single new 747 – they're still being built, although only for a few airlines – cost more in 2017 than a dozen 747s cost in 1970.

[3] Boeing had built about 1,500 747s as of mid-2015. Although its usefulness has been supplanted by more fuel-efficient jumbo jets, some airlines are still flying 747s.

[4] Source: Office of Technology Assessment, based on Federal Aviation Administration and National Transportation Safety Board data, as quoted in Safe Skies for Tomorrow: Aviation Safety in a Competitive Environment, an Office of Technology assessment publication.

[5] The domestic passengers total is from a chart titled "Passengers – All Carriers – All Airports" on this Department of Transportation website: https://www.transtats.bts.gov/Data_Elements. aspx?Data=1. The worldwide travel total is from an International Civil Aviation Organization news release titled "Continued passenger traffic growth and robust air cargo demand in 2017." It can be found at this ICAO link: https://www.icao.int/Newsroom/Pages/Continued-passenger-traffic-growth-and-robust-air-cargo-demand-in-2017.aspx.

Bigger planes can give the airlines more profit per mile. A 747 can hold close to 500 all-economy-class passengers, although more normal seat configurations keep the passenger total to between 325 and 400.

Insurance brokers predicted two crashes in the first 18 months of use of the 747, but those did not happen. The 747's safety record was perfect for years.

The first of the jumbo jets to crash wasn't even a 747. It was an Eastern Airlines L-1011 that crashed into the Florida Everglades while on a final approach to Miami International Airport on a December night in 1972. The cause was ruled to be pilot error after it was found that the cockpit crew had been distracted by a malfunctioning indicator. Ninety-nine people died in that crash and 77 lived – a horrible statistic, but no more than have died in crashes of standard jets.

The first jumbo-sized disaster happened on March 3, 1974, when a fully loaded Turkish Airlines DC-10 crashed after takeoff from Orly Field near Paris, killing 346 people. A faulty cargo door had collapsed, resulting in a drastic depressurization that froze the controls of the plane and caused it to nosedive into the French farmland.

Boeing's turn was to come later in 1974, when a Lufthansa 747 crashed on takeoff from Nairobi, Kenya, on November 22. Fifty-nine people lost their lives, while 98 survived. Nearly 18 months later, on May 9, 1976, an Iranian Air Force 747 transport broke apart during a thunderstorm over Spain, killing 17 crew members. Only in the Turkish Airlines crash was the casualty total above that of crashes of standard-size jets.[6]

None of this was on Caroline Hopkins' mind as she and Warren Hopkins boarded the Pan Am plane. Getting settled in for a flight on such a fine airplane – and in first class, yet – can be just plain fun. Some airlines gave their first-class passengers slippers to wear while on board. Others put pianos in the lounge. Still others would give their guests a hot towel before takeoff and landing, all of which added to the image they worked so hard to maintain: that flying is a special experience.

---

[6] In August 1985, the single-plane record was set when a Japan Airlines 747 smashed into a mountain, killing 505 passengers and 15 crew members. Four passengers survived.

Caroline Hopkins reported later that she always had a clear goal about where she will sit in an airplane. She said it may have been a result of her fear of heights, or her own caution. But after she and her husband made their booking through the American Express Travel Service, she wrote to Royal Cruise Lines in San Francisco and asked for airline seats near an exit. The line wrote back promptly, confirming that Warren and Caroline Hopkins would be in seats 5-A and 5-B, on the left side of the aircraft as one faced the front. That left only Row 6 between the Hopkinses and the cabin entrance door.

As Warren and Caroline Hopkins boarded the flight that night at JFK in New York, they encountered a minor problem: a man and a woman were already sitting in 5-A and 5-B. The Hopkinses produced their tickets, and the two were shooed away by a flight attendant. The other couple disappeared into the second-level lounge.

Warren Hopkins took off his tie, coat, and vest, and those items were moved to a closet by one of the flight attendants. In the middle of this process, he realized he'd forgotten to take his house keys out of his pants pocket to put in his already-stowed carry-on case, something he always did while traveling. "Oh well," he shrugged, and left the keys in his pocket as he settled into his seat with several magazines.

Five days later, those keys would be the only house keys remaining in the Hopkinses' possession. Caroline's had melted into uselessness in the raging fire that would soon happen.

Caroline Hopkins hung up her coat, too, but then got restless. "I think I'll go up to the lounge for a while before takeoff," she told her husband, and slid past him from her window seat into the aisle and made her way to the circular stairway.

Much to her surprise, Mrs. Hopkins found every seat in the second-floor lounge was occupied. She did not realize then, but was told later, that the cruise line was flying some of the Golden Odyssey crew members to Las Palmas and had nowhere else to put them on the full plane. Among the 28 passengers in that area were the couple who had been in the Hopkinses' seats.

Caroline stood, confused, for a moment before noticing that the door from the lounge into the cockpit was wide open. The new crew members, replacing the ones who had flown the plane to New York, were just getting settled into their seats.

Caroline got inquisitive.

Second Officer George Warns, sitting nearest the door on the right-hand side of the cockpit, looked up as Caroline peeked in.

"Would you mind?" she asked. "I've flown on 747s before, but I've never seen the inside of a 747 cockpit."

Warns shrugged and looked at the man in the front left-hand seat, Captain Victor Grubbs. "Sure, it's all right," Grubbs said, and Caroline stepped into the cockpit to look around for a few moments while the men ran through checklists and got their seats adjusted.

The cockpit, surprisingly small given the size of the rest of the aircraft, was shaped like the inside of a car, she thought. Captain Grubbs sat in the driver's seat, front and on the left. First Officer Robert Bragg was on his right. In front of them were control panels with dozens of indicators. Each pilot had a steering wheel shaped like a car's steering wheel, but smaller and with the part between 10 o'clock and 2 o'clock removed. Between the two pilots, where a car's front-seat storage console would be, were the throttles for the 747's four engines. Each pilot had several pedals on the floor, too.

In back of Bragg, sitting sideways at a small table and in front of another display with dozens more indicators, was George Warns, the flight engineer. His controls and indicators continued from the panels in front of him onto the ceiling of the cockpit.

Mrs. Hopkins thought the windows – the windshield was divided into two windows, one each in front of Grubbs and Bragg – seemed surprisingly small. In back of Grubbs were two "jump seats," as they are known, one behind the other, and both were empty.

As Mrs. Hopkins stood, a young ground crew member in fatigues stepped into the cockpit with a slip of paper in his hand, which he handed to Grubbs. "We put in thirty-three thousand gallons, sir," he said politely to the captain.

Thanking the officers, Mrs. Hopkins stepped back out of the cockpit into the lounge, and then went downstairs to her seat. She slid past her husband into her window seat. "Nothing going on up there?" he asked idly.

"I went in the cockpit," she told him, with no small amount of plea-sure, and gave him a brief description of her little adventure. He raised his eyebrows, expressing some hope that she hadn't gotten in the way.

It was a natural reaction. Most passengers are quite willing to accept the distance that exists between themselves and the crews of the planes on which they travel. That deferential attitude is not accepted readily by everyone, though. As one flight attendant of that era said sarcastically, "The pilot is God. There's nothing a pilot ever does that's wrong. That's the image of pilots."[7]

She said that with some resentment. In the 1970s, flight attendants were closer to being the sexy waitresses of the skies than being the first line of passenger safety. They were a group usually taken for granted by pas-sengers and even the airlines, most of which had age and weight limits on their flight attendants – an attitude that now, in the 21st century, seems bizarrely archaic, as well as downright insulting. Some airlines dressed their attendants in sexy clothing, like hot pants. Jokes were offered, stories told, and movies were made about the high-flying, yee-haw lifestyle of flight attendants. Required to be on board by Federal Aviation Administration safety regulations, the first flight attendants in the 1930s were licensed nurses. But flight attendants at many airlines in the 1960s and 1970s were listed under the marketing department, not the operations department. That contributed to the heightened sensitivity of flight attendants about their professional role, several of them told the authors privately.

It was during the later 1970s, though, that this attitude gradually began to change, encouraged by the flight attendants themselves. Some flight attendants became more aggressive about explaining what they correctly believed was their most important function on board an airplane – provid-ing safety information.

"Safety has always been shoved into the background, and airlines have been more service-oriented," commented Carmen Azzopardi a few years after the Tenerife cash. She was health and safety director for the Independent

---

[7] The person who offered this quote – a flight attendant – will remain unidentified as a courtesy to her.

Union of Flight Attendants through the early 1980s.[8] The IUFA represented Pan American's flight attendants before all of Pan Am's operations were folded into several other airlines in the early 1990s.

"That's the attitude that they give to passengers, that the flight attendants are there for their service," Ms. Azzopardi said. "And, consequently, they totally neglect any idea of the safety aspect of flying."

What she was saying was that flight attendants were not viewed as authority figures in the cabin – although the attendants were, and still are, the crew members closest to the passengers and have information that can be life-saving.

"Without the authority of one of the cockpit crew, it can be difficult and sometimes impossible for flight attendants to give out the information that they carry regarding evacuations and oxygen-mask usage, and on which they base a good portion of the prestige of their jobs," Azzopardi said.

"The glamour days are over, long gone," added Del Mott, former safety director for the Association of Flight Attendants, which represents nearly 60,000 flight attendants across the country from 16 different airlines. Mott gave numerous interviews in the years after the Tenerife accident, insisting that safety be given a higher priority for passengers.

"We want to be considered trained safety experts," she stated a few years after the Tenerife crash. "We don't want our recurrent training to contain a 15-minute lecture on when we're supposed to wear our gloves. We don't want 'We really move our tail for you' advertising campaigns, and spending four hours out of the total eight we're supposed to have in recurrent training just on service. We specifically want emergency safety training. But because we're under [the] marketing [department], marketing's prime concern is to sell seats on an airplane."

It is true, flight attendants have readily acknowledged, that airline travel is safe, and remains so. But Mott raised the possibility of being in an emergency – perhaps a crash, perhaps an emergency evacuation – without well-trained flight attendants.

---

[8] Interview with Jon Ziomek. The quotes from Del Mott are also from an interview.

"If you have three flight attendants who are baton twirlers in the back of that airplane," she suggested dryly, "you're in deep trouble if you have an accident."

It's a paradox. Through the advertising campaigns of the airlines in that era, the baton-twirling cheerleader image was what the flying public came to expect of flight attendants. Mott's reference to a "We really move our tail for you" advertising campaign, with its implied Playboy Bunny image, was a reference to a slogan actually used in a 1970s television commercial for Continental Airlines, which can still be seen on YouTube.[9]

Those flight attendants attempting to take their safety role seriously ran into resistance – not only from their own companies, but also the flying public. Carmen Azzopardi said she could remember many flights during which she would start the safety briefing with the standard, "Ladies and gentlemen, may I have your attention, please?" only to find that few, if any, of the passengers were paying any attention. In those cases, she said, she would stop the briefing and start all over again.

"Ladies and gentleman, may I have your attention, *please*? This is very important! I want you to look up to the front of the cabin, and you're going to see the most important person on this aircraft to you because it is that person who is going to assist you in an emergency situation."

One can imagine how jarring that would have been to passengers who were used to giggling flight attendants who fall behind in the instructions and are pointing out the emergency exits while the senior flight attendant is already talking about the oxygen masks.

There were no such giggling flight attendants on Pan American Clipper 1736 when it pulled away from the gate at 3 a.m., more than an hour late, as the Hopkinses recalled. The new crew, several passengers from Los Angeles later noted, seemed quiet and serious. Partly, it was the lateness of the hour. The two pursers, Dorothy Kelly and Francoise de Beaulieu, and the nine flight attendants ran through the safety briefing so efficiently that the Hopkinses later couldn't even remember it being given.[10]

---

[9] Continental Airlines merged with United Airlines in 2010.
[10] "Purser" is a designation for the senior flight attendants in a crew.

That kind of reaction illustrates the failure of the safety briefing for many passengers, some of the more militant flight attendants would say. Anyone who traveled in the 1960s and 1970s would have seen the attendants demonstrate the location of the emergency exits with a gentle wave of both arms simultaneously, pointing in a vague direction around the wings and the rear of the plane. That wave was universal to all flight attendants – almost all of whom in those days were women – because the gesture was thought to be the best way to point out the exits while continuing to look feminine.

Decades later, this situation has barely improved. The FAA's Civil Aerospace Medical Institute, known as CAMI, has reported to the FAA that *60 percent* of surveyed air passengers admitted to paying little or no attention to preflight safety briefings, and the other 40 percent had little knowledge of safety procedures.[11]

"In its safety studies and accident investigations, the NTSB continues to find that passenger attention to safety information is declining," the FAA memo summarized.

Meanwhile, the flight attendants union, the AFA, is more focused on safety than ever. Candace Kolander, who spent 20 years as the union's air safety, health and security coordinator (she took a similar position with the Air Line Pilots Association in late 2017), gave the example of the pre-flight check that flight attendants do with passengers who sit in exit rows. ("Are you with me? Can you handle the door if it needs to be opened in a hurry?")

The AFA, she said in an interview, had for years taken a position that flight attendants should get a verbal confirmation from these passengers that they understood their responsibilities. Although this doesn't seem like a major request, it was resisted because airlines are trying to make takeoff preparations as efficient as possible.[12] But that small but significant "Hey,

---

[11] A Federal Aviation Administration memorandum, "Recommendations for PED Usage Onboard Airliners," dated Sept. 16, 2013, summarizes more than a dozen studies about passenger attention to safety, or lack of it. The memo cites the CAMI information noted here. The author of this memo is listed as "Manager, Protection and Survival Research Laboratory, AAM-630." The memo is addressed to the Portable Electronic Device (PED) Aviation Rulemaking Committee (ARC).

[12] Many airlines now charge more money for seats in the exit rows – not because they're putting a price on the honor of the seat and its responsibilities, but because there's more legroom in the exit aisles.

this is important" warning has now become a standard part of the pre-takeoff process.

That was one step in the right direction. But a 2015 conversation with AFA officials revealed continuing deep frustration about the general issue of safety. Flight attendants know they're against not one but two powerful forces: an existing excellent safety record, plus the fear by some passengers of even thinking about a possible accident. And now, as we move further into the 21st century, there's a third force: more passengers are distracted by their own cell phones and tablets.

In 2013, the union lobbied hard for stronger onboard restrictions on "personal electronic devices," as mobile phones and tablets are generically called. Their concern is that passengers will miss important information during the safety briefing because they're finishing a last email or text before takeoff.

"Using these devices is going to distract people, especially in packing things away" before takeoff, said Dinkar Mokadam, the union's OSHA specialist. When the FAA was considering the implementation of a 2013 Civil Aerospace Medical Institute study, "We were strongly on record" as supporting the improvement of passenger safety awareness, he said.

The CAMI report, which called for less use of personal electronic devices, was not adopted by the FAA.

The airline industry has even been prodded by Congress. After several airlines announced they would be reducing the size of basic economy section seats in the next few years (travelers now have to buy a premium economy seat to get the same room they used to get in regular economy seats), Congress's 2017 funding bill for the FAA called on the agency to study and set a minimum safe-seat size. This was done not because cramped seats are a comfort issue, it was done because the larger number of passengers getting out of smaller seats could result in more difficult evacuations during an emergency. The bill had the strong support of the flight attendants union.[13]

---

[13] This amendment to the funding bill, proposed by U.S. Rep. Steve Cohen (D-Tenn.), had originally failed. But, following several early 2017 airline incidents involving passengers getting into onboard arguments with crew members, Congress approved the amendment.

Generally, the FAA, trying to find a happy medium between frightening passengers and encouraging the presentation of useful information, has encouraged airlines to get more creative in the way they present safety information because of this truth:

"The airplane passenger who has paid attention to the safety information available, and has developed a plan for what she or he would do to get out of an airplane in a hurry, is better able to handle an emergency situation without becoming confused or panicked," said the 2013 FAA memo, quoting several previous studies.[14]

Those are very important words, of course. But just what would get passengers to pay better attention to the safety briefing? Maybe having a passenger participate in the briefing? "That's problematic," Kolander said. Passengers aren't even allowed to stand while a plane is moving, and during taxiing is often when the briefings are given. So the effort continues to get passengers to put down their cell phones. Some airlines have tried humor, including animation and cartoons, in their video safety briefings.

Again, the desire is to get people's attention without scaring them. One possibility for holding passenger attention would be to explain the reasons behind some of the existing rules. That could increase the rules' acceptance. Those who fly have heard countless times, "Please make sure your tray tables are returned to the seatback in front of you, and your seats are in their upright position, and that all carry-on luggage is securely stored under the seat in front of you or in the overhead racks."

But how many of us have stopped to wonder why those chores have to be done before every takeoff and landing? We've heard the spiel so often that it has become just one more unexplained rule. So some of us perfunctorily give our bag a kick or move the seat halfway up and see if we can get away with it.

In fact, those chores are long-standing FAA safety requirements, and there's an important reason for them. They're intended to ensure that the passengers in the inside seats away from the aisle, closer to the windows,

---

[14] The logic in this point seems clear, and there are many sources for it, but here's a good one: Dan Johnson, *Just in Case: A Passenger's Guide to Airplane Safety and Survival* (New York: Plenum Publishing, 1984).

have as clear a path as possible to the aisle if an emergency evacuation is necessary. A bag on the floor or a seatback flopped all the way back will interfere with an evacuation.

Nine times out of 10, of course, it won't matter. It might not even matter 999,999 times out of a million.

But Pan Am Flight 1736 was one in a million.

CHAPTER 3

"Would you care for a drink?"

Dorothy Kelly, the chief flight attendant in Pan Am 1736's first-class section, bent over the Hopkinses as they flipped through some magazines. Dark-haired and attractive, Kelly made an attempt to project a pleasant demeanor, but she was also contending with unpleasant news: her husband, a pilot for Pan American, had been temporarily laid off just the day before. Because of the airline's seniority rules, younger pilots were occasionally put on unpaid leave if Pan Am's routes weren't filled enough to keep all of the pilots busy.

That was not a good way to start a workday, which was already difficult because in Kelly's case, it had begun at two o'clock in the morning.

"I think a beer would taste nice," Warren Hopkins said, looking at his wife, who agreed. Kelly nodded and walked back to the galley. Then she stopped, remembering what the flight attendants who left the plane in New York had told her: this was a charter flight, so the passengers had been given coupons that were to be exchanged for drinks on board. She walked back to Warren and Caroline Hopkins.

"Could I have drink tickets from you?" she asked.

The Hopkinses were confused. "What do I need drink tickets for?" Caroline asked, smiling. "And what are they?"

"Well, you need coupons to get drinks on this flight," Mrs. Kelly explained patiently.

"We weren't given any drink tickets," Warren replied. Not wishing to make an issue out of it, he reached for his wallet. "What do I have to do?" he asked quietly. "Should I buy some?"

"Bull!" came a surprisingly abrupt comment from a woman sitting in back of Hopkins. "You don't have to buy any drink tickets," she said, raising her voice, to Warren Hopkins's chagrin. "Here, take some of mine." She pulled a roll of coupons out of her purse like a string of sausages.

"Just a moment," said another nearby passenger. It was Jim Naik, one of the executives of Royal Cruise Lines. Sitting across the aisle, he'd overheard the confusion. "Here, let me give you some coupons." Naik introduced himself. He gave Kelly coupons for the beers and handed over a roll of coupons to the Hopkinses. He explained that the escorts were supposed to hand out the tickets to passengers as they boarded, but somehow the Hopkinses had been missed.

They started chatting. Naik, 37, of Cupertino, California, was on vacation with his wife, Elsie. He was born in India, his wife was from West Germany, and they had met at Golden State University in San Francisco when Naik was studying for his master's degree in business administration. They had two daughters back in Cupertino, 8 years old and 7 years old.

Naik had been with Royal Cruise Lines for two years as vice president of finance. He didn't normally go on tours and wasn't an official escort, but he thought he should intervene about the drink tickets, he explained with a smile.

"Well, we appreciate it very much," Warren Hopkins acknowledged. They exchanged information, Hopkins explaining that he owned a meat distribution company, selling meat to restaurants in the Chicago area and on the East Coast. Caroline's father had been in the same business, as the founder of the E.W. Kneip Co. meat distribution firm. They had two daughters, both of them in college.

Their chat became a conversation circle. Naik introduced the cruise director, Beau Moss, who was sitting in the middle of the first-class section. Despite the lateness of the hour, few people felt like resting, and it was pleasant to make friends at the onset of the trip, which the easygoing Hopkins had no trouble doing. Naik and the Hopkinses made pledges to have dinner together on the ship, and then Naik went back to his seat while Hopkins chatted with Moss about cameras. Moss, it turned out, was a camera buff who had brought along a new camera that he'd just purchased.

Next to the window, Caroline Hopkins took a blanket and pillow from one of the flight attendants and curled up. She found herself quickly drifting off – unusual for her. But with the quiet nearby voices of her husband and Beau Moss, the lights of the cabin turned low, and the reassuring hum of the engines, she slipped into sleep. The vacation was starting out just fine. Now, she thought as she drifted off, if only the weather would get better. New York's weather hadn't been what one would order for a celebration.

Although…a surprising number of Clipper 1736's passengers were indeed celebrating something.[1] In economy class, David Roberts and his wife, both 31, from Bakersfield, California, had been married only three weeks. This was their honeymoon.[2]

Several other couples were celebrating their marriages, too. Lottie and Fred Jamieson had been married only five days when they left their tiny desert community of Borrego Springs for Los Angeles International Airport early on Saturday, March 26, to catch this flight. What made their marriage unusual was that Jamieson was 72 years old and his new bride 58.

The former Lottie Quince, a divorcee, had met Jamieson in Borrego Springs, a desert resort town with a population of about 2,000, similar to the better-known Palm Springs. She was a well-known local artist specializing in scratchboard art, a process in which carving is done on a chalk-covered surface to achieve a woodblock-print or engraving effect. Her works had been shown in a number of art exhibits in the area.

Fred Jamieson was a Canadian who had co-owned and managed several movie theaters in Calgary, Alberta, and later a shopping center, before retiring to Escondido, California, in 1971. With a partner, he owned an avocado grove.

A lonely widower when he met Lottie, Jamieson was happy with his new friend. The two got along so well that they decided to start a new life

---

[1] Many of the people described in this section were killed. As a courtesy, real names are used only for survivors, or if there had been significant media attention on an individual after the crash.

[2] Much of the information in this section was taken from later media reports.

together. Just days after Lottie won first and second prize in the scratch-board art division of the Borrego Springs Art Guild show, the two were married, on Tuesday, March 22, in Indio, California.[3]

Perhaps the choice of a cruise was easier for older people, as Mrs. Hopkins had pointed out earlier in the evening to her husband, but the Jamiesons were hardly the only older couple on their honeymoon.

Alfred Herb, 67, and the former Eileen Swanson, both of University City, California, had been married February 5, just six weeks earlier. Herb was a retired Navy commander who, the previous June, had retired from his second career as a social services worker with the San Diego County welfare department.

Eileen had lived in Peoria, Illinois, for much of her early life and moved to California around 1960 when she married a Los Angeles city planner. She had been widowed three years when she met and fallen in love with Al Herb.

The Herbs may have known another former Peorian who was, coincidentally, on the same flight – Frances Hammond.

Miss Hammond, 70, was a spunky woman who had spent 46 years teaching kindergarten in the Peoria school system, retiring in 1972. Despite her age, she'd gotten interested in getting more education and had worked for, and received, a master's degree from Illinois State University when she was 59.

Albert and Florence Trumbull of La Mesa, California, had married the previous August. They had taken several vacations together since then, so this wasn't their honeymoon. But they, too, were older newlyweds – he at 72, she at 71.

Walter and Beth Moore of San Francico were yet another older couple on board who had married relatively recently. Both had been widowed in recent years. They had met in San Francisco among a mutual circle of friends, fallen in love, and married on October 22, 1975. Beth had at first insisted that she didn't want to remarry – she was 66 at the time – but had changed her mind after spending time with Moore.[4]

---

[3] The names of this couple have been changed for the same reason explained earlier.
[4] Mrs. Moore was interviewed several times by Jon Ziomek.

Others had different events to celebrate. Enid Tartikoff, a booking agent with Royal Cruise Lines, was marking her 50th birthday on this soon-to-be-dawning day, March 27. She and her husband, Jordan, had been on previous Royal Cruise Line trips but had never been on the popular "Mediterranean Highlights" cruise before.

Irma Calandra of Fresno, California, was celebrating her 54th by taking the cruise with her husband and their good friends, Dominick and Elizabeth Guerriero. Calandra had another reason for going, he kept telling the Guerrieros. He said he had spent much of his service time during World War II in Casablanca and was looking forward to revisiting that Moroccan city. There were surely a few jokes about the Humphrey Bogart-Ingrid Bergman film, *Casablanca*, as they got comfortable in their airplane seats.

Kathryn Barth of Escondido, California, had just retired from her husband's company, F. J. Barth Co. Inc., a securities systems firm, and she and her husband had decided to mark the occasion by taking a cruise. Mrs. Barth was 65, her husband 71.

Younger couples had things to celebrate, too. Robert Efird and his wife, Karen Anderson, of Seattle, were marking their 10th wedding anniversary. Both were doctors.

And there was another medical team on board. Maurice and Virginia Tyler were retired dentists who had spent their careers checking children's teeth for the Los Angeles public school system. This was their first cruise, and they were going on it with some neighbors, Walter and Irene Vedder, from down the street in Rancho Bernardo, a San Diego suburb. The Vedders belonged to a travel club in the community, and Irene had achieved some fame by having some of her poetry published locally.

There were young people on the flight, too. Joani Holt Feathers[5] and her then-boyfriend, Jack Ridout, who were sitting directly in front of the Hopkinses in 4-A and 4-B, were 29 and 33 years old, respectively. Across the aisle from them were Penny Quade, 26, and her sister, June Ellingham, 20.[6] Near them were Roland (known to his friends as Bo) Brusco, 29, and

---

[5] At the time, Ms. Feathers was known as Joan Holt. Her name changed years later following a marriage. For consistency's sake, from this point she will be referred to as Joani Feathers.

[6] Because of subsequent events, these names have been changed.

his wife, Terri, 25, of Seattle. Lynda Daniel, traveling with her parents, Jack and Patricia, was around 20. Perry and Trudy Johnson of Santa Monica, California, had brought along their two daughters, Monica, 15, and Lisa, 12. And most of the plane's flight attendants were in their twenties.

But they were the exceptions, as Warren Hopkins had noticed the previous night in the JFK terminal.

In addition to the older couples, there were several widows on board, including Lorelle Shute, 55, of Fresno, who was traveling with a divorced friend, Catherine Ellis of Pinedale, California, also 55. They were making their second trip together, having taken a cruise to Alaska the year before.

So it was a predominantly older crowd of people on this trip: couples, widows and a smattering of younger people. As dawn rose in the east, everyone on the plane relaxed and looked forward to what was shaping up as an interesting two weeks. Some people slept, others read, still others talked among themselves. The giant jet cut through the air, rushing its passengers toward the rising sun.

CHAPTER 4

The airports for Las Palmas and Santa Cruz de Tenerife, the two largest cities in the Canary Islands, are busy on Sundays almost year-round. Sunday is a standard day for beginning or ending cruises or beach vacations, and the Canary Islands offer good opportunities for both. The two airports are the focus of activity for these resort towns, which derive a major portion of their income on tourism.

Las Palmas, the chain's largest city with the largest airport, is located on Grand Canary Island. Santa Cruz de Tenerife is on the island of Tenerife, less than 100 miles away. Thousands of people move in both directions – coming in and going out – through the airport terminal buildings. Those just arriving are pale-skinned and excited, eager yet a bit uncertain as they look around them at the palm trees and the island's surprisingly high mountains. Outgoing passengers are tan and tired, weighed down by hats, trinkets, and perhaps a box or two of figs or avocados that they may try to sneak past the customs agents.

In recent years, nearly 10 million tourists have visited the Canary Islands annually, the vast majority of them passing through these two airports.[1]

With so much activity, there would be no special attention paid on Sunday morning, March 27, 1977, to two young men who walked through the Las Palmas terminal, one carrying a suitcase, the other empty-handed. They were unsmiling and nervous. With all the noise from the

---

[1] The numbers are from the Canary Islands tourism website. The Spanish tourism office in Chicago reported the total was around 500,000 in 1977.

public address announcements, greetings being exchanged, goodbyes being offered, and the general hustle and bustle of a busy airport terminal, no one would notice that the suitcase carried by one of the two men was ticking.

The men stopped when they got to the florist shop on the terminal's main floor, not far from the front door to the building. Near the shop was less pedestrian traffic, and the two were able to stand briefly, one man setting the suitcase down as if to rest. Then the pair walked out the front doors of the terminal building, leaving the suitcase on the floor near the florist shop. It sat there, unnoticed, by the hundreds of people moving through the building.

* * * *

Gordon Brown got up early on Sunday morning, March 27. He had slept well in his hotel the previous night and expected to sleep just as well aboard the *Golden Odyssey* for the next 12 nights.[2] Brown had spent the last two days sightseeing around Grand Canary Island. This afternoon, he would go to work. His wife, Jean, was at that moment five miles above the Atlantic Ocean and headed in his direction, riding aboard Pan Am's Clipper 1736. She was escorting 37 residents of the Leisure World community who had booked their passage on the *Golden Odyssey* through the Browns' travel agency, Good Time To Travel, in Laguna Hills, California. Their friends from the community would be enjoying themselves while the Browns would be on the job, checking bookings and accommodations and acting as informal cruise directors and activity coordinators for their group. "There's no leisure for us in this Leisure World," Jean Brown had kidded.

Gordon Brown was another of the travelers who had been unable to get on board Flight 1736 because it was completely booked. At least one of the Browns was required to be on the flight to act as the group's escort, so Gordon and Jean had decided between themselves who would be the escort and who would travel alone. "If you don't mind, Jean," Brown had suggested to his wife, "I'd like to go ahead early. I'll meet you there." Although Brown had traveled extensively, he had never seen Grand Canary Island.

---

[2] Gordon and Jean Brown were interviewed by, and corresponded with, Jon Ziomek.

So he explained to his wife that he'd like to fly over early and look around. Mrs. Brown, a genial 58-year-old with a cheery, high voice, readily agreed.

Brown had arrived on Grand Canary Island on Friday, March 25, and spent that day and Saturday touring the area. He was impressed with the beauty of the island, which has the largest city in the chain, Las Palmas, with 350,000 residents at the time. (By 2018, the population was closer to 400,000.) Grand Canary Island is only the third-largest in the chain, after Tenerife and Fuerteventura. Almost circular in shape, Grand Canary occupies 522 square miles of land and has a startling variety of scenery that even includes sections of desert – tourists can ride camels imported from Africa – not far from green mountains that rise more than 6,000 feet above sea level. The odd mix of terrain and altitudes allows for a cornucopia of crops, ranging from banana trees growing on the hills near the ocean to coffee plantations inland, along with almond, sugar cane and tomato farms.

The city of Las Palmas itself has an old section with some buildings dating back to 1497, and it's said that Christopher Columbus may have stopped there on his voyages to the New World. The entire chain of seven islands was called "The Fortunate Isles" in antiquity – there are references to them in ancient Greek literature. Explorers of various nationalities claimed the islands in succeeding years – Arabs, Italians, Portuguese – but they were conquered permanently by Spain in 1496. By then, they were known as the Canary Islands – not for the little yellow birds, although thousands of them flit around the island chain – but for the wild dogs that used to roam on them. (*Canis* is "dog" in Latin.)

The original Canary Islands inhabitants are thought to be of northern African stock. But following the Spanish conquest, the indigenous residents gradually merged with settlers, and there is now little to distinguish native Canaries, as the residents call themselves, from those of Spanish descent. Only one group has had any success establishing a historical identity – the Guanches, who originally lived mainly on Tenerife and spoke their own language.

Although the Canary Islands are known mainly as a tourist destination, they also have a political history. They were used as a place of exile for political prisoners during the rule of Spanish dictator Primo de Rivera in the 1920s, and by Francisco Franco as a base from which he began his eventually successful revolutionary Nationalist uprising against the then-Spanish Republic in 1936.

There has been so much mixing of the residents and settlers that it has been argued there is not much basis for a movement to separate the island chain from Spain, which still governs the islands more than 500 years after its conquest. However, some of the Canaries residents in the later 20th century wanted independence from Spain – or at the least more attention from the Spanish government. According to Spanish media reports from the 1970s, perhaps 10 percent of the islands' 1.2 million residents were militant in those days about what they felt was a lack of concern from Madrid. Among this 10 percent, the most militant among them organized themselves in 1964 into the Movement for the Self-Determination and Independence of the Canaries Archipelago (MPAIAC, using the Spanish acronymn).

MPAIAC's leadership was carried out for years by Antonio Cubillo, himself a native Spaniard. A former labor lawyer, he lived in the Canaries before jumping bail following a charge of agitation, as it was known, and escaping to Algeria. Cubillo explained MPAIAC'S position in nightly shortwave radio broadcasts from Algeria. Cubillo wanted an independent Guanche republic that would join the Organization of African Unity, a quasi-United Nations of African countries.

Cubillo's position was that the Canary Islands residents were originally an African people who were colonized against their will and maintained themselves as a distinct race from the mainland Spaniards. His problem was to convince native Canary residents that they were different enough to justify having a separate nation. MPAIAC's influence was said to be low, according to Spanish media reports, but Cubillo succeeded in establishing a political consciousness among some of the chain's residents, who were sensitive about such problems as the then-privately owned water supply in the islands. And unemployment was high enough in the 1960s and 1970s to keep many residents, seeking an answer to such problems, tuned in to Cubillo's radio broadcasts.[3]

---

[3] "Canary Islands Independence Movement," Wikipedia.com.

But enough public apathy existed on the islands to result in Cubillo's group trying more severe methods of attention-getting than occasional radio speeches...

...such as bombs. During the autumn of 1976, more than a dozen bombs were detonated in front of public buildings in cities on the islands, with MPAIAC claiming responsibility. It was an effort similar to the Puerto Rican independence group FALN, which set off explosives in public buildings across the United States through much of the 1980s. Although bombing buildings did succeed in drawing attention to their respective political movements, the public relations value of bombing a building was then, and still remains, highly questionable.

In that era, terrorist organizations were not as intent on killing innocent civilians as they have become.

At any rate, during the winter of 1977, the leaders of Cubillo's organization decided to place an explosive at the busiest airport in the islands: Gando Airport in Las Palmas, on Grand Canary Island. Another attention-getter.

So it was that on Sunday morning, March 27, 1977, the two young men walked unnoticed through the terminal of Las Palmas's Gando Airport and placed their suitcase by the florist shop. They were gone from the terminal by 11:30 a.m.

About 40 minutes later, Gordon Brown walked into the terminal through the same big glass doors the two MPAIAC men had used earlier. Brown was accompanied by two escorts from Royal Cruise Lines. All of them had taken a taxi together from the harbor, a distance of about six miles.

The day was sunny, with a temperature in the mid-60s Fahrenheit. It was a good day for a tour of the island, followed by the cruise departure, which was exactly what had been arranged for the passengers of Clipper 1736.

Brown and his companions were early – the Pan Am jet was not due until 1:15 p.m. But better early than late, they figured, and thus had arrived at the airport with plenty of time to spare, chatting among themselves about the day's plans.

As they walked up the steps of the terminal to the glass doors, the telephone was ringing at the main Gando Airport switchboard. When the operator answered the call, she heard a man speaking in a low and threatening voice, saying bombs had been placed in the airport terminal bulding, and they were set to explode. The building should be cleared at once. Then the man hung up.

The operator immediately disconnected her line, then, as fast as she could, opened another line on the switchboard and called the local office of Iberia, the Spanish national airline. The manager who answered the phone heard a nervous operator talking in rapid Spanish, explaining that she'd just gotten a bomb threat for the airport and that the caller had said something about two bombs. The Iberia agent acknowledged the call and told her to hang up. He'd call airport security in the airport manager's office, he told her.

As the Iberia Airlines representative was talking with the airport switch-board operator, Brown and the Royal Cruise Lines officials entered the terminal. They had just passed the florist shop and were headed toward the Pan Am ticket counter when a roaring explosion suddenly blasted through the entire terminal building. People screamed, and everyone flinched and ducked as glass shattered and flew across the concourse. Smoke billowed through the area, and several people immediately fell to the floor. A young clerk in the flower shop, struck by several pieces of flying glass, became a sobbing mass of bloody cuts before passing out from the shock of her injuries. A section of the ceiling came crashing down only a few feet in back of Brown and the other men, splattering plaster as it fell.

"Did you hit the floor?" Brown was later asked. "No, we hit the door!" he answered. He and his companions, unhurt, turned and ran out of the front entrance. There was confusion and disorientation as others ran out of the building behind them, while about eight people remained inside on the floor, bleeding and moaning or crying.

Meanwhile, the Iberia ticket agent had just gotten through to the air-port security officer inside the control tower. "We've had a threat of some bombs planted in the terminal," the Iberia official said. "I know!" the security officer yelled into the phone. "The first bomb has already exploded!"

Police were called while the airport managers huddled together, con-ferring on what to do about the threat of a second bomb. Outside the building, passengers and visitors milled around on the driveway and near the parking lot, uncertain where to go. The conference among officials inside yielded first one result, then another.

It was initially decided to load outgoing passengers on planes in a staging area several hundred yards away from the main terminal building. That would keep the terminal vacant while police searched it. But what to do about arriving planes?

The minutes crawled by: 12:30 p.m., 12:45 p.m., 1 p.m. Several thousand feet over everyone's heads, at 1,000-foot intervals, jets were ordered into racetrack-shaped holding patterns in the sky while the airport managers considered their next action. One possibility was to land the planes and have everyone disembark well away from the terminal. But ambulances were even at that moment rushing the eight wounded individuals to area hospitals. There could be no chance taken that another bomb was anywhere in the vicinity. And officials may have been considering an additional bit of information: the Canary Islands depend heavily on their public image. Just how would it look to arriving tourists to unload their luggage on an airport taxiway, with a nearby terminal building that had been closed because of a terrorist bomb? No, those airplanes circling overhead would have to land somewhere else until the situation could be cleared up. Send them to Tenerife, only 59 air miles to the west. Everyone could wait there for an hour or two while the mess got cleaned up and the building checked for more bombs.

Police were dispatched to the waiting passengers near the building, and the decision to close the airport was explained. There would be no arrivals for an indefinite period, everyone was told. Those waiting for incoming planes or planning to board a departing plane should call the airport after a few hours to get an update.

Brown and his companions shook their heads and grumbled. "Let's go back to the ship," Brown suggested, so they climbed into a taxi, still buzzing among themselves about the explosion.

High above, Jean Brown was sitting in seat 37-C of Pan Am Clipper 1736 and perhaps at that very moment peering out of her window down on the island, wondering what the problem was. Why were they circling and not landing?

Well, her husband told himself, as he and his companions returned to the *Golden Odyssey,* at least he'd have something exciting to talk about with his wife when she finally did land.

CHAPTER 5

It had started out as a routine flight. KLM Royal Dutch Airlines 4805, a chartered Boeing 747 from Amsterdam's Schiphol Airport, was carrying 235 passengers to Las Palmas in the Canary Islands for a week of sunshine and fun. Once there, the plane would pick up a load of vacationers who had just concluded their holidays and return them to Amsterdam.

There and back. Strictly routine.

But it didn't happen that way because of the bomb at Las Palmas. KLM's flight crew, especially the pilot, had every right to be displeased with the way the day was going. They didn't need delays – they'd taken off from Amsterdam a few minutes late, although the flight had been able to make up that time in the air.

But another delay could be a serious problem for this captain, Jacob Louis Veldhuyzen van Zanten, one of KLM's top pilots. One month past his 50th birthday, van Zanten had accumulated a significant 1,545 hours of flying time in 747s.[1] Blond, handsome, successful, and confident, van Zanten was the man airline officials had chosen to introduce KLM's pilots to the intricacies of flying the jumbo jets. He spent hundreds of hours in the KLM 747 simulator with other pilots, explaining procedures and running them through simulated flights. Jacob van Zanten was one of the airline's stars – he'd even been featured in photos acompanying some of KLM's

---

[1] Second reference in Dutch is to use two last names: Veldhuyzen Van Zanten. For normal U.S. style, van Zanten will be used.

print advertisements in magazines and newspapers around the world, smiling at potential passengers.

"KLM. From the people who made punctuality possible," read the headline of those advertisements. There, in the center of the two-page ad, was Captain van Zanten, his Nordic features beaming at the readers. He was in his uniform, with gold bars on his shoulders to signify his rank. Underneath were the words, "The reliable airline of those surprising Dutch."

And now, as his plane circled above Las Palmas, perhaps van Zanten looked at his watch. Things weren't so reliable now, as the crew waited for instructions from the airport managers.

Van Zantzen's First Officer was Klass Meurs, also one month past a birthday – his 42nd. Meurs lived in Heemstede, near Amsterdam. Although he was an experienced flyer, with 9,200 hours of flying time prior to this flight, Meurs had a total of only 95 hours in 747s – not even two months' worth. Any uncertainties he may have felt about flying in the jumbo jet were probably relieved by the confidence oozing from the man on his left.

By contrast, Second Officer and Flight Engineer Willem Schreuder, 42, of Voorburg, the Netherlands, was much more experienced with 747s. He had amassed 543 hours in them and had even put in more total flying time for KLM than Van Zanten, with 17,031 hours, compared to the captain's 11,700 hours. Van Zanten was the senior officer, but the amount of time that he'd spent in the simulator as an instructor in recent years had caused him to slip behind some of the younger officers in route flying.

The 747 they were flying was called *The Rhine* (named for the major Western European river) when it rolled off the Boeing Aircraft Co.'s assembly line in the autumn of 1971. Before leaving Schiphol Airport at 10:20 a.m. that morning, the plane's airframe had made 5,200 takeoffs and, of course, the same number of landings in the five and a half years since it had been built. It had a total of 21,195 hours in the air.

For this flight, the entire plane had been chartered by Holland International tour lines.

Shortly after 1 p.m., the instructions came from Gando Airport's control tower: all incoming planes were being diverted to Tenerife's Los Rodeos Airport, approximately 20 minutes' flying time to the west. The diverted flights would have to wait there until Las Palmas officials could reopen Gando Airport.

Perhaps the mood changed just about then, as the instructions were transformed into action in the KLM cockpit. The crew reset their navigation system – a computer that helps fly the plane to specific targeted radio beacons – and then pulled the plane out of its holding pattern to swing west and head for Tenerife. There was no doubt about it now – they and everyone else would be running very late. The casual chatter between crew members may have slackened, the humor coming less easily. And van Zanten had another pressure on him: as chief pilot for KLM, he was intensely aware of a KLM work rule – it was even a Dutch law – forbidding any overtime for flight crew members. The rule was a safety measure, to ensure that overly tired personnel weren't handling the controls of jets with hundreds of vulnerable passengers on board.

If their stopover at Tenerife wasn't too long, there'd be no problem, van Zanten knew. More than a couple of hours, though, and they'd be cutting it close. He banked the plane and picked up the aircraft's public address microphone to explain to the passengers what was happening, while Meurs began looking for the Los Rodeos charts in the pilots' airport and runway chart book.

* * * *

In a holding pattern several thousand feet above the KLM flight, another Boeing 747 was circling – Pan Am 1736. It was an older plane than KLM 4805, having been brought out of the Boeing hangar in early 1970, the very first year of 747 deliveries. Since then, the airframe had logged 25,725 hours in the air and made 7,195 takeoffs. Coincidentally, the name of the jet – the Clipper *Victor* – was the same as the first name of its pilot, Victor Grubbs, of Centerport, New York.

Grubbs, 56, was an experienced pilot who had put in 21,143 hours in the air during his Pan Am career, 564 of them in 747s. He was in good spirits on this flight. He'd just passed his latest mandatory medical checkup the previous Wednesday.

Sitting to Grubbs's right was Robert Bragg, the first officer. Bragg, 39, of Howard Beach, New York, was a regular in 747 cockpits – he had a whopping 2,796 hours in them, out of his total flying experience of 10,800 hours.

Second Officer George Warns of Blairstown, New Jersey, was 47 years old and also experienced in 747 operations. He had 559 hours of time in the air with the jumbo jets out of his total of 15,210 flying hours with Pan Am.

After the six-and-a-half-hour flight from New York, the Pan Am crew members were not exactly thrilled when the Gando Airport controllers radioed the delay and diversion. "Can't we stay in a holding pattern until the airport reopens?" Grubbs had asked the tower, but received a "no" because no one knew how long the delay would be. It was explained to Clipper 1736's crew that a bomb had gone off in the terminal building. But after some consultation among themselves, the crew members decided to tell the passengers as few details as possible – perhaps thinking, with some justification, that a full account of the news would be too upsetting.

So Captain Grubbs broke into the conversations and the card games going on in the cabin to announce that "a plane was stalled on the runway" at Las Palmas, causing a diversion to Tenerife. But he also called the cruise director for Royal Cruise Lines, Beau Moss, into the cockpit to tell him that the tower had said something about a bomb in the terminal building. Moss thanked him for the information, left the cockpit, and returned to his seat – but on the way, he stopped to tell Jim Naik, the cruise line's vice president. Naik, in turn, got up and strolled over to the seats of Warren and Caroline Hopkins, both of whom were reading just then. He told them the real reason for the delay. They expressed appropriate surprise. "I hope this isn't going to cause any problems with the cruise, Jim," Warren Hopkins said. "Oh, I don't think so," Naik answered reassuringly. "They'll get it straightened out soon."

Naik then moved around the cabin and mentioned the bomb to another couple with whom he'd chatted earlier, Edward Hess and his wife, Mary Kay, of Phoenix, Arizona, who were sitting at the right-hand front of the first-class section. Thus, despite the caution of the crew, word rapidly spread through the cabin about the bomb. Back in the cockpit, the crew changed course to follow KLM 4805. Clipper *Victor* pulled out of its holding pattern and aimed for Los Rodeos Airport on Tenerife. From here on, Pan Am 1736 and KLM 4805 would be drawn closer and closer together, until their paths would literally, and disastrously, cross.

CHAPTER 6

The island of Tenerife, shaped like a lamb chop, is the largest in the Canary Islands archipelago, at 785 square miles. As with the other islands in the chain, the terrain changes dramatically for such small islands, with mountains, green hills, and valleys, even sections of desert, plus a beautiful coastline with black and gold sand beaches.

The most dominant feature of Tenerife is an enormous mountain, Pico de Teide, "the Devil's Peak," which rises 12,250 feet above sea level and is often snow-capped – unexpected for an island known as "the Eternal Spring."

The mountain affects island life. For one thing, it's a natural location for a cable car ride, and that's what was built there for tourists. So the mountain has been a source of revenue for Tenerife.

But the Devil's Peak also has a negative effect. The mountain's height prevents prevailing ocean breezes from reaching the southern portions of the island. Thus the north side of the island is much more humid than the south and occasionally gets weather that's downright unpleasant.

According to the Spanish government's department of tourism, the month of March sees an average of only five rainy days in the Canary Islands, with an average temperature of around 65 degrees Fahrenheit.

Pico de Teide throws those figures out of kilter for Tenerife. The ocean winds blow wet clouds against the mountain, blocking out the sun, and when the breeezes die down, the clouds slide down the mountain and create fog. It doesn't happen often. But it happens often enough.

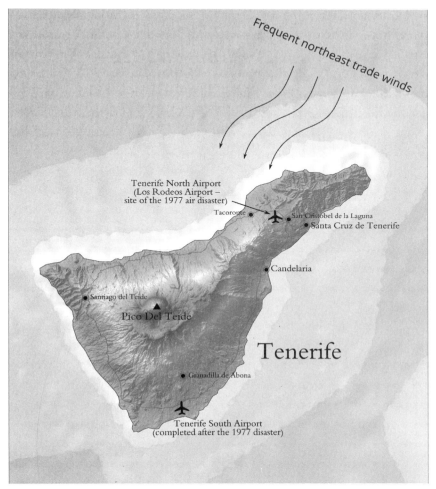

After a terrorist bomb exploded in the terminal at the Las Palmas airport, Pan Am 1736 and KLM 4805, along with other scheduled flights, were diverted to Los Rodeos Airport on Tenerife. They were told to wait at Los Rodeos until the Las Palmas airport re-opened.

The Tenerife airport, Los Rodeos, was built on the north side of the island, about five miles inland from the capital city of Santa Cruz de Tenerife. The city sits on the northeast corner of the island, atop the bone of the lamb chop, to continue the metaphor. Laurel, walnut, almond, eucalyptus, and walnut trees grow alongside washed main streets with white and brightly colored buildings. Banana plantations and vineyards lie on the outskirts of the city, which, along with the ancient Spanish fort of San Cristobal, overlooks Tenerife harbor.

To get to Los Rodeos airport from downtown in 1977 required a ride up winding roads into the hills in back of the city, perhaps stopping for a quick look at the monument to General Francisco Franco, a former governor of the island who began his 1936 Spanish revolution here and eventually became Spanish prime minister.

The Los Rodeos airport was not large: not only did it have just one runway, but pilots criticized it because the runway was not well excavated. There was a hump on the runway so that it was difficult to see one end of the runway from the other end. The fog sometimes made that view impossible. The runway ran east-southeast to west-northwest, or 120 degrees to 300 degrees on a compass. A taxiway ran along the northeast side of the runway, with four exits of varying angles connecting the runway and the taxiway.

The small terminal building sat near the northern end of the taxiway. In 1977, there were no connecting jetway tunnels. Passengers boarded or disembarked using stairway ramps brought to the planes. Inside the terminal was a waiting area large enough for a few dozen black vinyl two-seat couches, with a souvenir stand and a Red Cross station, a refreshment counter, and a number of ticket counters to handle the airlines servicing Tenerife.

Much of the air traffic coming into Los Rodeos consisted of charter-operated jumbo jets. Given the airport's size, the introduction of jumbo jets a few years earlier had made the process of loading and unloading passengers more difficult. On Sundays, when some vacationers were leaving and others were arriving, the terminal building resembled a stadium hallway during the Super Bowl.

Not only was the airport crowded, but it had a bad safety record. In 1956, an Avianca Airlines plane dropped part of a wing on a house nearby, killing one person. There was one accident a year at Los Rodeos from 1965 through 1968, killing a total of 98 people. The worst was in 1965, when an Iberia airlines flight collided with machinery on the runway and 60 people were killed. On June 9, 1970, the provincial government decided to build a new airstrip, bigger than Los Rodeos, to be located down the Autopista del Sur highway from Santa Cruz de Tenerife. That would put it on the south side of Pico de Teide mountain, away from the fog. The new airport was to be called, simply, Sur (south) Airport.

Moving Tenerife's flight operations was an excellent idea. In addition to the tricky weather conditions at Los Rodeos, there were homes near Los Rodeos that sat close to the fence at the edge of airport property. Those residents were not happy about the noise from the airport and the jet fuel fumes.

After the government's decision to build a new airport, the plans were formalized and the site officially chosen. In 1972, after 200 million pesetas were allocated for the new airport's construction, a chartered Spantax Airlines flight full of German tourists plummeted to earth just after takeoff from Los Rodeos when it was caught in crosswinds, killing 155 people. This disaster vigorously renewed the uproar for the new airport.

Ground was broken for Sur Airport, and the new runway was completed and paved by 1974, but by 1976, public attention was waning again. There were rumors that local hotel owners were subtly pressuring for a slowdown of the new airport's completion because it was so much farther away from Santa Cruz de Tenerife – in heavy traffic, the drive could take an hour. Tourists, on whom so much of the island's economy depended, could get irritated with a long ride to or from the airport and not spend as much money, or perhaps not come back at all.

Whatever the reason, by early 1977, the second phase of construction – completing the terminal building – had not yet begun. Therefore, no bigger, fogless airport was yet available, nearly seven years after it was decided that Tenerife needed one.

So it was that on Sunday afternoon, March 27, 1977, KLM 4805 came in for a landing at Los Rodeos Airport, touching down at 1:38 p.m. on Runway 30 (300 degrees on a compass).

Captain van Zanten taxied his plane as close to the terminal as he could get and parked near other, smaller jets that were bringing in fresh new tourists and taking tired ones out.

Photo courtesy of Gonzalo López

This calm photo of Los Rodeos Airport is in stark contrast to the chaos of March 27, 1977. The runway, taxiway and four turnoffs are clearly visible. The KLM plane taxied from the near end of the runway to the far end before turning around and attempting to take off up the runway. The taxiway wasn't used because parts of it were blocked by other airplanes.

At first, he announced to the disgruntled passengers that everyone would have to wait inside the plane until they received permission to fly back to Las Palmas. About 20 minutes later, however, apparently after checking with the control tower and being told there was no word from Las Palmas, van Zanten changed his mind and told the passengers they could leave the aircraft and wait in the departure lounge.

Shortly after 2:15 p.m., Pan Am Clipper 1736 touched down on the Los Rodeos runway and pulled onto the taxiway before parking near a British Airways 707 and a Spantax Airlines DC-8, several planes down from the KLM 747 and farther from the terminal building. The engines were stilled, and a quiet settled over the cabin as the passengers gazed out onto startlingly green and beautiful hills that rolled up to Pico de Teide mountain.[1]

---

[1] Spantax ceased operations in 1988.

"We may be here as long as one hour, ladies and gentlemen," Captain Grubbs announced. "Because of the congestion in the terminal already, we're not going to be able to permit anyone to leave the immediate area of the aircraft" – a statement that was greeted with boos and grumbling, which Grubbs couldn't hear because the cockpit was one floor away from the main passenger cabin.

However, he added, obliviously talking over the booing, "I've requested that a ramp be placed alongside the aircraft so that those who wish to stretch their legs may stand on the stairway or alongside the plane at the bottom of the stairs."

"Want to get some air, Caroline?" Warren Hopkins asked, gesturing at the door.

"When they open the thing, I sure will," his wife said, laughing. "My seat is really sore."

So was everyone else's on the plane. The Hopkinses and other New York passengers had been sitting for nearly seven hours, which was bad enough. But those who had flown from Los Angeles had been in sitting positions, except for occasional leg stretching in the aisles or bathroom trips, for 12 hours.

One older passenger in particular, who had boarded in Los Angeles, had suffered from all that sitting: Ethel Simon, a member of the Leisure World contingent along with her husband, Meyer, had developed leg cramps during the flight that had caused her to suddenly cry out in pain, startling everyone within a few rows. She had been regularly pacing up and down the aisles since then, trying to work out the spasms.

Some of those on board had been in the air even before the charter flight left from Los Angeles. Ralph and Ruby Koslosky, for example, had flown from Anchorage, Alaska, to get the Los Angeles charter. Edward and Jeannette Bolles had flown from Honolulu, as had Catherine Seacrist. Mrs. Seacrist, the previously mentioned widow, had retired to the island of Maui in 1970 from Reno, Nevada, after her husband passed away. To get to Los Angeles for the charter flight, she had to take a local airline from Maui to Honolulu, then a connecting flight to Los Angeles in time for the Pan Am charter. Her total flying time up to this point was close to 18 hours, not counting the hours of layovers in between.

So for many of the Pan Am passengers, it felt good, indeed, to stand up and walk around after the engines had stopped turning and a quiet had settled into the cabin. Caroline Hopkins took advantage of the open-door opportunity several times. The outside air was chilly but refreshing. The first time she stepped out, she could see blue sky. But on her second trip to the ramp, about 45 minutes later, she saw that their New York weather had followed them. The sky was filling up with ever-thickening clouds, the wind had picked up, and the temperature seemed to be falling.

Caroline watched with some curiosity as airport minibuses shuttled back and forth between the nearby KLM 747 and the terminal building, taking passengers to the building and then going back for more. They didn't seem to be unloading any luggage, so Mrs. Hopkins assumed, correctly, that the KLM flight was also here temporarily, but its captain had decided to let the passengers keep themselves occupied in the terminal. She watched with some envy for a while, feeling a bit like a prisoner, but then was chased back inside by the increasingly chilly wind.

She took her seat and flipped through a copy of *Gourmet* magazine, with its glossy photographs of elegant dishes and well-appointed dining tables. Would that her own culinary abilities were up to the standards of the magazine, she thought. Then she decided to write a letter to each of her two daughters.

Putting down the magazine, she requested some Pan Am stationery from one of the flight attendants and wrapped her feet in a blanket while the doorway, just one seat row away, remained open and the chilly breeze swept in. The older woman and young companion who had been sitting behind the Hopkinses had given up fighting that draft, being even closer to it, and had gone upstairs to the lounge. Warren Hopkins continued a chat with Jim Naik, the cruise line executive, about cameras. They were almost drowned out by an increasingly boisterous card game nearby. Joani Feathers and Jack Ridout, in 4-B and 4-A, were playing gin rummy with Terri and Bo Brusco, in 3-B and 3-A. The group members were betting imaginary money, and Feathers was now several thousand dollars ahead of everyone else. Brusco and Ridout were combining the game with a chance to talk about flying, having discovered that each was a pilot – Brusco had flown helicopters during the Vietnam War, and Ridout held a private pilot's license. Their combined conversations about flying and gin rummy became louder, getting to the point that Hopkins and Moss had to talk louder to continue their own chat.

Feathers and Ridout, both divorced, were enjoying a vacation together.[2] They had met several months earlier in San Diego when a mutual friend introduced them. Feathers was a former police officer from Phoenix who had moved to San Diego several years before and gone into interior designing. Young, blonde, and attractive, Feathers was impressed with Jack Ridout's self-confidence, of which he had plenty. Ridout ran a company he'd founded, EJR Corporation, which was involved in a variety of enterprises: land development, manufacturing plastic table tops for Jack-In-The-Box restaurants, boat parts, and others. The company's motto was "Every day you see something we make."

Ridout was a millionaire at the age of 33, and his demeanor was one that oozed self-assurance. He'd even been a hero a few years earlier, jumping into the Pacific Ocean to rescue a seven-year-old girl who'd gone into water over her head. Then there was the time he'd pulled a friend out of a dangerous rocky cove when Ridout was only 12. And there was a closet full of skeet-shooting medals and other medals for marathon boat racing. "Jack always knows what he's doing," friends said about him.

Ridout and Feathers had been relaxing together one Sunday afternoon about six weeks prior to this trip when Joani had looked up from the travel section of a newspaper and said it would be nice to take a cruise. Ridout considered the idea, then said, "You find a nice one and come up with your bucks. If you can put the deal together and get first-class cabins, A-deck cabins, fine, I'll go. I could use a vacation, anyway."

Feathers had done just that, booking them onto the "Mediterranean Highlights" cruise and getting first-class air tickets. She was thorough. She had plenty of self-confidence herself and appreciated it in others. Feathers

---

[2] This information is from interviews after the crash with Ms. Feathers and Mr. Ridout.

had been the seventh woman ever hired by the Phoenix police department to serve on its force. Pert and smart, she had worked as a radio dispatcher for the department before being accepted as a regular patrol officer. Feathers had met and married one of the officers and had a daughter from the marriage. But while she was in Phoenix, her life had been dealt a shockingly severe blow when her father was murdered by her stepmother. The woman was sent to prison, but in the succeeding year, Feathers lost her taste for police work. Although she had been raised in Phoenix, she had been born in San Diego, and as her marriage broke up, she decided to return to her birthplace. Her biological mother, who had divorced her father many years before, still lived there. Feathers had worked only a few months as an interior designer for a company called Design For Living when she was introduced to Ridout by her boss, Steve Lyman, Ridout's friend.

Feathers and Ridout were pleased to be sitting in back of the Bruscos. They, too, had noticed the relatively small number of young people on board and had quickly introduced themselves at Los Angeles International Airport. The friendship developed on the flight until the gin rummy game turned it into a loud and enthusiastic frolic, with yells of pleasure and lots of laughing. Bo Brusco's mother, Cleo, sat across the aisle from her son, occasionally watching the game and vicariously enjoying the fun.

The Bruscos were from Oregon, where Bo helped his father in a tugboat operation hauling timber from the woods of the Northwest down the Columbia River. But Roland Brusco Senior wasn't along for this cruise; he'd stayed at home while his wife, son, and daughter-in-law enjoyed themselves. They'd parted rather abruptly on the morning everyone left – when asked if he wanted to have breakfast with the family before they went to the airport, Brusco Senior turned them down because he would have had to move his car.[3]

Next to Cleo Brusco was Penny Quade, who was traveling with her mother, Margaret Ellingham, and her sister, June Ellingham. Mrs. Quade had left her husband, Dennis, back in Visalia, in Northern California, to come along with her mother, who had wanted to get away with her girls. Mrs. Ellingham's husband, James, a paving contractor, had stayed home.

---

[3] This information is from later media reports.

All three were sitting in the first-class section because Mrs. Ellingham had taken two cruises before this one with Royal Cruise Lines. As a reward for her loyal patronage, she had been given first-class air accommodations. Joani Feathers had a memory of Mrs. Ellingham enjoying the flight and the first-class accommodations. Caroline Hopkins remembered Mrs. Ellingham because of the woman's eye-catching black pantsuit. Penny Quade sat in 3-J next to the window, with her mother in back of her in 4-J, and June on the aisle in 4-H.

By coincidence, a former customer of June's was also on the plane. June worked in a savings and loan association in Visalia, and one of her customers was Marianne Jakoubek – who, at that moment, was sitting farther back in the plane with her husband, Robert. They were a friendly and interesting couple. Robert Jakoubek, 67, had recently purchased an authentic Chinese junk and was refurbishing it with the intent of sailing it down the Pacific Coast and through the Panama Canal.

Two rows behind Mrs. Ellingham and her daughter were Jim Naik and his wife, Elsie. Their location put them across the aisle and back one row from the Hopkinses. Mrs. Naik remained in her seat next to the window, 6-J, during most of the flight and during the waiting period on Tenerife. Naik tried to keep busy, moving around the cabin. He stopped to chat with the Hopkinses several times and also talked with Edward and Mary Kay Hess.[4]

At a permanent card table in the middle of first class was Beau Moss, the cruise director, who also spent the flight and waiting time chatting with passengers. While the plane waited on the taxiway at Tenerife, Moss would occasionally jump up, grab a big straw hat and put it on his head, then pick up the microphone for the airplane's public address system.

"The *Golden Odyssey* is a beautiful ship," he would coo to the passengers. "The most modern conveniences...there'll be a party with the captain tonight to welcome you all aboard." He would mug and grin his way through each announcement, leaving those around him smiling and laughing.

---

[4] Jim Naik was interviewed by Jon Ziomek after the crash.

53

Others in first class included a newlywed couple, Fred and Lottie Jamieson, in 1-A and 1-B; Mary and Richard Bowman of Cerrito, California, who sat directly in back of the Jamiesons; Ed and Mary Kay Hess, across the aisle from the Jamiesons in 1-H and 1-J; John Amador, a U.S. Immigration and Naturalization agent from Marina del Rey, California, and a friend, Harry Harper, sitting in back of the Hesses, in 2-H and 2-J.7

In back of the Hopkinses were Linda Daniel and Elsie Church, in 6-B and 6-A. Then there was a space for the door, and in back of that were Linda's parents, Jack and Patricia. Behind them, in 8-A and 8-B, were Cynthia and Maurice Magante of Sacramento, California.

Sitting with Beau Moss at the center table was Enid Tartikoff with her husband, Jordan. She was the Royal Cruise Lines booking agent.

An hour went by with no word from the captain or the airport. Naik told the Hopkinses that everything was being considered: bringing the ship to Tenerife, or even taking the entire group of cruise passengers back to Las Palmas on a ferry. But it seemed simplest just to wait until Gando Airport on Las Palmas was reopened – it really should be any minute, he was sure.

The quiet that had settled in the cabin – except for the card game up front – had given way to restless pacing, staring at the ceiling or out the window, and tempers that were beginning to fray.

Back in economy class, David Alexander, 29, was doing his best to keep busy. He was traveling alone, sitting in 30-C, on the left-hand aisle. Alexander was a microwave technician for Teledyne Corporation. A quiet, bespectacled man, his hobby was photography. He had, of course, brought along his camera for the trip and kept it around his neck. He'd stepped off of the plane and onto the staircase a few times to look around and even snapped a few shots. He took a photo of the other nearby 747, a KLM plane.5

Alexander chatted with the pleasant couple sitting immediately to his left, in 30-A and 30-B, Eddie and Lydia Ronder.6 They even gave Alexander some Tylenol tablets when the wait got to be too much for him and he

---

5 This information is from interviews with David Alexander. Years after the crash, Mr. Alexander changed his last name from Wiley to Alexander. To be consistent, this book will use David Alexander.

6 This is a pseudonym to spare surviving relatives unnecessary pain.

developed a severe headache. In front of Alexander was Norman Williams, a business college administrator traveling with a colleague from the school, Ted Younes, in 28-C. Next to Williams and closer to the window were a mother-daughter combination whose combined age looked to be more than 150 years, Alexander figured.

Across the aisle from Alexander were Grace Ellerbrock, in 30-D, and her husband, Byron, in 30-E. The Ellerbrocks had switched seats with another couple when they'd boarded in Los Angeles because they had wanted to be on the inside of the plane rather than in window seats. The Ellerbrocks were now sitting next to Albert and Florence Trumbull, in 30-F and 30-G, the older couple who had gotten married just the prior summer.

In the four seats in front of the Ellerbrocks and Trumbulls were four friends from Kelowna, British Columbia: Ted and Brenda Freeman in 29-D and 29-E, and Roy and Aya Tanemura in 29-F and 29-G. [7]

Both couples had traveled extensively, although this was their first trip together. Tanemura, 60, had a land development business in which his wife was a full partner. They were active in the Kelowna Lions' Club. Aya had been president of the Lady Lions, and Tanemura was one of the senior members of the Lions – next year, in fact, he was scheduled to move up to governor of the district Lions organization. They were also active in their local Buddhist church, where Aya again had gotten involved in leadership – she had served as president of the Kelowna Buddhist Women's Association for years. Their religion had a strong effect on them. Buddhism emphasizes internal peace, strength, and emotional equilibrium. [8]

"Someday we must part," Mrs. Tanemura had often told her husband, expecting, for some reason, that she would die first. "When that time comes, you must be brave and carry on."

Despite their many activities, the Tanemuras found time for travel. Their children – one boy and one girl – were grown and had left home. The Tanemuras had traveled to many places around the world: Asia, Europe, Hawaii, Australia, and New Zealand. Visiting with the Freemans a few months earlier, they had joked about how there wasn't much left to visit.

---

[7] The real names of the Freemans have been changed for reasons that will become apparent shortly.
[8] This information is from an interview with Roy Tanemura after the crash.

"How about a cruise?" Ted Freeman, 56, a chiropractor, had suggested. Both he and his wife were excited about the idea of going on a cruise with their friends. "A cruise in the Mediterranean," he had said. The Tanemuras were not sure. Actually, they'd been thinking of confining their travel to North America.

"I haven't seen all of Canada," Tanemura said, uncertain. "I've been as far as Montreal, but I haven't seen much of it beyond that. Maybe we should try a tour just in Canada."

But after further discussion, the Tanemuras gave in to their friends. This would be their last trip abroad for awhile, they told each other. After this one they'd stick to traveling North America.

A few rows back were Paul and Floy Heck, two more of the group from Leisure World. [9] Mr. Heck, 65, a retired machinery buyer, sat on the aisle in 34-D and carefully studied the emergency evacuation card at every opportunity. He hated flying and was afraid of the process. He studied the evacuation card with care.

"If we have trouble, go that way," he told his wife, 70, sitting next to him. He gestured at the emergency exit in front of them, on the left side of the cabin. Next to them, in 34-F and 34-G, were another husband and wife from Leisure World, Jim and Betsy Dickens. [10] The two couples were friends. It was natural, when each couple decided to take a spring vacation, to take a cruise together.

In front of Richard was Ethel Simon, the woman whose leg cramp had startled everyone when she reacted with a yell of pain. Three rows in back of Mrs. Simon and her husband, Meyer, was Jean Brown, who had booked her trip through Good Time To Travel, the travel agency she and her husband, Gordon, ran in Leisure World. Mrs. Brown sat in 37-C, next to a retired Army colonel, Mike Jones, and his wife, Dahlia. [11] While chatting with the Joneses, Mrs. Brown learned that they had retired to Petaluma, California, north of San Francisco, in 1967 when Jones retired from the Army after 30

---

[9] The Hecks originally told the author they would prefer to remain anonymous. Both have since passed away. Their information is taken from newspaper accounts and from *Just In Case* by Daniel Johnson.

[10] These names are pseudonyms.

[11] These are pseudonyms, too.

years of service.[12] Now 63, he had served on the Petaluma Planning Commission for seven years and had been chairman since 1971. Mrs. Jones, 57, was an avid gardener and a former president of the Petaluma Garden Club and Northern California District of Garden Clubs. Although they had traveled extensively during Mike Jones's career, they had never been to the Mediterranean and were thrilled about the upcoming cruise. Now they laughed about the fact that they were stuck on another island less than 100 miles from the ship.

Three rows in front of them, by the window, in 34-A and 34-B, were retired Admiral Walter Moore and his wife, Beth. They, too, were bored, which they tried to overcome by reading and chatting. With her shoes off and feet stretched in front of her, Mrs. Moore worked on her needlepoint.[13]

Two rows in front of them, in 32-A and 32-B, and sitting just one row in back of the emergency exit, were Tony and Isobel Monda, yet another retired military couple.[14] Mrs. Monda had brought some reading, a religious booklet from the church a friend of hers attended back in San Diego. It was filled with parables, homilies, and religious stories. Mrs. Monda found it mildly entertaining. She admitted to not being particularly religious – but that was probably why her friend kept sending her these pamphlets, she figured with a smile. She and her husband had been almost out the door of their home the previous day, Saturday, on their way to the airport when she had looked around for something to read on the plane. Her eyes fell on the booklet on a coffee table, and she picked it up and put it in her purse. Actually, Tony ought to be the one reading it, she thought, looking at him next to her. He's the religious one in the family.

Which indeed he was. The origin of his devotion went back to an incident in World War II, when Monda was a young sergeant leading a squad of riflemen in combat near the German-Belgian border in late 1944. They had worked their way through a small town, firing at the retreating Germans. When Monda's troops finished clearing the town, they began

---

[12] This information is from interviews and correspondence with Jean and Gordon Brown.
[13] This information is from an interview and correspondence with Beth Moore.
[14] This information is from an interview and correspondence with the Mondas.

regrouping to rejoin their company – just as the Germans began lobbing mortar shells into the middle of the troops.

Monda took cover under a nearby jeep, where he stayed while the barrage continued. The mortar shells crunched into the earth with flat, hard explosions. Fragments from one shell blasted into Monda's chest, but they were so tiny and his own tension was so great that he didn't notice the wound until the barrage was over and the troops were again moving. Looking down at his shirt, Monda was shocked to find that the khaki had turned red from his blood oozing through the material.

Being a rifleman in an infantry company, Monda didn't need any reminders of the fragility of his mortality. But the sight of his own blood stirred a resolve in him that day in Belgium as he reached out for a larger meaning for the miserable nightmare he was struggling through.

"This is it, boy," he told himself. "If I ever come out of this war alive, I'm going to church every Sunday for the rest of my life."

He survived that war and the next one, too – the Korean conflict – and he kept his pledge. Every single Sunday, even while in the Army, Monda managed to find a priest. Every single week for 32 and a half years.

Until today.

The Mondas had now been on the airplane for more than 13 hours. It was getting to be late Sunday afternoon, local time. Monda couldn't go to church on the plane, obviously. Perhaps he could find a priest on board the ship. After having kept his vow fighting his way through two terrible wars, Monda had no intention of breaking it when he was on vacation.

CHAPTER 7

The 235 passengers from the KLM 747 were allowed about two hours inside the terminal building at Los Rodeos Airport before they had to return to their airplane. Some headed for the refreshment counter; others browsed through the souvenir and magazine displays. Still others just strolled through the building and struck up conversations with passengers from other flights.

When the passengers had unloaded at the terminal from their mini-buses, they had been given transit passes to expedite their reboarding later. One of the people handed such a pass was Robina Monique van Lanschot, 25, a hostess for Holland International, the agency that had chartered the plane.

Miss van Lanschot was about to become an unusual statistic. She made a seemingly innocuous decision that would, in just minutes, save her life. And then it would bring her nightmares and notoriety.

What Miss van Lanschot did was to decide not to get back on board the KLM plane. She had a home on Tenerife, for one thing. She had a boyfriend, Paul Wessels, on Tenerife whom she wanted to visit. Also, as a hostess for Holland International, much of her work was here on the island of Tenerife. Although she was supposed to accompany the flight to Las Palmas, she thought it would be simpler to have a friend send her luggage back from Las Palmas while she remained on Tenerife.

Miss van Lanschot had been strolling through the terminal building before deciding on her course of action. She turned around, walked back to the flight attendant who was issuing transit passes, and handed hers in. Along the way, she asked another of the Holland International hostesses, Yvonne Wessels (sister of van Lanschot's boyfriend), to join her – but Yvonne decided to get back on board the plane.[1]

So Miss van Lanschot then tracked down Nicole Kloet, another of the Holland International hostesses on the flight, and asked Miss Kloet to send her luggage from Las Palmas. Miss Kloet agreed to do so. Then Miss van Lanschot went to a telephone and called her boyfriend. By 4 p.m., when everyone else was reboarding the KLM plane, the two of them were far away.

---

[1] Forty years after the crash, Robina van Lanschot recalled these details in an interview in the *El Mundo* newspaper: "Robina: I was wondering: Why am I not dead?" by Ana Maria Ortiz, March 26, 2017. Here's the link: http://www.elmundo.es/cronica/2017/03/26/58d54e9522601d58468b45e4. html. Ms. Lanschot eventually married Paul Wessels and raised three children.

CHAPTER 8

Sitting inside a stationary airplane for hours on end is a contradiction in concepts. It negates the need for the airplane. Why sit in an unmoving transportation device when you can do your waiting more comfortably elsewhere?

By 4 p.m. at Los Rodeos, irritation was rising in the Pan American plane. Passengers were pacing the aisles or flipping through already well-thumbed magazines, or talking in increasingly cranky tones with other passengers, or napping fitfully, or staring at the ceiling. Even the card game in first class had broken up.

Beau Moss was doing his best to divert everyone. He circulated among the passengers, periodically donning his straw hat, then using the public address microphone to talk cheerily of the coming cruise. "Maybe they'll bring the ship over here to Santa Cruz de Tenerife," he suggested at one point. The idea had been quickly rejected by cruise officials, though, because Las Palmas was on the far side of Grand Canary Island, and the sailing time between the ports of Las Palmas and Santa Cruz de Tenerife was nearly three hours.

So the waiting went on. The last bags of peanuts from the plane's galley were distributed, as were the remaining sandwiches and snacks. The flight attendants served drinks – and more drinks. A number of passengers drank beer, soda water, pop, anything, out of boredom, and as a result, the flight attendants developed a minor problem, but one that increased the irritation level even more: an ice cube shortage. Everyone was rationed to one cube per glass.

Caroline Hopkins continued her letters to her daughters, filling them with every detail of the day's events.

Aboard the KLM plane, the crew didn't have to contend with restless passengers. But close to 4 p.m., everyone who had visited the terminal was reversing the process by which they had gotten off: waiting at the terminal for one of the minibuses and then being shuttled back to the base of the stairway leading up to the jet's doorway. But the reboarding was delayed even more because two of the passengers' children couldn't at first be found – they'd wandered through the terminal on their own before KLM staff members and the parents tracked them down.

While the KLM passengers strolled through the airport, Captain van Zanten and his crew had waited patiently in the KLM cockpit for news from Las Palmas. It had not come. From the cockpit windows, van Zanten could easily see the heavy clouds and wisps of fog that were moving in, rolling across the hills around the airport. More problems.

Sometime after 3 p.m., van Zanten left the cockpit and hiked over to the terminal building's operations room. From there, he called KLM's operations headquarters in Holland and reminded the officials of his crew's schedule problems. They'd all been on duty for seven hours at this point, he told them. The operations officials told him there'd be no problem if he could get off the ground in the next hour or so. If not, van Zanten should call back and something else might have to be arranged – like sending an entire new crew to Tenerife.

Walking back to his plane, van Zanten was surely concerned about the time problem, regardless of the assurances from KLM operations. Van Zanten was described later by a colleague as "a serious and introverted individual but with an open-hearted and friendly disposition," and the serious side of his personality may have been starting to dominate as the time problem got worse.[1] He had more than 200 passengers who wanted to start their vacations (not counting the newly departed Robina van Lanschot)

---

[1] "Disasters in the Air," by Jan Bartelski, quoted on Wikipedia's "Jacob Veldhuyzen van Zanten" page. The author was a professional acquaintance of van Zanten.

and another load of passengers waiting at Las Palmas who wanted to get back to their lives in Amsterdam. And he wanted to get back himself – to his wife and two children in Sassenheim. His crew members were all married; they had families they expected to see tonight in time for dinner. Instead, everyone, including the passengers, was facing the possibility of a night in a hotel on Tenerife.

Five of the nine flight attendants aboard were standby flight attendants, which meant that they were only called in occasionally to fill in for the regular attendants. So they were all in a hurry to get back home to their families, too: Mrs. M. Tom-Karsebloom, 35, of van Zanten's hometown of Sassenheim; Mrs. M. Viergever-Drent, 29; Mrs. J. Schuurmans-Timmermans; Mrs. W. Keulen, 20; and Mrs. J. van Staveren-Marechal, 32.

Mrs. Marechal was even standing in for a stand-in. According to later Dutch media reports, a friend and fellow attendant had been asked to take the place of another attendant on this trip, but, after initially agreeing, had canceled because she wanted to stay home with a sick child. So Mrs. Marechal went in her place. Dutch media reports stated after the crash that the friend who had stayed home with a sick child was afraid to answer her phone because she feared it was KLM calling her back to duty.

And there were the passengers. They all would be late in getting to their destinations, and that would foul up hotel reservations. Then the passengers would blame the airline for cheating them out of a few hours on the beach, or shopping, or doing whatever else they were going to do at the onset of their vacations.

"From the people who made punctuality possible." Captain van Zanten surely didn't need reminding of that right now.

By 4 p.m., the worrying must have stepped up significantly. Perhaps van Zanten was thinking about what he could do to expedite things. What if they finally did take off, got back to Las Palmas, and there was another delay of some kind? They'd used up quite a bit of fuel on the run down from Amsterdam. The tanks had enough fuel to get the plane back to Amsterdam, but what if there were more delays and holding patterns – or, the worst possible situation, if Amsterdam's weather was so bad they had to go to an alternate airport?

Captain van Zanten decided to take an action that might save time later. He would refuel right now, while they were sitting and doing nothing anyway. He radioed the tower to request it. The operation would take about 30 minutes, he figured.

Shortly later, passengers sitting on the left side of the Pan Am plane saw several gasoline trucks driving down the taxiway apron to the KLM plane.

The refueling operation began. Anyone could understand the thinking that led up to this decision to refuel. Perhaps, if there were any criticism of the decision, it could be that van Zanten didn't make the decision soon enough. If he'd decided to tank up as soon as he had landed, the refueling operation would have been completed by now. But then again, everyone had originally thought the wait at Tenerife would be a short one.

At any rate, yet another painful coincidence now happened. Only a few minutes after the refueling began, van Zanten got word from the control tower that Las Palmas's Gando Airport had reopened. Despite a careful search, no second bomb had been found, and the terminal had been cleaned up. Airlines could now resume their regular schedules. There may have been a round of frustrated profanity in the KLM cockpit at that point. Van Zanten, having already started the refueling operation, decided to continue it and just hope that the weather would remain good enough to get off the ground when they were finished.

When Captain Grubbs and the Pan Am crew got the news that Las Palmas was open, they immediately radioed the ground controller in Tenerife's control tower, Fernando Hernandez-Abad Gonzalez, for permission to start their engines.[2] Hernandez-Abad had bad news for the Pan Am crew: KLM was now refueling, and its position on the taxiway apron was blocking Clipper *Victor*. The taxiway, not wide enough for a 747 to turn around, was jammed with more than half a dozen airplanes in front and in back of both 747s. There was only one way to go – forward, past the terminal building to the northwest end of the taxiway, then onto the runway apron, and finally onto the runway.

As soon as KLM left, anyway.

---

[2] The Spanish custom of two surnames is shortened to the first surname on second reference. Thus, Fernando Hernandez-Abad Gonzales will be referred to as Hernandez-Abad.

Grubbs grabbed his microphone and called the KLM cockpit. "How much longer are you going to be with that refueling?" he said abruptly.

The question was audible on the KLM cockpit radio because both airplanes were using the same frequency, 118.7 megahertz.

"About twenty minutes," van Zanten answered.

"Pan Am, did you copy?"[3] the ground traffic controller, Hernandez-Abad, asked the Pan Am crew on the same radio frequency.

They acknowledged van Zanten's answer, but Grubbs, impatient, wasn't about to accept that as the only solution. He sent his first officer, Robert Bragg, and Flight Engineer George Warns out of the plane to pace off the clearance alongside KLM in order to determine if the Pan Am plane could squeeze past the KLM jet on the taxiway. They needed a lot of room – about 140 feet, allowing for the wheels and the wing on one side. Grubbs had no intention of sitting around this airport any longer than he had to. Besides, he could see for himself that the weather was getting worse. There was occasional light rain plopping down on the windshield now, in addition to the increasing fog.

The two came back in five minutes. Couldn't do it, they said, easing themselves back into their cockpit seats. They were less than 20 feet short – but short, nonetheless. If the Pan Am crew tried the maneuver, they'd risk driving their 340-ton vehicle onto the soft dirt and grass adjacent to the taxiway and then not being able to get back onto the concrete.

So, they waited. Meanwhile, smaller planes in back of KLM 4805 did have enough room to squeeze by, and several of them did just that – moving along the taxiway past KLM, past the terminal to the end of the taxiway, then taxiing down the runway.

Grubbs had another idea, perhaps recalling how interested Caroline Hopkins had been during her peek inside the cockpit the previous evening in New York. He announced over the loudspeaker that anyone who was interested could come up and have a look at the cockpit. The flight attendants would help maintain order among those who wanted a quick mini-tour. It was a fun idea, and a lot of people took Grubbs up on it,

---

[3] Asking someone if they "copy" a message is shorthand in official radio lingo. The person is being asked if they understood the message.

creating a "people jam" that extended through first class and up the lounge stairway, through the lounge and into the cockpit. Because the only way up to the cockpit was also the only way down, the jam was in two directions. A number of people from the middle and rear of the plane used the first-class washrooms while they were waiting to see the cockpit, which then made it more difficult for those in the front of the plane to use their assigned toilets.

At this point in the wait – shortly past 4:30 p.m. – the cockpit voice recorder transcripts begin for the conversations in each cockpit. While other planes began their taxiing and takeoffs, the two jumbo jets sat. Aboard both the KLM and Pan Am planes, the crews were chatting – among themselves on the Dutch plane, and to the visiting passengers on the Pan Am plane.

Judging by the remarks, the mood in the Dutch cockpit wasn't as relaxed as it was in Clipper 1736. They talked shop – and they talked about the weather.

"This island is a lot prettier than all of Las Palmas," First Officer Klass Meurs offered idly. He spoke in his native Dutch.

"What I saw of it, yes," someone else observed dryly. Another sarcastic voice added, "And always nice weather." From their vantage point, the weather was obviously terrible.

"Nice in the sunshine," Meurs replied, still trying to be pleasant. Others muttered "Ja" ["Yes"] in agreement, temporarily giving up on their wisecracks.

Van Zanten was familiar with the island's odd weather conditions, as influenced by the dominant mountain, Pico de Teide. "Yes, on the south side the sun shines, guaranteed," he noted.

Second Officer Willem Schreuder, the flight engineer, interrupted to announce how the refueling was doing. "Eight tons more [to go], guys," he said.

They started swapping stories of bad-weather flights they'd had in the past. Captain van Zanten told his story first.

"We went into Shannon [Ireland]. It was rather shitty weather," he said bluntly to begin his anecdote. The others exchanged murmurs of recognition. "We saw the runway at two hundred feet or so," he continued, meaning that the runway hadn't become visible through the fog until the plane was only 200 feet above it. The pilot of the next plane in, using a superior tone that thoroughly irritated van Zanten, had told the tower that "contrary to KLM," he could see the runway much sooner. "Shithead," the captain now said, with dismissive irritation.

"At a hundred and fifty feet?" someone else cracked.

"Yes, no, much sooner than that," Van Zanten said, continuing the story. Then he delivered his punch line. "Well, no wonder, man," he radioed back to the following plane, "we burned quite a big hole for you in it [the fog]."

"Ja," Meurs answered, acknowledging the righteous attitude his pilot was feeling.

"'Contrary to KLM,'" Van Zanten repeated in English, mocking the unnamed pilot. Another voice said only, "Limey," a derogatory suggestion that the pilot of the other jet must have been British.

They continued their conversation, talking about their own plane and its flight plan as the minutes ticked on.

Back in the Pan Am cockpit, the crew was chatting with the passengers who stood for a few moments in the small enclosure. Patiently, Grubbs explained to each one about the delay at La Palmas.

"It wasn't much fun coming in here, was it?" one passenger asked.

"Well, you know, we didn't know why we had to land, except they just ordered us down," Grubbs answered. "We told them that we could hold and wait until they, ah, if we, hoped that the field would open like it actually did because we had plenty of fuel." His explanation, a bit confusing, was to say that he'd have rather put the Pan Am plane in a holding pattern over Las Palmas because his jet had plenty of fuel.

"We had no idea how long it would be," one passenger said.

"This is the explosion on the plane?" said another passenger, who had misunderstood the location of the explosion.

"No, it was an explosion in the terminal over there," Grubbs answered, "and, ah, I suspect with the unstable, ah, political situation in the motherland over there that they were just a little edgy. And they ordered everybody...they just ordered us out of the air."

A stream of passengers continued into the cockpit, exchanging a sentence or two with the crew before moving back out. "You know, I can congratulate you folks, that you kept your cool and got us all in," one said.

Grubbs laughed. "I guess," he acknowledged modestly, then commented, a bit slyly, "Well, gee, you know we thought we would be gone an hour ago, but all of a sudden, he's got two big truckloads of gas," a reference to KLM. "But we did talk to him, and he said in a half an hour he'd be gone, and we're gonna be right behind him."

"I'll be derned," the passenger answered. "How long did it take you to learn all of this?"

"Oh, about a week," Grubbs answered, and the cockpit filled with laughter. Flight engineer Warns couldn't resist running with the joke, too. "It was 10 days, wasn't it?" he added. "I was a slow learner." They all chuckled again.

"Thank you all; it was a new experience," said another passenger of his peek at the cockpit.

"Thank *you*," Grubbs replied, and then, once again, went into his explanation. "If they would have let us circle at, about three times up there... we had plenty of fuel to do it and requested permission, but they said, 'Nope. Land.'"

In the middle of this general patter, the crew was joined in the cockpit by two more Pan Am employees who had flown specially from Las Palmas. Just as Holland International's Robina van Lanschot had made an impulsive decision that would remove her from the events of this afternoon, these two men took seemingly insignificant actions that put them right in the middle of what was about to happen.

The two were Juan Murillo and John Cooper. Murillo was Pan Am's Madrid operations supervisor, in charge of all charter flights. He and Cooper, a Pan Am mechanic from England, had flown to Las Palmas in order to meet Clipper 1736's expected arrival, and they would be in charge of servicing the plane for its return trip. In fact, they were in the operations room at Gando Airport when the bomb went off. After finding out what had happened, Murillo decided to fly to Tenerife to meet the Pan Am plane, and then hop a ride on it back to Las Palmas. Cooper joined him.

At 4 p.m. they left Las Palmas on an Iberia turboprop plane, just when Gando Airport was reopening. At 4:25 p.m., they landed at Tenerife and were put on a specially assigned minibus, then taken straight from their plane to Clipper 1736. Hooked into the plane's communications system via headset while standing outside the plane, Cooper talked to the cockpit crew.

Grubbs, continuing his chatting with the passengers, turned to those standing in the cockpit to say, "They've sent some people since we've been here; they've flown over on another carrier to see if they could help us get out...the Pan American people from Las Palmas...he can tell us what really happened when he gets on board." There was a friendly chuckle all around.

Then he continued his verbal tour of the cockpit for the passengers, pointing out the various systems and what they were for, explaining how the controls worked to turn the plane. He even used the KLM nearby as a model to point out the 747's fifth engine, which sits high up on the tail. It's used to provide electrical power to the interior of the plane while it is on the ground.

Cooper and Murillo by now had climbed into the plane but had to wait for a few minutes in the first-class lounge because of the crush of passengers trying to get a look at the cockpit. First Officer Bragg stepped outside the cockpit to greet them, while Grubbs went on with his tour. A passenger asked what had happened to the other planes that had been parked nearby. Grubbs told him, "They were smaller, so they could get by him [they could slide past the KLM without driving off the taxiway], but we, unfortunately, are both big ones." They'd have to wait until the KLM jet was finished refueling, he said. His chatter was peppered with occasional references to KLM and the fact that it was holding up their flight's departure.

"We only have to go fifty-four miles, if we ever get started here," he sighed at one point. (The actual flight miles totaled 59.)

"Well, what happened over there in the other airport?" another passenger wanted to know.

With the patience of a saint, Grubbs again went through his explanation. "The only information we got was an explosion in the air terminal there," he repeated. "And they were afraid of another one, and 'cause we told 'em we had plenty of fuel, we asked them if we couldn't circle there...."

Back in the KLM cockpit, the conversation had turned to the subject of airline regulations about overtime. The crew started figuring when they would get out of La Palmas for the return to Amsterdam.

"Half an hour on the ground more, then one hour over there [at Las Palmas], including one hour ground time," Meurs, the first officer, calculated. "Then you're gone at eight o'clock."

"Right," van Zanten acknowledged. Someone else then muttered, "But that means nothing."

It turned out there was confusion about how much active-duty time was actually permitted under the airline's rule. The crew members started wondering if they were already playing with the fates.

"I'll look out for myself," van Zanten said. "No messing around with me."

Another crew member suggested sarcastically that when they finally got back to Amsterdam, "You phone [Hans] Raben [the director-general of civil aviation in the Netherlands at the time]. Then you can tell [him] in person" that the flight had been late.

Meurs had an anecdote to tell. He recalled flying with a fellow KLM pilot on a freighter flight from Amsterdam to New York. They had "delay and delay at Schiphol," the Amsterdam airport, before finally departing.

"Eventually we went through to Montreal," Meurs related. "We had eighteen hours, fifty-four minutes of flight time. We thought we could go to nineteen hours."

"Nineteen hours," another voice repeated.

"Later on, this appeared not to be true because you can only go nineteen hours if you have a rest seat in the back. We had a freighter, and it was not there."

There was silence as they all digested this bit of information.

"Well, they obviously forgave us," Meurs continued.

Captain van Zanten started chuckling at the idea that Meurs had been only six minutes under the maximum duty time. "Eighteen hours, fifty-four," he repeated.

"But what are the repercussions if you…" Schreuder asked, his voice trailing off.

"You'll face the judge," a voice said. KLM's pilot overtime rules had been codified into Dutch law.

"Definitely," another voice added.

"Of course," the captain noted, "you cannot think you are also going to get some..." the punishment wasn't spoken out loud: jail time.

"Yes," Schreuder added, picking up the thread. "Then you are hanged from the highest tree."

"Ja, ja, ja, ja," Meurs agreed quickly.

"And of course you can forget the company backing you," van Zanten said.

"Don't you know it," Schreuder stated. The tone of the conversation had turned unpleasant.

"Is it a question of fines or is it a question of prison?" Schreuder asked, after a moment.

Meurs had become certain. "Yes, that would mean imprisonment," he said.

Van Zanten was not quite so sure. "At any rate it would mean revocation of your license for quite a while, and that means money," he commented.

"Not for me," Meurs said tellingly, "because the BOM [basic operating manual for the airline] states I have to obey captain's orders first...."

"Yes, yes, now, I won't give you such an order," van Zanten said with reassurance. He fully intended to get his crew back to Amsterdam before any hassles about their extra duty time.

Their conversation trailed off. A flight attendant then came into the cockpit. Meurs asked, "Is that movie finished downstairs or not?" The passengers had been watching a film after they reboarded. "Yes, it was finished quite a while ago," was the answer.

There was more silence, and then van Zanten noted they were almost finished with the refueling. "Fifteen hundred liters more," he observed.

The flight attendant was still in the cockpit. "Are you still tanking?" she asked. "Yes, fifteen hundred liters more," Schreuder repeated.

"We are not quite there yet," van Zanten remarked.

There was more silence, then one of them, heaving a sigh, and possibly looking out the window at the fog, commented, "Goddamn, I can do without Las Palmas."

They chatted idly a little more before Schreuder finally announced, "The fuel is in." An airport employee stepped into the cockpit to announce the same thing. "Goodbye," he said, using English.

"Thank you," he was told.

Captain van Zanten chuckled. "We hope we go now," he said, also in English.

"Sorry you've been delayed," the employee said.

"No, it is okay, is not your fault. Thank you very much, you did a good job," Van Zanten told him politely.

"Nothing could be done," the employee said about the delay. After an exchange of farewells, he left the cockpit and the crew began preparing to get underway. They kept talking as they started to check their equipment. One of them said there was half an hour of holding time at Las Palmas. They complained to one another again about the weather, and the possibility of being stuck either on Tenerife or in Las Palmas. If they couldn't land at Las Palmas – assuming the weather was the same as on Tenerife – they might have to go to Casablanca, one suggested, or simply back to Amsterdam, without ever getting the passengers to their vacation spot.

Then they began their crew briefing:

"Take off on Runway Three-zero, normal crew coordinates," van Zanten began, reverting to English, the official language of international aviation. The others listened intently as their work began again.

Back in the Pan Am cockpit, crew members were still gabbing among themselves and making an occasional crack about KLM holding them up because of its refueling. That got the crew talking about the supersonic Concorde jet, which – according to Warns, the engineer – burned up about 4,200 gallons of fuel an hour, a staggering rate that was about twice that of a Boeing 747. At that time – 1977 – the supersonic Concorde had been in commercial jet service for only about one year.[4]

---

[4] Development and use of the Concorde, a British-French cooperative project, ended in 2003. The plane traveled at up to twice the speed of sound, or about 1,500 miles an hour. It could fly from London to New York and land at a New York time earlier than the London time when it had departed. One Concorde crashed in 2000, killing 100 passengers and nine crew members. The then-Soviet Union also used a supersonic jet, the Tupelov 144, for passenger and cargo travel, but after several crashes, the Tupelov 144s were taken out of service sooner than the Concorde.

"I haven't been on it yet. It's a very small airplane," Warns commented. "It could cruise way above fifty thousand [feet]."

"They only carry a third the people" of a jumbo jet, Grubbs noted.

"Yeah, I know, it's just all fuel," someone else remarked.

"Right where you're standing now, in a Concorde you couldn't stand up [straight]; you'd be like this," Warns said, apparently hunching over. He started a comparison. "When you walk into the door and head for the cockpit…"

"…You'd be on your knees the whole way," Grubbs finished, generating a laugh.

"You know Mayor Beame?" Warns continued, referring to the then-mayor of New York City, a diminutive man. "It's built for him. Fits old Abe." The remark brought another round of laughter.

The passengers kept coming in. One remarked jocularly, keeping the good mood going, "This has been a good trip, especially [because] it hasn't been rough for the last four hours," a gentle tease about them sitting on the ground for so long.

Grubbs chuckled, and then heaved a sigh. "I'm 'bout ready for the sack," he said idly. "Yeah," Warns grunted in agreement.

By now it was 10 minutes before five o'clock. In the KLM plane, Captain van Zanten had completed his refueling and was about to start his engines. However, the pilot of a Sterling Airways flight then interrupted their conversation on the ground controller's radio frequency.

"Sterling one-one-zero will be ready to start in 10 minutes," the pilot told the ground controller, Fernando Hernandez-Abad Gonzales.

"Ah-ha, that's him, he's going to be ready to start in ten minutes," Grubbs said, catching only the latter part of the radio transmission and thinking the news was about KLM.

"Good," someone said.

"Let's see where he's going," Grubbs said. Because of KLM's lengthy refueling, Grubbs was under the impression that van Zanten might be flying straight back to Amsterdam.

"Tenerife, KLM Four-eight-zero-five is ready to start," Captain van Zanten then radioed to Hernandez-Abad.

"Ah-ha, he's ready," Grubbs said, pleased.

Hernandez-Abad, in the control tower, wasn't sure which plane had just called him.

"Station calling to report," he responded – a shorthand way of asking which plane had called him. The KLM crew member – possibly Meurs – stated again: "KLM Four-eight-zero-five for Las Palmas, ready to start."

Hernandez-Abad heard him that time. "Roger, Four-eight-oh-five, you are cleared to start."

"Thank you very much," Meurs radioed back politely.

Bragg and his Pan Am crew wasted not a moment.

"And Clipper one-seven-three-six, ready to start," Grubbs radioed to the tower seconds after KLM's transmission.

"Roger, one-seven-three-six. Ah...stand by," Hernandez-Abad answered.

"Okay," Grubbs acknowledged. They greeted one more passenger, Charlotte Baldwin of Washington, D.C., a travel agent, who introduced herself to the crew while a flight attendant passed around cups of coffee. After quick introductions, Baldwin left the cockpit and the crew began its prestart checklist, making sure the plane's computer guidance system was set properly. They reviewed other checkpoints, such as making sure the "No Smoking" and seatbelt warning lights had been turned on.

Someone, apparently the flight attendant who had delivered the coffee, gazed out the cockpit window. "Is it raining out there?" she asked. "Is that rain or fog?"

Grubbs obediently flipped on the windshield wipers, only to see very little of the moisture removed. "That's fog," he said.

In the passenger cabin, purser Dorothy Kelly picked up the public address system microphone. "Ladies and gentlemen, you will notice that the captain has turned on the 'No Smoking' sign at this time. Please refrain from smoking. Please make sure that your seat belts are fastened, your tray tables are closed, and your hand-carried luggage will be stowed beneath the seat in front of you...."

Back in the middle of the economy section, Lydia Ronder turned to David Alexander and asked if he wanted to switch to her window seat before the plane took off so that he could get a few more photos. No,

Photo courtesy of David Alexander

Pan Am passenger David Alexander took this photo from the open doorway of his plane just minutes before KLM – seen two jets ahead – and Pan Am were given permission to start their engines and begin taxiing.

thanks, he replied. The fog was too heavy for photos just then. His decision to remain in his aisle seat may have saved his life.

In first class, Caroline Hopkins finished the letter to her daughters. "At last," she wrote. "We're moving."

Back on Grand Canary Island, aboard the *Golden Odyssey*, the captain of the ship had gotten a telephone call from the airport. The Pan Am jet would be taking off soon, he was told. Gordon Brown got the word from the captain, and with several escorts from the ship, they all hurried down the gangplank and jumped in a cab. Then they sped out to Gando Airport to wait for the arrival of the plane.

CHAPTER 9

B y 4:50 p.m., visibility on the runway had fallen to 2,000 meters – not quite two-thirds of the runway's length. With the temperature at a humid 50 degrees Fahrenheit, the fog was increasing by the minute. Only 12 minutes later, by 5:02 p.m., visibility had dropped all the way down to 300 meters – the minimum required for international takeoff clearance. But just prior to that, the fog had been blowing in and out, first blocking the views of the nearby hills, then clearing enough that distant homes on the hillsides could be seen.

Refueling of KLM 4805 was finished at 4:54 p.m. local time, with the jet taking on 55,000 liters of fuel, or about 15,000 gallons. This made Captain van Zanten's plane about 50 tons heavier – a small but eternally significant increase of about 15 percent. A heavier plane requires more runway to take off, as well as more speed. And yet another painful coincidence fell into place this day.

Van Zanten had his first officer, Klass Meurs, radio the control tower for permission to start engines and begin taxiing. Meurs did so, receiving instructions to move past the terminal building to the end of the taxi apron and then swing around onto the runway. KLM 4805 followed the instructions, doing as other jets had done a few minutes before. Their instructions were to enter the runway going southeast, taxi all the way down to its end, turn around and then take off in the opposite direction they'd taxied. Four smaller jets had already done exactly that after Gando Airport had been reopened. The first one had probably already landed at Gando by now, after the short hop from one island to another.

The KLM plane swung slowly around the end of the apron, then onto the runway, heading down the asphalt.

As KLM taxied past the terminal building – moving in the opposite direction it had faced while sitting near the building – some of those on board may have given a friendly wave or two in the general direction of the terminal. They'd had a couple of hours of wandering around inside the building to chat with some of the other passengers or local employees, making a casual acquaintance or two.

With the departure of Robina van Lanschot, who had decided to remain on Tenerife, the passenger count on KLM 4805 had been reduced to 234, with the crew total remaining at 14. Among the passengers were six babies-in-arms, 25 small children, and 14 teenagers. The rest were adults. Most of the passengers were Dutch, but there were also four Americans aboard: Mrs. Terry Twist and her infant girl, Melissa; and Don and Jane Gilles, all of Rochester, New York. The adults were all employed in Amsterdam.

How does someone react after waiting a long time for something to happen and finally getting what they have been waiting for? A gradual easing of the tension, the shoulders relaxing as people lean back. The earlier irritation, following the lengthy delay, is defused.

From the terminal building, watching the KLM jet as it taxied by was Manuel Fandiño, a Spanish freelance photographer who was vacationing on Tenerife but had decided to hang around the airport that afternoon. He was curious about KLM 4805 and Pan Am 1736, never having seen a 747 before. So he watched both planes from the terminal's big glass windows. He had his camera with him.

At 4:58.14 p.m. (14 seconds after 4:58), First Officer Meurs radioed the control tower to remind the traffic controller that, in order to take off, KLM would have to make a tricky 180-degree turn when it reached the end of the runway. For the jumbo jet, that would not be easy. The maneuver is called a "backtrack."

"Approach [a term for the controller], KLM Four-eight-zero-five on the ground in Tenerife," Meurs said, by way of identification. "KLM...

ah…Four-eight-zero-five, roger," the air traffic controller, Fernando Azcunaga, acknowledged. At this point in the process, Azcunaga had taken over for the ground controller, Fernando Hernandez-Abad Gonzales.

"We require backtrack on one-two for takeoff Runway Three-zero," Meurs said.

That sentence, confusing to the general public, was verbal shorthand among these flying professionals. When Meurs said that his plane would have to do a backtrack on "one-two for takeoff Runway Three-zero," he was talking about a maneuver on the same runway. The numerical designation for a runway changes based on the direction a plane is going on that runway. Runways are designated by degrees of the compass, so Runway One-two is 120 degrees around the compass from due north. Therefore, following the compass in a clockwise direction, 120 degrees points in an east-southeast direction. Runway Three-zero is 300 degrees on the compass, which is the opposite of east-southeast – it's west-northwest. The KLM plane was taxiing east-southeast but would reach the end of the runway, do its backtrack by turning around and reversing its direction, and then take off heading west-northwest.

"Okay, Four-eight-zero-five," Azcunaga acknowledged. "Taxi…" he paused briefly to consider how the jet might avoid the backtrack maneuver, then continued, "…to the holding position Runway Three-zero, taxi into the runway, and…ah…leave runway third to your left."

Shorthand again. This time, the controller, trying to help the pilots, was telling KLM 4805 to turn off the runway onto the third taxiway turnoff.

Each of the taxiway turnoffs connects the taxiway with the runway. By turning off the main runway onto the taxiway, KLM 4805 could taxi down the taxiway instead of the runway, then swing onto the runway with a bigger arc. The swooping turn would be an easier maneuver than coming to a complete standstill and then turning the plane around in an about-face.

In the cockpit, the crew acknowedged the controller's suggestion but immediately got confused about which turnoff he had told them to take. "Roger, sir, entering the runway at this time and the first taxiway we, we got off the runway again for the beginning of Runway Three-zero," Meurs radioed back to the tower.

The controller heard Meurs say "first" instead of his instruction to take the "third" turnoff. Instead of correcting the misunderstanding, he returned to his original instruction.

"Okay, KLM eight-zero...ah, correction...Four-eight-zero-five. Taxi straight ahead...ah...for the runway and...make...ah...backtrack."

Why Azcunaga didn't correct the taxiway turnoff number in his conversation with the KLM crew isn't known. Perhaps he thought it would be too complicated to get that straightened out. Also, from where he was positioned, the fog may have made it impossible to see if the third turnoff was cleared of airplanes.

The weather was getting worse by the minute. That made things unpleasant enough. But van Zanten was also getting testy. There would be little wonder if First Officer Meurs found the situation uncomfortable: bad weather plus a crabby boss sitting three feet to his left.

Van Zanten was about to demonstrate his distraction. The KLM cockpit had radioed to the control tower that it had swung onto the runway and was heading down Runway One-two, which had been acknowledged by the tower. Then, just 24 seconds after the KLM jet had been told, first, to get off the runway at the *third* exit, then *not* to do that, van Zanten asked the tower if he was supposed to turn off the runway at the *first* exit.

"Approach [the pilot's designation for the control tower], you want us to turn left at Charlie One taxiway, Charlie One?" van Zanten asked in his transmission. "Charlie One" was aviation terminology referring to the C-1 exit from the runway.

"Negative, negative," the controller repeated. "Taxi straight ahead... ah...up to the end of the runway and make backtrack." The controller could now hear for himself that the KLM crew seemed distracted.

The order was accepted again by KLM. "Okay, sir," came the response at 4:59.39. This exchange seemed to sink in, and there was silence as the KLM plane continued to move slowly, at about six miles an hour, down the runway. It was now well past the terminal building.

Looking out her passenger window on the left side of the Pan Am plane, Caroline Hopkins and her husband, Warren – and others sitting on the jet's left side – could see the KLM jet taxi slowly by, its green "KLM" letters visible on the tail through the fog.

At almost exactly 5:00 p.m., Pan Am Clipper 1736 was given permission to start its engines and contact the tower for taxiing instructions. The four giant Pratt and Whitney engines – each so big it could hold a motorboat – whined into life, one by one, their high-pitched screams cutting through the foggy air.

"Tenerife, the Clipper One-seven-three-six," First Officer Robert Bragg said into his radio to the control tower, by way of identifying the jet he represented.

"Clipper One-seven-three-six, Tenerife," replied Azcunaga, the same controller who was guiding KLM 4805.

Again, this was aviation shorthand. Bragg asked for the attention of the control tower by stating the airport name first: "Tenerife." Then he followed with who was talking to the controller: the crew in Pan Am Clipper 1736. The controller responded the same way. He first identified the aircraft to which he was speaking – "Clipper One-seven-three-six" – followed by his own identification, the Tenerife control tower.

"Ah…we were instructed to contact you and also to taxi down the runway. Is that correct?" Bragg asked.

"Affirmative," the controller responded. "Taxi into the runway and… ah…leave the runway, third, third to your left."

Once again, the controller was going to try to divert a plane onto the third turnoff. This would clear the runway for KLM 4805's takeoff, and also make it easier for Clipper 1736 to make the big turn from the end of the taxiway onto the runway.

"Third to the left," Bragg acknowledged. "Okay."

And at 5:02.16 p.m. local time, Pan American World Airways Clipper 1736 was on its way, too.

CHAPTER 10

Yet another of the painful ironies of this day was that instructions which at first sounded simple became, on later examination, subject to several interpretations. The air traffic controller had specifically told KLM to turn off the runway at the third exit to the left, but the crew had twice gotten that mixed up. The controller had then apparently given up and told them to taxi down to the end of the runway and turn their plane around.

Now, he told the Pan Am crew to turn off the runway at the third exit. Bragg, the first officer, acknowledged this, and after he did so, Second Officer George Warns added his confirmation. "Third, he said," Warns stated helpfully. And still another voice in the cockpit – either Grubbs or one of their two jump-seat passengers, Juan Murillo, or John Cooper – added "Three," just as "-rd one to your left" came back from the tower.

The mood was reasonably light in the Pan Am cockpit. Despite the hassles of the delay, there did not exist the uptightness that had apparently settled into the KLM cockpit. The Pan Am crew members were so loose, in fact, that although the word "third" had just been spoken five times in the last 14 seconds and "three" said once, plus one partial transmission of the word "third" over the radio, Grubbs didn't quite catch it. Like van Zanten in the KLM jet, Grubbs thought the tower controller had said "first" exit. "Third," if said quickly and casually, does indeed sound like "first" because of the identical "ir" sound in the middle of each word.

"I think he said 'first,'" Grubbs then said to Bragg. Bragg was willing to check. "I'll ask him again," he said. Then, almost musing to himself, Bragg added, "left turn." There wasn't any dispute about the left-turn part of the instructions, at least. That both the KLM and Pan Am captains thought the controller had said "first" indicates that the word perhaps hadn't been pronounced in perfect English.

The crew members were then preoccupied looking out the windshield as they swung onto the runway and began taxiing slowly down it, following the KLM plane. Weather conditions continued to deteriorate, with visibility at just 300 meters, which pulled an observation from Grubbs.

"I don't think they have takeoff clearance minimums anywhere right now," he offered. Then, a few seconds later, he decided to chat with his two jump-seat passengers, Murillo and Cooper, in the rear of the cockpit.

"What really happened over there today?" he asked, throwing the question over his right shoulder. His question was a reference to the earlier airport shutdown at Las Palmas, from where the two cockpit visitors had just arrived.

Murillo leaned forward. "They put a bomb in the terminal, sir, right where the check-in counters are."[1]

"Well, we asked them if we could hold [maintain a holding pattern in the air while waiting for clearance to land] and...uh...I guess you got the word, we landed here," Grubbs responded chattily, repeating his explanation for the umpteenth time.

The visibility through the fog was changing by the minute. At 5:02 p.m. it was down to 300 meters, less than one-tenth of the length of the 3,400-meter runway. Eight minutes later, at 5:10 p.m., enough fog had blown away to change the visibility to 1,000 meters, according to a Spanish weather station report. One thousand meters of visibility would surely have been enough to prevent what was about to happen – but by 5:10 p.m., it was too late. Yet another brutal coincidence had just fallen into place.

Because both planes were on the same radio frequency, each could hear what the other jet's crew members were saying to, and being told by, the controller in the control tower.

The verbal exchange about the bomb at Las Palmas was not transmitted over the radio but was recorded on the cockpit voice recorder that's carried

---

[1] Others said the bomb was just outside the terminal concourse flower shop.

on every commercial airliner. In the 1970s, the device recorded 30 minutes at a time. Thus, after accidents, the verbal exchanges prior to the accident could be studied for clues as to why failings occurred.

After the collision and fire that was now only a few minutes from happening, the cockpit voice recorders from both jets were recovered by investigators.[2]

"KLM Four-eight-zero-five," the tower called at 5:02.49. "How many taxiway...ah...did you pass?"

If the weather hadn't been foggy, of course, the controller wouldn't have had to ask that question. But the fog had become so thick that he couldn't see either plane, and the airport had no ground radar.

"I think we just passed Charlie Four now," was the reply. That was the last turnoff before the end of the runway.

Possibly because of the earlier confusion about turnoffs, the controller decided to remind the KLM crew of his revised instructions. "Okay...at the end of the runway make a one eighty and report...ah...ready...ah... for ATC [air traffic control] clearance," he said.

The KLM crew members surely listened carefully because there was some background conversation in the tower that was picked up during the radio transmission, making it difficult to hear the message.[3]

Some linguists have suggested that the word "Okay" may be the most commonly used word in the world. Its exact derivation is unknown, although the most likely explanation, according to Fowler's *Modern English Usage,* is that it is a 19th-century misreading of an abbreviation of "all correct." Its origin is the United States, but there are few countries in the Western world where it is not used.

One longtime commercial pilot complained about this after the Tenerife crash, noting that many controllers at international airports in the 1970s would give an "Okay" in their speech as any one of three uses: a comment,

---

[2] They're part of what are sometimes referred to as "black boxes," although the containers are actually orange. The other onboard recording device is the flight data recorder, which records technical changes in an aircraft's operations. For example, these recorders helped determine that the May 2016 crash of an EgyptAir jet into the Mediterranean was caused in part by an onboard fire.

[3] One later report stated that a soccer game was playing on a radio in the control tower, which contributed to the tower's background noise, adding to the difficulty of hearing radio transmissions.

an interjection, or a sign of approval. [4] On this day on Tenerife, the controller had just used it as an interjection, sticking it into his conversation merely as a way of saying that he had understood what was told him, and *not* that he was giving approval. In just a few minutes, that would become sickeningly, disastrously important.

Back in the Pan Am cockpit, the crew members were trying to figure out which exit they were supposed to use in order to move off of the runway onto the taxiway. They peered out the window and also kept their pilots' chart book open to a diagram of the Tenerife airport.

"The first one [the first turnoff from the runway, which was marked as C-1] is a ninety-degree turn," Bragg noted.

"Yeah," Grubbs grunted. Bragg may have spelled out the angle as simply a way of identifying the turnoff, but certainly the crew members weren't eager to take that one. They wouldn't have liked swiveling the 747 through a hard left turn, then a hard right turn in order to move down the taxiway. The second and third turnoffs, though, were even worse – they were 135-degree turns back toward the terminal building.

"Must be the third…. I'll ask him again," Bragg offered.

"Okay," Grubbs agreed.

While they were discussing it, KLM's van Zanten had just radioed the tower, asking why the lights that run down the middle of the runway were off.

Meanwhile, conversation continued in the Pan Am cockpit. "We could probably go in…it's…ah…" Grubbs started to say, apparently willing to try the first turnoff.

"You gotta make a ninety-degree turn…" Bragg reminded him.

"Yeah," Grubbs said again.

Bragg wanted to make his point, so he kept talking. "…Ninety-degree turn to get around this," he said, and then pointed on the map to a turnoff farther down the runway. "This one down here, it's a forty-five." Possibly thinking that he was pointing to the third turnoff, he was in fact looking at the fourth turnoff, which was a comparatively shallow turn of 45 degrees from the Pan Am's line of travel, and therefore easier for the jumbo jet.

---

[4] Jon Ziomek interviewed a senior Pan Am pilot (not Grubbs).

He picked up the microphone and called the control tower. "Would you confirm that you want the Clipper One-seven-three-six to turn left at the *third* intersection?" he asked, continuing the confusion, and drawing out the key word.

"One, two," Grubbs counted idly.

"Third one, sir. One, two three – third, third one," was the firm response.

An unidentified voice in the Pan Am cockpit kiddingly counted one, two, four.

Grubbs was pleased about the acknowledgement. "Good," he said, continuing the confusion about the turnoffs.

"Very good. Thank you," Bragg told the tower.

"That's what we need, right, the third one?" Grubbs said to his first officer.

Warns counted in Spanish. "Uno, dos, tres," he said. Grubbs was amused and repeated it. "Uno, dos, tres," he said, too. "Tres...uh...si," he added, perhaps drawing grins from others.

"Right," Grubbs said, thus concluding a lengthy series of exchanges between the crew and the tower.

"We'll make it yet," Warns commented, and the crew then began reviewing their checklists for takeoff.

Meanwhile, KLM 4805 had reached the end of the runway and the crew was preparing to wheel the plane around for its backtrack. This was the point at which Captain van Zanten radioed the control tower to ask about the runway lights – just as the Pan Am crewmembers were talking about their proper exit off the runway onto the taxiway. Because of the fog, van Zanten figured he was going to need those lights to keep his jet properly positioned on the runway during the takeoff attempt.

The controller didn't answer KLM's question immediately. While he was checking on the state of the runway lights, he decided to check in with the Pan Am crew again because he couldn't see their plane at all.

"Clipper One-seven-three-six, report leaving the runway," he said. Even though his words, on paper, look like a statement, he was using aviation shorthand to ask the crew *if* Pan Am had left the runway and made it onto the taxiway.

"Clipper One-seven-three-six," Bragg responded, but then continued with Grubbs. By simply stating Pan Am's flight number, Bragg meant to acknowledge the implied question in the controller's transmission: yes, they would tell the controller when they'd turned off of the runway. But is it possible that van Zanten thought Clipper 1736 was *confirming* it was already off of the runway?

At 5:04.26, Clipper 1736 passed what its crew thought was the first turnoff. "There's One," Bragg said, looking past Grubbs out the window to the left. "There's One," Grubbs agreed, and then added, by way of identification, "That's the ninety-degree." Then they returned to their checklists. "Weight and balance finals?" Bragg asked.

They finished their checklists. "Taxi check is complete," George Warns summed up. They moved on. "Takeoff and departure briefing?" Bragg asked.

"Okay," Grubbs said, continuing his relaxed manner. "It'll be standard. We gonna go out there – straight out there till we get to three thousand five hundred feet, then we're gonna make that reversal and go back out to fourteen [meaning 14,000 feet altitude]."

The controller didn't, right then, repeat his reminder to Pan Am's crew about telling him when they had turned off of the runway. Flipping through some written memoranda in the tower looking for an answer to KLM's question, he found one about the runway center lights. He decided to call both 747s at the same time, thus saving himself a transmission.

"KLM Eight-seven-zero-five," he said, getting the aircraft's flight number wrong, "and Clipper One-seven-three-six, for your information, the centerline lighting is out of service."

In the KLM cockpit, van Zanten radioed back, "I copied that." Despite the use of an incorrect identification number by the controller, KLM's cockpit crew knew he meant them because there were no other KLM planes at the airport.

Once again, Bragg repeated his plane's flight number. "Clipper One-seven-three-six," he said – another shorthand acknowledgement of what had just been transmitted.

But Grubbs didn't like that news. "We got centerline markings only," he told his crew, referring to the announcement that the runway lights were off. "They count the same thing as.... We need eight hundred meters [visibility] if you don't have that centerline."

He interrupted himself to note that they were passing the second turnoff on the left. "That's two," he pointed out.

The second turnoff was a steep angle away from their current direction, as was the third turnoff. But Warns and Bragg, looking at their airport guide, noticed that the fourth turnoff was only a 45-degree turn onto the taxiway, which would have been comparatively easy for the plane.

"Yeah, that's forty-five there," Warns agreed.

"Yeh," Grubbs grunted.

"That's this one right here," Bragg said, apparently pointing to the runway chart.

"I know," Grubbs agreed.

"Okay," said Warns. "Next one is almost a forty-five... huh...yeh."

Grubbs: "But it goes...ahead, I think it's gonna put us on the taxiway."

Warns: "Yeah, just a little bit...yeh."

Another unidentified crew member: "Okay, for sure."

They were now realizing they were confused about which exit they'd been directed to take because the fourth one was the most logical exit for them. But the controller had repeated himself several times, saying they should take the third exit, which required a turn of 135 degrees away from their current direction.

Perhaps they found it hard to believe the controller hadn't wanted them to take the simplest turnoff onto the adjacent taxiway.

Bragg was still studying the chart. "Maybe, he...maybe he counts these as three," he said, gesturing again to the chart. So many planes were clogging the first exit that perhaps it was not to be counted. What appeared on their chart as the third exit had an exceptionally steep 135-degree turn. Could the controller have possibly meant their 230-foot-long, 340-ton 747 should use that exit? If so, they'd have to slow down, then put their giant aircraft into a sharp left turn. Then, at the end of the turnoff lane, they'd have to make the same steep turn in the other direction onto the taxiway in order to continue moving and get in back of the KLM jet for takeoff.

They muttered among themselves about which turnoff was which. "I like this," Grubbs said sarcastically. They looked at the chart and then out into the fog. At that point, "We couldn't see *any* taxiways," Warns recalled later.[5] At this exact moment, the KLM jet had completed its 180-degree turn and was now pointed straight up the runway, aimed nose-to-nose at the Pan Am jet but separated by almost 2,000 meters of runway. Because of the fog, though, each jet was completely invisible to the other. Even their headlights, switched on as soon as the engines went on, were unable to pierce the fog.

The KLM jet shuddered as Captain van Zanten held the brakes after the turn was complete, but only for two and a half seconds. They had just finished their own takeoff checklist and were ready for takeoff. Van Zanten released the brakes and began advancing the throttle, and KLM 4805 began moving forward.

"Wait a minute," First Officer Meurs protested. "We don't have an ATC clearance."

Van Zanten didn't need this from a man who'd flown a total of only 95 hours in 747s. Anyway, he was in a hurry. Everyone was in a hurry. The fog was worse. The hour had grown late.

"No, I know that. Go ahead, ask," van Zanten said hurriedly.

At 5:04.44, which was just when the Pan Am crewmembers realized they were confused about their position on the runway, Meurs radioed the tower. "Uh, the KLM Four-eight-zero-five is now ready for takeoff...uh... and we're waiting for our ATC clearance."

In a few seconds, the air traffic controller would give KLM its flight instructions, which is *not* the same thing as takeoff permission. That would not have come until the controller said this: "KLM Four-eight-zero-five, you are cleared for takeoff." Which he didn't say.

"KLM Eight-seven-zero-five..." [getting the number wrong again], the controller droned, as he began issuing instructions for the plane to follow

---

[5] "The Deadliest Plane Crash," a PBS *Nova* documentary, 2007.

after it had left the ground. "…Uh, you are cleared to the Papa beacon [a radar coordinate several thousand feet past the end of the runway]. Climb and maintain flight level nine-zero [9,000 feet]…"

Perhaps, looking through the cockpit window and seeing that visibility was at an absolute minimum, the tension increased even more for van Zanten, Meurs, and Schreuder. Van Zanten may have been so distracted by his desire to get up and away from the island that he reacted instinctively when the controller said KLM was cleared to the radar beacon. The controller's statement did imply takeoff permission – although without granting it exactly.

"…right turn after takeoff, proceed with heading zero-four-zero…" the controller continued.

Captain van Zanten had been a flight instructor with KLM for 10 years, recently returning to active flying after spending several months as a pilot instructor. That meant he'd accumulated hundreds of hours in flight simulators, in which pilots are trained. In a simulator in the 1970s, no one played the controller's part. The instructor acted as the controller, giving students their clearances for various actions: landings, takeoffs, simulated emergencies.

Perhaps that is what began rising to the surface of his consciousness. Perhaps.

"…until intercepting the three-two-five radial from Las Palmas VOR," the controller finished.

Seven-tenths of one second before the controller had finished his instructions, van Zanten acknowledged them – but not on the radio, only in the cockpit – with a quick "Ja." The fact that he said that before the controller had finished indicates he was impatient, and the fact that he said it only in the cockpit indicates he was distracted.

Meurs, following correct procedure, now began reciting the instructions back to the control tower to make sure everyone in the KLM crew had understood them. Van Zanten sat next to Meurs, right hand gripping the throttles for the engines, left hand on the steering column. Was he paying attention to what was said? Was he reverting to his instructor pilot role? What was on his mind at that moment?

Los Rodeos Airport
March 27, 1977

More than half a dozen planes clogged the taxiway apron in front of the terminal.

KLM 747

PAN-AM 747

PAN-AM 747 TAXIS

KLM 747 TAXIS

RUNWAY

C-1

C-2

C-3

C-4

TAXIWAY

TERMINAL

PLANES COLLIDE

KLM 747 makes a U-turn at the end of the runway and begins its takeoff roll.

KLM's pilots tried unsuccessfully to lift off after they saw the Pan Am 747 through heavy runway fog. The Pan Am crew tried unsuccessfully to steer off the runway onto the grass when they saw the approaching KLM 747.

Note: Diagram is not to scale.

N

DIAGRAM BY MARK MEYER

Diagram courtesy of Mark Meyer

Here are the details of the crash, presented visually.

"Ah, roger, sir," Meurs began. "We're cleared to the Papa beacon flight level nine zero...."

Captain van Zanten was perhaps thinking of how he wanted to get his passengers to Las Palmas so they could get off the plane with their luggage and head for their hotels. Or about his responsibility as KLM's chief instructor pilot in setting a good example by getting his passengers to their destinations before the weather shut down the airport, thus saving KLM's schedule for the day, and those of many employees.

So, at 5:06.11, while his co-pilot was in the middle of clarifying their flight instructions from the control tower, before anyone had been given takeoff clearance, Captain van Zanten pushed the throttles forward. "We gan," he said in Dutch. ["We're going."]

KLM 4805 was taking off.

CHAPTER 11

A t 5:06.09 p.m., following standard procedure, KLM co-pilot Meurs began repeating the flight instructions for KLM 4805 to the control tower. He had barely gotten one sentence into them when Captain van Zanten started opening the engine throttles.

"Ah, Roger, sir," Meurs said. "We are cleared to the Papa beacon flight level nine-zero...[the throttles began revving at this point]...right turn out zero-four-zero until intercepting the three-two-five," which was a designation for another radio beacon.

"We are now at takeoff [or "taking off]," Meurs concluded.

Even after replaying that last sentence numerous times on the cockpit voice recorder, investigators from Spain, Holland, and the United States weren't sure whether Meurs had said KLM was "at" takeoff, or "taking" off. "At" takeoff would imply the jet wasn't moving, but was ready to. "Taking off" would imply movement right then. Possibly Meurs spoke in that semantically awkward way because he was flustered by the action of his pilot in opening the throttles. Neither he nor van Zanten had asked for – nor had they been given – takeoff permission. As explained in the previous chapter, the air traffic controller had given KLM clearance *only* for its flight path.

Maybe that's what Meurs *wanted* to do: ask the control tower for take-off permission. As a new pilot in the 747 cockpit, and especially with his former instructor sitting next to him, Meurs would have been sensitive to correct procedures. He'd demonstrated this a few minutes earlier, when

KLM was first told it could enter the runway to begin taxiing. Van Zanten had released the brakes and immediately pulled the plane onto the runway, while Meurs had gone ahead and repeated to the ground controller the taxi instructions they'd just been given.

The plane was now rolling at about 30 miles an hour through the fog, a movement that had been initiated when van Zanten announced [in Dutch], in the middle of the flight instructions, "Let's go...check thrust."

Possibly Meurs threw a quick glance at his captain. First, van Zanten had seemed as if he wasn't even going to wait for the flight path clearance; now he wasn't waiting for takeoff clearance. There he sat, one of the chief pilots for the entire airline – how could Meurs question the man who had certified him to fly in 747s only a few months earlier?[1] Meurs had said only about 20 minutes previously, during the chatter among the crew members as they had sat near the terminal during the refueling, "The Basic Operating Manual states I have to obey captain's orders first."

What could Meurs do now? His newness, his uncertainty, his respect for the captain, his repeated use of "sir" on the radio in the last few minutes – all, in retrospect, indicate a possible lack of self-assurance to speak out and question his commander.

The runway began to move more quickly under their wheels. In front of them was grayness – just fog and the runway markers.

The controller had no idea what had just happened. To him, "We are now at takeoff" was an imprecise way of saying that KLM 4805 was *ready* for takeoff, not that the plane was rolling down the runway – which the controller couldn't see because of the fog. (The new airport being built on Tenerife, Sur Airport, was to have ground radar. Ground radar at Los Rodeos would have shown the KLM plane was moving.)

Meurs' announcement, "We are now at takeoff," started at 5:06.15, concluding at 5:06.17. The controller was so unaware of what KLM was doing that he matter-of-factly answered again with that casual Americanization,

---

[1] Ripley, *The Unthinkable*, 74. Ripley also quotes Roger Shaw, an FAA pilot trainer, as saying, "In the early '70s, the captain was God. Now a lot of people send their pilots to charm school, if you want to call it, so that they can create a climate where everybody feels that, if they see something they don't like, they can discuss it."

"Okay." Then he said, "Stand by for takeoff. I will call you" – the most disastrously misunderstood eight words in the history of aviation.

In the the United States in the late 1970s, an air traffic controller who told a flight crew to "stand by for takeoff" could be reprimanded or even suspended. The reason is that, even though "stand by" had begun the controller's transmission, the rest of his phrase ("...for takeoff") might precipitate an automatic response by a pilot. Or worse, some kind of radio interference might prevent the pilot from hearing all parts of the command, especially the "stand by" part.

According to U.S. procedures, the proper way for a controller to instruct a pilot would have been to say, "Taxi into position and hold," or "Hold your position until further notice." There is no ambiguity about the word "hold." The word "clearance" would not have been spoken until the clearance was actually being given.

In that way, no words are used that could be misunderstood. The pilot is being told directly to wait. The overall result: no situation in the United States would have been similar to what was now unfolding, horribly, on Tenerife. But in 1977, international aviation regulations were different from those in the United States.

It is of small consolation to the many victims of this day that the Tenerife accident prompted a serious review of, and eventual changes in, international aviation procedures.

So even though controller Azcunaga had just responded to Meurs's "We are now at takeoff" comment by casually telling the KLM crew to "stand by," his words were only barely audible. The reason for the difficulty in hearing those words was because at the same instant the controller was saying them, the Pan Am crew members were reacting to what they had just heard on their own radio – that KLM was ready for takeoff – and they wanted to make sure everyone knew they were still on the runway.

Grubbs, hitting his radio transmission button first, said, "No, uh..." While Bragg hastily added, "And we're still taxiing down the runway, the Clipper One-seven-three-six..."

This meant Azcunaga in the tower and Bragg in the Pan Am cockpit were talking at the same time over the airport's common radio frequency. The controller's request to KLM that it stand by for takeoff clearance occurred from 5:06.18 to 5:06.21 p.m. Grubbs and Bragg began their transmissions less than two seconds after the controller started to talk. Grubbs took just a moment to say, "No, uh," but Bragg's transmission ran slightly longer than Azcunaga's, to 5:06.23.

The result was that, for about two and a half seconds after Meurs had announced his plane was "at takeoff," there was a jumble of voices on the radio. The multiple transmissions were the apparent cause of a shrill noise, known as a heterodyne, which was recorded on the KLM cockpit recorder and which came out of the KLM cockpit radio. This noise lasted three and three-quarter seconds, ending at 5:06.23, and enveloped the transmissions from the control tower and the Pan Am cockpit. That noise covered all the transmissions except Azcunaga's "Okay" and the end of Bragg's identifying code. And yet another horrible coincidence fell into place.

Later testing, though, would show both the Pan Am transmissions were *still audible* – although just barely – in the KLM cockpit. But one has to remember KLM's pilot was distracted, determined to get out of Tenerife. He may have thought he'd seen a slight break in the fog, enough to turn off the windshield wipers, according to a later examination of the data recorder, so he was ready to go. His mindset was such that he could not take the time to strain to hear a noise on the radio that sounded like talking. He'd certainly heard Azcunaga's "Okay," though.

But apparently, the message from Bragg never registered with van Zanten, nor did the order to "stand by" from Azcunaga. And if it did register with Meurs, he never indicated it verbally. Neither he nor Schreuder, the flight engineer sitting in back of Meurs, said anything just then.

And if the controller's, or the Pan Am crew's, words registered with van Zanten, they did not make enough of an impression to make him stop what he was doing. By now, his jet was moving at about 75 miles an hour and the ground was becoming a blur. The jet plunged ahead into the gray fog, its headlights piercing a few hundred yards before dissipating into the swirling grayness. Another chance to save 583 lives had just gone by.

Yet there would be three more.

Several seconds after the Pan Am crew's warning that they were still on the runway, at 5:06.25 the air traffic controller, Azcunaga, decided to check in again with Grubbs and Bragg to make sure he'd understood them.

"Roger, Papa Alpha One-seven-three-six, report the runway clear." It was the same instruction he'd issued a few minutes earlier, although worded differently.

Once again, that was professional shorthand. Here's a full sentence interpretation of what Azcunaga had just said: "Pan American One-seven-three-six, tell me when you're off the runway." To the layman, Azcunaga's actual transmission ("report the runway clear") almost sounded as though the tower were asking the plane's crew to confirm that the runway really was clear right *then* – but he was actually *asking* them to let him know when the runway *became* clear.

Pan Am responded. At 5:06.29, Bragg said, "Okay, we'll report when clear," a transmission in which the word *when* takes on a painfully important meaning.

"Thank you," the controller said.

"Yup," Bragg acknowledged casually.

To the Pan Am crew, they were saying that they would let the tower – and by extension, the KLM crew – know *when* they were off the runway.

Again, the KLM cockpit voice recorder has nothing indicating that van Zanten comprehended what had just been said on the shared radio frequency.

But what about the other two pilots in the cockpit? Perhaps Meurs heard that completely clear transmission and looked at van Zanten, who was guiding the plane down the runway at a speed now approaching 100 miles an hour. Yet, again he hesitated, and the next chance to avoid the coming catastrophe went by.

But someone else in the KLM cockpit spoke up – a man who had more hours in KLM cockpits than even Captain van Zanten. It was Willem Schreuder, the flight engineer, who at 53 was older than Van Zanten, too.

About half a second after the tower said, "Thank you," to Pan Am, Schreuder leaned forward and shouted to van Zanten in the now-noisy cockpit, "Is his er nist af dan?" ["Is he not clear, then?" or "Is he not off there?"] This was the second of the final three opportunities.

Van Zanten was looking ahead while glancing at the indicators in front of him: speed, exhaust pressure ratio, flaps…distracted, he didn't quite hear Schreuder. "Vat zeg je?: ["What did you say?"] he asked Schreuder, using up another couple of seconds. The plane was now moving at more than 100 miles an hour.

At 5:06.34, Schreuder repeated his question, this time louder, and it became the final chance to prevent the world's worst aviation catastrophe. "Is his er niet af, die Pan American?" ["Is he not clear, the Pan American?"]

Before Schreuder had even finished asking his question, the pilot answered emphatically, at 5:06.35, "Ja wel!" ["Oh yes!"]

Now it was Schreuder's turn to be puzzled and disturbed. Van Zanten was so sure, he surely thought to himself. But that hadn't been what Schreuder thought he'd heard on the radio.

At 5:06.43, Meurs announced they'd reached their "V-1" speed, about 150 miles an hour, the speed at which they would be unable to stop without running off the end of the runway. That meant they were now committed to a takeoff attempt.

And so, on this dreary afternoon on a faraway island where no one wanted to be to begin with, hundreds of people were all about to become victims: of bad weather, bad luck, and bad vibrations.

The horrible ifs:

▶ If Pan Am Clipper 1736 had left the United States at its originally scheduled departure time, it might have been in front of KLM 4805 at Tenerife and wouldn't have had to wait for the Dutch plane to take off.

▶ If the MPAIAC organization had not made the Las Palmas airport a terrorist target, the jets would not have been diverted to Tenerife.

▶ If the telephone threat to the Las Palmas airport switchboard had contained the word "bomb" instead of its plural, airport officials wouldn't have feared the possibility of a second explosion and may not have diverted aircraft to Tenerife.

- If Tenerife's taxiway had been larger, Pan Am 1736 would have been able to swing around KLM 4805, or there would have been enough room for the Pan Am jet to have been towed to a clear section so that it could take off in front of KLM 4805.

- If Captain van Zanten had not decided to refuel at Tenerife, his plane would have been tens of thousands of pounds lighter. It wouldn't have needed as much runway for a takeoff, and it would have been able to climb faster, resulting in a near miss instead of a collision. Also, KLM would have been leaving about 30 minutes earlier – a time of less fog and better visibility.

- If Pan Am's crew had insisted on waiting on the taxiway until KLM 4805 had taken off, or had been told to do so by the controller before entering the live runway, the collision would not have happened.

- If the garbled transmissions to the KLM cockpit had been clearer, the plane might have been able to stop its takeoff.

- If the air traffic controller had spoken more emphatically to KLM 4805 in telling it to hold its position before takeoff, without using "okay," the KLM crew might not have begun its takeoff roll.

- If Pan Am's crew had left the runway on the difficult C-3 exit, it might have steered the plane clear by the time KLM 4805 came by.

- If van Zanten hadn't been so distracted about overtime rules, he would have been more aware of what was happening right in front of him.

- And if van Zanten had accepted the flight engineer's shouted question about the Pan Am plane's position, KLM 4805 would have canceled its takeoff roll and been braking when the Pan Am jet came into view through the fog.

No one was considering any of this in the Pan American cockpit, of course, as the plane continued to taxi down the runway. The pilots were as casual as they had been all afternoon. As they taxied, waiting for what they thought was the correct turnoff onto the taxiway, they heard Meurs tell Azcunaga in the control tower that the KLM plane was ready for take-off. Grubbs and Bragg had responded immediately, Bragg telling Azcunaga they were still on the runway.

Not being aware of the interference that had garbled their message on the KLM cockpit radio, the Pan Am crew believed Bragg's message would leave absolutely no doubt about their position. Then, several seconds later, Azcunaga had asked them to tell him when they got off the runway. Obviously, this was so that he could give the "You are now cleared for takeoff" instruction to the KLM flight. "Yup," Bragg had said cheerily.

Then they talked among themselves again, and their resentment at being held up earlier by KLM came out. After all their waiting for KLM 4805, now it was having to wait for them to get out of the way.

Grubbs correctly interpreted Meurs' message about being "at takeoff" as an indication that KLM was in a hurry.

He mocked them by saying to his colleagues at 5:06.32, "Let's get the hell out right here – get the hell out of here," and chuckled. The others understood he was making fun of the KLM plane and joined in the razzing. "Yeah, he's anxious, isn't he," Bragg added.

But while they were talking, they missed C-3, the runway exit they'd been told to use.[2]

Warns added a comment: "Yeah, after he held us up for an hour and a half, that bastard," he said with some disgust, overstating the delay.

"Yeah, that prick," Bragg said, irritated.

"Now he's in a rush," Warns added.

At 5:06.38, as Warns was adding his own sarcasm, Grubbs looked up from his instruments and peered through the windshield. By now they were almost halfway between C-3 and C-4. The fog actually did seem to be lifting a bit. In another three minutes, in fact, it would have cleared enough so that visibility would be recorded by the airport's weather observer as about

---

[2] Chief U.S. investigator Douglas Dreifus of the National Transportation Safety Board was later asked if the Pan Am crew had deliberately gone past C-3, planning to use C-4 because the angle was shallower. His reply was that he was convinced the crew had simply not seen C-3 in the fog, which by this point was extremely heavy. "We couldn't see any taxiways," Bragg confirmed years later.

1,000 meters on the runway. That, too, would have been enough to avoid what was just about to happen.

But what Grubbs saw when he looked out the window made him forget about refueling delays, about exits and runway charts and sarcasm and tours of the cockpit and everything else.

He saw the headlights of KLM 4805.

Perhaps, for the first moment, Grubbs assumed the plane was stationary. "There he is," Grubbs announced to the others. The remark may have been made casually, as one would point out a landmark by the roadside. But as he stared into the fog along with the other crew members, whose attention had been drawn by their chief's remark, it became immediately obvious that KLM 4805 was *not* standing still. It was speeding down the runway directly at them.

"Look at him," Grubbs suddenly gasped. "Goddamn!...that...that son of a bitch is coming!"

"Get off! Get off! Get off!" Bragg screamed, as much at his own captain as the KLM plane. Each of them yanked his steering wheel as hard as he could to the left, and Grubbs threw the throttles open so quickly that their own takeoff warning horn sounded. Bragg had a later memory of screaming, "We are still on the runway!" and Grubbs believed he said, "What's he doing? He'll kill us all!" Neither of those statements appears on the official cockpit voice transcripts, possibly because the warning buzzers were drowning out other sounds, possibly because those words were screamed in the crew members' minds.

Grubbs threw the throttle open as hard as he could, but a 340-ton machine can't move quickly in that situation. They were only able to get their 747's speed up to 19 miles an hour.

Instinctively, they all ducked.

In the KLM cockpit, they were now nearing takeoff speed, and Meurs and Schreuder could hope they'd soon be up and off the runway, and that Captain van Zanten was correct that the Pan Am jet wasn't on it. At 5:06.43, six seconds before impact, Meurs announced, "V-1," meaning that the plane was now going too fast to abort its takeoff. Van Zanten began easing the steering column back, and the nose of the KLM jumbo jet rose a few feet into the air. The pilots couldn't see the ground directly in front of the plane and instead were staring into a gray mist.

No one will ever know who first looked up from the KLM control panel and out the windshield – perhaps Schreuder, sitting sideways in back of the pilots and monitoring his own instruments, never did at all – but whoever did must have been squeezed down to his soul by the sight of a giant airplane directly in their path. Instinctively, Captain van Zanten yanked the steering yoke back so hard, thereby lifting the nose even further into the air, that the lower part of the jet's tail cut a groove into the runway behind them. There was time left only for a primal moan, an expression of banal profanity that would become van Zanten's final words: "Oh Godverdomme…" ["Oh Goddamn…"]

The steering yoke jiggled uncertainly. The plane tilted slightly to the right, then the left. Van Zanten fed the engines all the power he could. Maybe, just maybe they would get over the Pan Am jet. Why was it there?

At 5:06.49 and three one-hundredths of a second, Canary Islands time, KLM Royal Dutch Airlines Flight 4805 and Pan American Flight 1736, carrying a combined total of 644 passengers and crew, collided and destroyed each other.

CHAPTER 12

Six seconds before the impact, Pan Am's Captain Grubbs and First Officer Bragg swerved their 747 to the left as hard as they could. But a 340-ton aircraft does not exactly respond like a sports car, especially when it's going only 19 miles an hour. Earlier so careful *not* to pull their plane onto the soft grass adjacent to the taxiway, Grubbs and Bragg now wanted nothing more than to get *onto* that grass.

Then they ducked.

Inside the cabin, the swerve felt like a sharp turn and nothing more. On the left side of the cabin, in seat 32-A, Isobel Monda looked out her window as the plane turned. She was oblivious, as were the other passengers, to the screaming in the cockpit.

"My God," she gasped, realizing how close they were to the grass, "the damn fool's going to run right off the runway!"

In the first-class section, on the right side of the airplane in 2-H, John Charles Amador looked out of his window as the plane turned sharply to the left. He saw a nightmare: a 747 airliner appearing through the fog and rushing, seemingly, right toward his seat. There was no time even to yell. He simply put his head down in his lap.

Now moving at more than 150 miles an hour, the KLM plane slashed into and partially over the Pan Am plane in about one second. There was a surprising lack of noise. To Warren Hopkins, it was as if someone had taken a long piece of adhesive tape and ripped it from the ceiling of the jet. Jack Ridout later remembered the noise of the air rushing, pulled by the KLM jet as it passed a few feet over his head. Thrash air noise, he said, describing it aeronautically, and it sounded "like a swarm of bees."

Joani Feathers remembered a snapping sound, like a twig being broken. Isobel Monda was convinced that the noise, to her a shuddering "thump," was the noise of the plane running off the runway onto the grass, just as she had feared. Jean Brown, in 37-C, remembered just a "loud noise." Florence Trumbull, in 30-G, had a distinct impression of the whiz of the KLM jet passing a few feet over the heads of her husband and herself. Ridout, too, remembered feeling a shadow.

And still others had their own comparisons: to Jim Naik, the sound was as though two buses had just bumped together.

No one, except for a few people sitting on the right side of the plane who coincidentally looked out of their windows just then, realized what had just happened. Some passengers didn't realize they'd been in a collision until hours later. They assumed that a bomb had gone off because there'd been talk of bombs earlier in the afternoon.

And then the Pan Am passengers looked up. Their 747 had just turned into a convertible.[1]

Captain van Zanten, in his last moments, had pulled so hard on the steering yoke that the lowest portion of the KLM plane's tail cut a groove in the runway 68 feet long. He gave the engines as much thrust as he could, and the KLM plane did lift a few feet into the air, but the Number 3 engine – the inside engine on the right-hand side of the plane, looking at it from the rear – caught the roof and rear section of the Pan Am jet's second floor and ripped off the lounge, just in back of the cockpit. In one second, it was gone, along with 10 people who'd been sitting in it. Portions of several bodies fell into the first-class cabin as the ceiling in that section opened up. The amputation of this portion of the Pan Am plane was so surgically precise that when First Officer Bragg reached over his head to pull the cockpit roof-mounted fire extinguisher handles for the four engines, he grabbed only the open sky.

---

[1] The details of the collision in this chapter and succeeding chapters are taken from various U.S. government documents about the crash.

After KLM's Number 3 engine removed the Pan Am lounge, the rear lower half of the KLM fuselage scraped against the upper portions of the Pan Am fuselage – but at an angle because of that sharp left turn by the Pan Am crew. The KLM jet slid along the Pan Am fuselage like two giant sticks being rubbed together to start a fire, which is exactly what happened.

Part of the top of the Pan Am fuselage peeled back like a giant sardine can, exposing the open sky to many of the passengers. The KLM jet's right-side landing gear blasted into the Pan Am fuselage several rows in back of the first-class section, pulverizing everything and everyone in its path. As the fuselage scraped over the top of the Pan Am fuselage, it found deficiencies in the metal that would never have appeared in normal service, and the fuselage began cracking into parts.

Although the nose of the KLM jet cleared the Pan Am plane completely, the rear portion of the KLM fuselage did not. The left wing and landing gear and left-side engines crashed into the rear of the Pan Am fuselage. According to later government reports, the backdraft from KLM's Number 1 engine somehow, horribly, sucked the people in Pan Am seats 47-E and 49-G directly out of their plane and carried their bodies many yards down the runway, where they were later found. The KLM's right-wing landing gear did the same to the body of the person in 21-H.

The rearmost part of the Pan Am plane, the vertical tail fin, was completely shattered by the KLM fuselage, which had some of its own underbelly metal and baggage compartment sections smashed or ripped into pieces and deposited around the Pan Am plane.

The exploding collision of the two giant jets sent a spray of metal fragments – including all four KLM engines and engine parts, parts of the KLM right wing, the two Pan Am right-side engines and engine parts, wing flaps, various sections of the KLM landing gear, pieces of the Pan Am tail, and several tons of sections of the top of the Pan Am fuselage and the bottom of the KLM fuselage – in all directions.

After it had passed through and over the Pan Am plane, what remained of the KLM plane stayed in the air for about 200 more yards before belly-flopping back onto the runway, approximately at the C-3 turnoff. It slid another 200 yards or so, curving as it skidded so that when it finally came to rest, it had turned itself around and was almost pointing back in the direction from which it had come. Its fuselage, too, had cracked into sections. The right wing had completely disintegrated; curiously, the left wing had remained relatively intact, except for the motors and landing gear.

Some of the KLM passengers may have survived the initial impact with the Pan Am jet, but there would have been instantaneous death with the crash-landing. The ripping apart of both planes opened the KLM plane's gas tanks and sprayed thousands of gallons of jet fuel over the runway. The fuel was ignited, resulting in raging fires of near volcanic proportions that totally consumed the KLM fuselage. There was no chance to escape that crematorium. No one, the charred bodies would later show, had even able to rise out of their seat. The temperature at the center of the flames reached 4,000 degrees Fahrenheit – easily hot enough to melt the metal of the plane's airframe.

On the Pan Am plane, flying metal fragments sliced into seats and people, cut into the sides of the plane, and caused other parts of the aircraft to buckle and collapse. Seats were tossed through the air. Oxygen canisters and fire extinguishers began exploding from the heat. The overhead luggage racks collapsed in several sections of second class, crushing those who had asked for window seats. In other sections, the luggage compartments did not collapse, and in fact provided shelter from the flying metal. Warren Hopkins was cut deeply on his forehead by flying debris; Caroline Hopkins received no such head wound, although she was sitting only inches from her husband. Jack Ridout, in front of Warren and Caroline, was hit so hard on the head by a metal fragment that he momentarily lost consciousness, but next to him, Joani Feathers' head was protected by the overlap of the luggage compartment. In the economy section, the collapsing luggage compartment fell on David Alexander's seatmates, the Ronders, while he, in an aisle seat, was untouched.

The flying metal fragments killed many on impact, stunned others, and caused still others to go into a mental freeze.

Beth Moore was mentally alert at the explosion, although she had been bent over, adjusting her bag – an action that may have saved her head. When she straightened back up, the collision had taken place and her husband, the retired admiral, had a severe gash on the top of his head that had stunned him.

The Mondas were unhurt by the metal fragments, possibly because they sat directly behind a group of lavatories that protected them from the incoming force of the KLM plane. The Trumbulls found debris tumbling into them; Albert Trumbull felt a live electrical wire from the ceiling fall across his arm, burning him and possibly shocking him into action.

Air traffic controller Fernando Azcunaga, in the control tower, had no further exchange with either plane after telling the KLM crew to stand by, and reminding the Pan Am crew to call him when they had cleared the runway. Shortly after his last communication with the Pan Am crew, he looked up in alarm at the sound, diffused by the fog, of an explosion. He could see nothing from the tower windows. The noise was followed by a second explosion only seconds later.

Perhaps the fuel tanks behind the airport buildings had just exploded, he thought with concern. Fernando Hernandez-Abad, the ground controller, was busy talking to a Luft Transport jet whose crew wanted to know when they could start their engines. [2] But then a British Airlines pilot called him to say, without specifying exactly where, that he had seen a fire on the runway. Azcunaga, Hernandez-Abad, and assistant controller Juan Benitez strained to see something in the fog.

While they looked, Benitez sounded a fire alarm and picked up a hot-line telephone to the airport firehouse. Fire Chief Ramon Castro answered.

Benitez told Castro to alert his men because a fire had been reported on the runway. They'd call back as soon as they could locate the fire, Benitez said. Castro ordered his 12 men – 11 firefighters and a foreman, Alfonso Cabello – to rush into their gear, while the control tower personnel struggled to find out where the fire was. Azcunaga, innocently hoping that the Pan Am or KLM crews might have seen something, called repeatedly and vainly to the two jets: "KLM, report…Clipper One-seven-three-six, report…Hello, KLM Four-eight-zero-five…Do you see a fire?"

[2] Luft Transport Unternehmen, or LTU, was a German passenger airline that operated from 1955 to 2011.

At about 5:08 p.m., just more than a minute after the collision, the fog cleared enough for the control tower personnel to see a bright light on the runway. Benitez called the firehouse again to report that the fire had been spotted "to the left of the parking area," meaning the parking area for planes on the taxiway. The firemen drove off in the department's four turret trucks, crossing the taxi strip on a diagonal and watching for the fire, the source of which still wasn't known.

As the firemen moved through the fog, they approached a bright light that was sending out heat like a blast furnace. Moving through the mist, they saw with horror that an entire jumbo jet – the KLM plane – had been enveloped in monstrous flames roaring more than 100 feet into the air. The fire was so all-consuming that only the tail fin at the rear of the plane's fuselage wasn't burning. The firemen jumped off their trucks and began spraying foam and water on the blaze.

Meanwhile, Santiago Gonzalez, airport services chief, had gotten a call in his first-floor office from the tower. At the time, all he was told was that "something strange" was on Runway 30. Gonzalez hurried out of his office, climbed into an airport car parked on the taxiway, and drove onto the runway, where he saw the flaming carcass of the KLM plane. He immediately turned around, drove back to the terminal building, and returned to his office, where he hastily began making telephone calls to other fire departments in the area.

According to the Spanish government report, firefighters found the KLM plane about 5:09 p.m. After working there for a minute or two, the men were distracted when a further clearing of the fog revealed another big fire raging several hundred yards down the runway. Thinking this was part of the plane they were now working on, foreman Cabello divided his 12-man force into two squads and sent one of them toward the second fire, with two water trucks.

It was about this time that photographer Manuel Fandiño, who had been hanging around the airport to take pictures, noticed the commotion and raced onto the airstrip on foot, bringing his camera with him. His were among the earliest pictures taken of the disaster.

Arriving near the second source of flames, the firemen were stunned to find a second Boeing 747 – the Pan American plane – burning ferociously, sending huge crackles of flame through the fog. But there were survivors milling around this wreckage, so the second group radioed back to the first, asking for reinforcements. Maybe there were others who could be saved. According to the government report, this was between 5:11 p.m. and 5:13 p.m.

The report said that one of the fires near the Pan Am plane was extinguished, preventing about 5,600 gallons of fuel from igniting. But the other fires were enormous, eventually burning themselves out by 3:30 a.m. the next morning. By then, 11,000 pounds of foam and 135,000 gallons of water had been used on the fires at the two jets by three fire departments: the airport's, and those of the city of Santa Cruz de Tenerife and San Cristobal de la Laguna, a nearby city.

The Tenerife disaster illustrated the need for a piece of technology that the Air Line Pilots Association had been advocating for years: radio transmitters on the tail of all planes, which would send a signal that could be picked up on fire equipment receivers. At Tenerife, that may have cut precious seconds or even a minute or so from the time required to locate the planes hidden in the fog.

The next day, the local newspaper, *El Pueblo*, ran an interview with a resident of one of the houses that adjoin the airstrip.

"It must have been around 5:15 in the afternoon," the man recounted. "I was at home, like most Sundays, in the garden of the cottage. Suddenly, I felt the windows of the house trembling, as if from an explosion. Instinctively I glanced toward the airport. It isn't the first time that there have been accidents there, and I was frightened. A few minutes later, I could see an enormous column of black smoke rising up, offering a violent contrast to the fog, which was hanging low over Los Rodeos. It seemed like an explosion from the gasoline supply tanks at the airport. Only half an hour later, I realized that an accident had taken place, for I detected the same smell of burned flesh as a few years ago, when one hundred fifty-five people lost their lives in a similar accident. And that macabre odor is not easily forgotten, no matter how many years pass."

CHAPTER 13

"*Disasters are predictable, but surviving them is not. No one can promise you a plan of escape.*"[1]

The ability to act quickly in a life-or-death situation can be acquired. It isn't surprising, for example, to learn that flight crew members are among those who keep the coolest heads in a plane crash. After all, that's part of their training. Being responsible for a specific task can take away the psychologically wrenching situation of going from benign indifference to deciding what to do, where to go, how to get out of the airplane, whom to save, and then acting – within seconds – on that series of decisions.

In the case of Pan Am 1736, as on every flight, all the attendants had their assigned stations at specific emergency exits. If an evacuation were to be required, the attendants would activate the emergency chutes that come from the bottom of the doorframe and then help the passengers out. The first officer was to check the passenger cabin while the captain remained at the controls.

The passengers were supposed to file in an orderly manner to the nearest exits and then slide down the chutes to the ground. In this manner, according to airline industry training exercises, an entire 747 full of passengers can be emptied in two minutes.

---

[1] Ripley, *The Unthinkable*.

But that kind of evacuation requires a healthy crew who can properly instruct the passengers on where to go and how to use the slides. It requires injury-free passengers who can move down debris-free aisles with decent speed. It requires functioning emergency exits and emergency chutes, an absence of panic, and – as will be explained shortly – an absence of another prevalent and dangerous form of behavior, "negative panic," in which passengers simply sit immobile and are unable to rise or respond in any way.

The evacuation of Pan American 1736 at Tenerife had none of those conditions.

First, none of the emergency exits opened properly. This wasn't a manufacturer's deficiency but the result of the smashing together of the two planes, which warped the fuselage of the Pan Am plane.

Also, more than half of the Pan Am passengers and nine of the 13 flight attendants were dead because of the collision, from flying metal, or from the landing gear of the KLM fuselage. About 100 passengers were injured – some slightly, others severely, with cuts, broken limbs, burns, and/or smoke inhalation. Many were too injured to move properly, or at all.

Plus, most of the passengers were middle-aged or elderly folks, who – no surprise – move slower than younger people.

Yet estimates by the surviving passengers suggest that about 100 people, perhaps more, were healthy enough to get out of the Pan Am plane. But only slightly more than half of that number did. Why? And how?

Crisis behavior was just emerging as a field of study in the 1970s. The earliest reports at the time showed that only certain categories of passengers would respond well in a crisis, such as people who have had training in crisis behavior, including flight crew members and members of the military (current and former).

"The military hones soldiers' cooperative instincts in an environment that has all of the required characteristics," Erez Yoeli and David Rand wrote in an August 2015 *New York Times* article about the nature of acting heroically: "Soldiers occasionally find themselves helping others at enormous personal risk; and they live, train and work together for relatively long periods, during which they have plenty of opportunities to observe whether a peer helps others without thinking."[2]

On Tenerife, this group included Warren Hopkins, an Army veteran of the World War II Pacific campaign. Hopkins, who'd been sitting in seat 5-B in first class, was the first person to get out of the Pan Am plane. When the sky, or more appropriately, the fog, appeared above him and his wife, a warning bell rang in Hopkins's consciousness. The cues of danger were there. Others in the cabin were getting the same messages. In fact, a number of men who had served in World War II were on board, among them Albert Trumbull, Walter Moore, Tony Monda, and Jordan Tartikoff. All were among the earliest responders.

But Warren Hopkins was the very first to act on his impulse. Unlike many other passengers, he didn't wait for the flight attendants or the captain to explain what was wrong. For reasons that he did not take the time to examine, he knew that he and Caroline had to get out of the plane immediately.

"Let's go," he commanded, turning to his wife and touching her arm. She was still noticing the suddenly changed condition of the plane's interior: shredded and curled wallpaper, the pastels and asterisks that airlines used in the 1970s to decorate their interiors, all of which suddenly looked like a child's papier-mâché project.

It took Warren just a few seconds to unbuckle his seat belt and move into the aisle, then step over debris that had landed there from the overhead compartments and from torn parts of the plane. He was now bleeding severely from the head because of a blow from falling debris. Caroline Hopkins had not noticed her husband's injury because he had turned away so quickly, and even he wasn't aware of it because he was focused on what he wanted to do.

Warren didn't notice anything that had fallen from the lounge upstairs, although another first-class passenger later remembered a body falling

---

[2] The Yoeli-Rand article appeared shortly after a dramatic example of this relationship of crisis behavior and military training. In August 2015, an attempted terrorist attack on a passenger train in northern France was prevented when several passengers, including two off-duty members of the U.S. military, subdued a gunman.

down, still strapped into its seat, looking undisturbed except for the lack of a head.

Because of his proximity to the exit door — it was just two rows in back of him — Warren was able to reach it in only a few steps, even with debris in the way. He passed the seat of the woman who had tried to give them the drink tickets in New York. That seat and the seat of her presumed granddaughter were empty. Perhaps they had gone up to the lounge before takeoff; perhaps they had plummeted through the floor, as several other people had done when the floor in some sections collapsed. Wherever they had gone, the Hopkinses never saw them again.

As he made his way down the aisle, Hopkins passed Enid Tartikoff and her husband, Jordan, who were sitting near him in 6-E and 6-F. He did not notice them because he was now focused exclusively on getting to the door. They were alive and unhurt but stunned, facing the empty seat of Beau Moss, who had gone up to the lounge before takeoff, a decision that had meant instant death when the collision happened.

Hopkins did not stop to reflect on their fate but stepped to the door — or, rather, where the door had been. Not only was the door gone, ripped off its hinges, but the collision had also removed the entire doorframe and surrounding fuselage section. A jagged outline of metal was all that was left to define that spot. There was no thought whatsoever of activating the emergency slide. He didn't see one, or a lever to activate it.

Assuming that his wife was standing right behind him — Warren hadn't looked back yet — he stood momentarily in what was left of the doorframe and looked out. The perspective was unique. Most Americans board planes through jetway tunnels and never see the outside of the plane except through a window. At Tenerife, the passengers had been allowed to stand several times on a platform outside the plane's front door. Now, however, there was no platform and no stairway. The left-side engines were still turning. Sparks were flying through the air from exposed electrical wires, and jet-fuel fires were just beginning to crackle under both left-side engines. The fuselage would soon begin to crack and sag down.

Some survivors would later say they felt as though they were in a disaster movie, as if real life had suddenly become unreal. Indeed, the scene was Dante-esque: gray fog was rolling in as orange flames shot into the air from underneath the huge silver wing that was now beginning to scorch and blacken. As he stood on his perch, though, Warren Hopkins could see green grass and gray runway only a few yards away, demonstrating how close Grubbs and Bragg in the cockpit had gotten to moving the plane off the runway before the collision.

Without the stairway in front of Warren to give him some perspective, the distance down to the ground was frightfully high, "like jumping off the top of a barn," he would later say. The actual distance was about 20 feet.

But with an urgency brought by the sight of the fire and the certainty that he must get away, Hopkins leaped into space. His body, with arms out and legs bent, flew in a parabolic arc, out and then down, down until he hit the ground, miraculously landing on the balls of his feet – although more on the left foot than the right. The impact severed two tendons and bruised bones in his left foot. He immediately fell to his hands and knees, losing one shoe and his wristwatch from the physical shock of the jump but not even noticing the sting of the landing.

For several seconds, and what seemed like minutes, Hopkins was now alone on the ground and almost underneath the plane, which was beginning to generate flames and black smoke. He turned around and looked up, fully expecting to see his wife standing where he'd just been. She wasn't there. In fact, no one was, and Hopkins felt terribly alone, standing next to the giant jet.

"Caroline! Caroline!" he screamed, trying to make himself heard over the still-whining engines.

Back inside the plane, Caroline Hopkins had reacted immediately when her husband said, "Let's go" – but she couldn't get her seat belt unfastened.[3] Still thinking calmly, the thought came into her head that she'd been on plenty of airline flights, had buckled and unbuckled her seat belt dozens of times. This was one time when she was in a hurry, but she couldn't get it unsnapped.

---

[3] "After preparation, the next best hope is leadership," Amanda Ripley wrote in *The Unthinkable*. "That's one reason that well-trained flight attendants now shriek at passengers in evacuations."

It has been suggested that seat belts on airplanes should be made to match those in cars, so that they can be opened by pushing a button, as opposed to releasing a flap. In a moment of extreme emergency on a plane, some people might instinctively revert to the more-common automobile motion, which could delay their evacuation by a precious few seconds. Perhaps that's what happened to Caroline Hopkins, she would later say.

Click. *Finally,* she thought, and stood on her shoeless feet (she'd removed her high heels after boarding), placing her right hand on her own seatback and left hand on that of Joani Feathers's seat in front of her. Now there was another problem. In the aisle, next to her husband's now-empty seat, were three people standing and talking in low voices – almost casually, Caroline Hopkins thought.

She wasn't the only person who couldn't get her seat belt unfastened. In front of Mrs. Hopkins, Joani Feathers was going through the same nightmarish process. Feathers later remembered her first reaction to the crash was expecting there would be another impact and immediate death.[4] So at first she sat, passively and calmly. Caroline Hopkins thought she saw Feathers reacting when Warren Hopkins said, "Let's go!" but Feathers later had no memory of that.

At that point, Jack Ridout, Joani Feathers's seatmate, regained consciousness after being stunned by falling debris. "This is it!" he announced sharply, helping to snap Joani out of her state. He unsnapped his seat belt and rose in one movement.

In times of extreme crisis, perhaps many of us fall back on banalities. Passenger Betsy Dickens said almost the same thing to her husband, Jim, in 34-G.[5] As remembered later by a survivor, she turned to her husband and announced, "I think this is it." The difference was that Ridout's "This is it!" was more of a call to action, whereas the elderly Mrs. Dickens's "This is it." was a statement of acceptance. The Dickenses did not make it out of the plane.

---

[4] This information came from interviews with Ms. Feathers and Mr. Ridout.

[5] This passenger's real name was changed as a courtesy to surviving relatives. The words were recalled by another survivor.

Ridout, now standing, noticed Feathers fumbling with her belt. He reached over and pulled her out from underneath it. They stepped with difficulty into the middle of the aisle, which was piled with coats, pillows, blankets, and parts of the overhead storage racks. Ridout looked out the right side of the plane and saw flames. Then he looked out the left side and saw that it appeared to be closer to the ground. (The fuselage was beginning to tilt that way.)

Ridout announced, "Those engines are going to blow! We've got to get out of here!" The two made their way down the aisle just as Caroline Hopkins got her seat belt undone and stood up.

Mrs. Hopkins turned to her right to move into the aisle. By now, Jordan Tartikoff, on the other side of the aisle, had risen from his seat and was tugging at his wife, trying to get her to stand. Mrs. Tartikoff was positive there would be an explanation coming for what had just happened, she later said, and refused to leave her seat.[6] Her husband had to forcibly pull her up.

Several other passengers were standing alongside the Tartikoffs. In an indelible image that Caroline Hopkins would remember with clarity years later, they appeared to be murmuring quietly to themselves as if they were discussing sports scores. "This is no time to wait for a bus," Caroline thought to herself. She hoisted her skirt, stepped up on her seat, and began clambering over the seatbacks in order to get to the doorway, which Joani Feathers and Jack Ridout had now reached.

Feathers now stood at the open doorway area with Ridout in back of her. Below her was Warren Hopkins, shouting, "Come on! I'll catch you!" – a generous but impractical idea, given the height. She hesitated, so Ridout gave her a shove and then turned away, looking for someone else to help. What he didn't notice was that Joani Feathers's skirt and slip had caught on an exposed wire sticking out from the fuselage, and she was suspended briefly, hanging from the plane at a gravity-defying angle.

Feathers managed to pull herself back to a standing position, then unsnagged her clothing from the wire. She turned back toward the ground.

---

[6] This information is from an interview with another passenger who spoke with Mrs. Tartikoff.

"I'd rather have a broken leg than burn to death," she told herself, and so she jumped. With excellent aim, she landed almost in Warren Hopkins' arms. Her impact with the ground was lessened because she landed partially on Hopkins's left foot, aggravating his injury. He remained oblivious to his injuries until hours later.

"Get away from here! Quickly!" Hopkins urged her unnecessarily. Feathers paused only long enough to look at the blood running down his face from his head injury. "Oh my word, he's hurt badly," she thought. But she took his advice and ran directly away from the aircraft as fast as she could. As were many other women on board, Feathers was shoeless, having slipped out of hers on board. She was, at the time, unaware of a deep cut on her right foot.[7]

Caroline Hopkins made it to the doorway just after Feathers had jumped. By now, perhaps 30 seconds had elapsed since the collision. Like her husband, she was momentarily awestruck by the perspective. The wing was so long that it looked like two wings. Then she saw her husband below her. "My God, you look so small," she thought. The distance down to the ground activated her fear of heights, and a wave of vertigo washed over her. To steady herself, she reached out and grabbed part of the ragged-edge fuselage metal, which opened a deep gash on the fourth and fifth fingers of her left hand. As with her husband and his foot, Caroline Hopkins didn't notice her own injury until later.

As she paused, she could hear explosions – a combination of exploding oxygen bottles and fire extinguishers, plus igniting fuel. She was frightened of the height, but the flames under the wing and the blasts ringing in her ears were a powerful incentive to get out of the plane promptly. She jumped but tumbled awkwardly down, her center of gravity horribly off balance, and she landed almost directly on her right shoulder and right side with a flat crack, snapping some shoulder bones and knocking the air out of her lungs. She lay on the ground dazed until Warren Hopkins rushed over to her and implored his wife to get up.

---

[7] The FAA's Civil Aerospace Medical Institute now recommends that women wear light flat shoes, such as gym shoes, when on flights.

The Hopkinses heard more small explosions as she lay on the ground, but she was immobile because of her loss of breath and the impact of her landing.

"We've got to get away from here!" Warren Hopkins insisted, grabbing her by her left arm. "I can't move," Caroline told him fearfully. "I can't stand up." She didn't know what was wrong, just that she couldn't get to her feet. She thought, with curious but probably accurate mental detachment, that she must be in shock. Warren began dragging her and quickly reached the wet, high grass next to the runway. Behind them, parts of the Pan Am fuselage were beginning to erupt in orange flames and loud explosions. Both Hopkinses were cut again and again by pieces of metal zinging through the air.

The action inside the cabin began speeding up. In first class, many passengers remained astonishingly calm – too calm, in some cases. Penny Quade, in seat 3-H, told her sister and mother to sit still and wait for the flight crew. She'd never flown before, and her uncertainty caused her to hesitate. She and her family wasted precious seconds, waiting to be taken care of. (Penny later would spend hours talking to the Hopkinses in their hospital room, reconstructing the moments after the crash.)

Enid Tartikoff was another who was reluctant to leave the plane, she later told David Alexander, another survivor. Only with great effort was her husband able to convince her to get up. Still another passenger tentatively asked the group in the cabin, "Are the stewardesses going to come?" "No, they're not!" Bo Brusco answered firmly, helping his wife and mother down the aisle.

Others began responding. Jim Naik, in 5-D, across the aisle from the Hopkinses, sat stunned for several seconds. He watched, horrified, as a headless body, still strapped into a seat, fell from the lounge above. He turned to his wife to say he wanted them to get out of the plane and touched her shoulder. She was unconscious. Her head fell sideways and blood oozed from a fresh head wound. Naik unsnapped his seat belt, stood up, and leaned over to unsnap his wife's belt – but then was knocked completely out of the plane by an explosion, one of many as the plane began disintegrating. Remarkably, he landed unhurt. He scrambled to his feet next to the plane, helplessly looking up at the fuselage and wondering frantically how he was going to get his wife out. With rising panic, he stayed below the plane as others jumped out. Then another explosion ripped through the plane. The fuselage cracked further, and Naik saw an object fall out of the plane. It was his wife, and she was alive but her body was smoldering. Naik raced over to her and pulled her, still unconscious, away from the fuselage.

Some of the passengers in first class tried to help others. Richard Bowman, 48, of El Cerrito, California, had been sitting in Seat 2-B with his wife next to him when the collision occurred. Bowman later told government investigators that it seemed to take about five to 10 minutes to get out of the plane, a time estimate no doubt magnified by the intensity of the experience. On the way out of the plane with his wife, Bowman and Edward Hess, from 1-H, helped several others through the rubble to the exit that Warren Hopkins had first used. Then they got out themselves.

The paradox of being one of the later passengers to get out of the plane was that, as the seconds ticked by, the landing gear of the plane weakened and the plane sagged closer to the ground, making the jump easier. But the interior of the plane became increasingly dangerous: the floor was collapsing and secondary explosions were sending debris zipping through the cabin. Although the first-class section was one of the last to be reached by fire, the smoke and fumes and heat increased with frightening speed. Ridout recalled trying to help a flight attendant inflate a rubber raft so the passengers would have something to jump into, but an explosion sent metal fragments whizzing through the cabin, killing her. Jack Daniel, from Seat 7-B, heard family friend Elsie Church calling for help and turned back to assist her, in the process telling his wife and daughter to leave the plane, which they did. There were more explosions, and Daniel's family did not see him or Elsie Church again.

Others fought their way out. Terri Brusco later recalled looking up and seeing one of the cockpit control panels visible through holes in the ceiling of the passenger cabin. Then she and her husband, Bo, began working their way through the debris toward an exit. As they struggled, Mr. Brusco guided his mother. Suddenly the older woman fell through a large crack in the plane's floor, completely disappearing from view. Terri and Bo

Brusco jumped out of the plane and, just as Jim Naik had, spent agonizing moments before finding the elder Mrs. Brusco underneath the plane, her body smoldering. They pulled her through the high, wet grass alongside the runway to extinguish the flames on her clothing.

Penny Quade and June Ellingham were behind the Bruscos and also had a mother to help. By now, the plane's fuselage had rolled slightly to the left as it sagged, making it difficult to stay oriented. The young women helped their mother pick through the rubble toward the opening, then the floor gave way completely. Mrs. Ellingham followed the elder Mrs. Brusco, tumbling under the passenger area into the plane's mangled lower level of metal, broken seats, wiring and support sections. Because of the tilt of the fuselage, the two daughters then had to walk along the left side of the plane's interior wall in order to get out. They jumped down from the plane. This time, no one appeared underneath.

Ridout himself left the plane after flinging the rubber raft out of the opening. Before jumping, however, he looked around for someone else to help. Spotting an apparently unconscious older woman still in her seat, he tried to pick her up – and found himself lifting two separated sections of her body. He turned away and jumped out of the plane, landing in the rubber raft. He scrambled out and ran over to Joani Feathers, waiting at a safe distance from the plane. They stood together, numb with emotion, watching the plane burn. "How stupid! How stupid!" they told each other.

Perhaps the last people out of the first-class section were Edward Hess and his wife, Mary Kay. As the flames in and around the airplane rose, turning much of the fuselage into an inferno, Hess pulled his wife to the edge of the plane's interior. She was at first trapped in the wreckage – then Mrs. Hess was boosted out of the plane by a push from an unknown person just before another explosion. Whoever gave her that life-saving shove apparently did not make it out of the plane.

The Civil Aerospace Medical Institute has determined that in an aviation emergency, passengers often aim for the exit they used to board the plane. In the first-class section of the Pan Am plane, that was an advantage because the best way out was through the section of the fuselage where the door had been.

But farther back in the plane, that instinct served no purpose. It would have been impossible for passengers in the rear of the cabin to work their way all the way forward to that same front door where everyone had boarded. In the economy section, everyone had to find his or her own way out of the plane.

After the impact, there were initial yells of fright and also encouragement, and perhaps a few moments of tenderness, as those resigned to their fates turned to their mates for comfort. "Let's not panic!" one person yelled, although, as will be discussed in the next chapter, that's not a common reaction.

Reconstructing the Pan Am economy section evacuation from interviews with survivors, we know this: there were three exit areas used: over the edge of the ripped fuselage near Isobel Monda's seat in Row 32, through cracks and breaks in the fuselage around Row 40, and through the roof just in front of the center lavatories. Most of those in economy class who survived were seated a few rows in front of to a few rows in back of the central section of lavatories – from approximately Row 28 to Row 35. In front of this section, the KLM jet's right-wing landing gear had smashed through. In back of the section, the KLM's left-wing engines and landing gear had struck the Pan Am plane.

Among the least hurt, and perhaps the least aware of what had happened after the impact, were Tony and Isobel Monda. In their seats in 32-A and 32-B, they were shielded from the KLM plane by the lavatories, which acted as a buttress for the roof in their section. Although the force of the collision knocked off Mrs. Monda's glasses, she still thought the plane had merely run off the runway. She sat still, trying to orient herself. Then she saw passengers scrambling for the emergency exit door one seat in front of her, and in fact, a line of people was beginning to form by it.

Still not aware of the extent of the emergency, Mrs. Monda calmly reached beneath the seat in front of her and pulled out her purse. She slipped her purse strap over her shoulder, then stood up. Having read the emergency instructions card and paid attention during the safety briefing by the flight attendants, she fully expected to leave the plane by the exit that others were already lining up to use.[8] She turned slightly as her husband rose, and they both took a sweeping look around the plane to their right and behind them.

It was then that they grasped the magnitude of what had happened. Mrs. Monda saw people lying sprawled in their seats, unconscious or dead. Many were bleeding. Fumes were appearing in the rear of the plane. Other passengers were shocked and unmoving, staring around them. The window on her left had been knocked out of the airframe, she suddenly noticed.

"They're not all going to get out," Mrs. Monda realized with a calmness that surprised even her. "But I am."

She started for the emergency exit, but her husband held her and turned her around. "No, this way," he said, and pointed toward the section of the fuselage where a window had been knocked out near their seats. The fuselage was cracked and open.

Mrs. Monda would later note that the window was knocked out just next to where she had placed the religious pamphlet earlier in the flight. "It was because God was there," she said.

Her husband, looking through the windows, could see and hear the engines still operating and, like others, was afraid of another explosion. While his wife was turning around, he reached under the seat and pulled out their carry-on bag, an action that prompted the man on Monda's right, Bennett Reynolds, a friend of the Mondas, to do the same.[9] By the time Mr. Monda had returned to a standing position, his wife had impulsively taken a flying dive out the window, head first, like a cartoon character.

"If I don't get ahold of something to turn around on, I'm going to be in trouble," Mrs. Monda thought to herself in mid-dive. Somehow she did, wriggling out onto the wing and turning herself around in order to get her feet under her. But then the slippery wing surface caused her to lose her

---

[8] Rehearsing the brain for a crisis is the best preparation for a crisis, according to many studies. For example, see Ripleu's *The Unthinkable*, or numerous articles by researcher John Leach of Great Britain.

[9] The flight attendants' union now strongly advises against this because it slows down evacuations. "We've seen an issue in carry-on bags in almost every single evacuation of the last few years," Taylor Garland, AFA public affairs spokeswoman, said in February 2018. Among other problems, she noted, rollaway bag wheels can rip the emergency slides. However, at this particular moment on the Pan Am plane, no warning had been given from the crew. And a number of passengers were unaware of the severity of the situation.

balance. She tumbled off the back edge of the wing to the ground, a distance of about 15 feet, landing terribly wrong, partly on her right foot and right arm, breaking both and cracking a rib as well. Unable to move, she lay on the runway, directly underneath the back edge of the massive wing.

Her husband, Tony, was next to climb out onto the wing. He moved a few feet farther from the plane on the wing before sliding down and off the back, throwing his bag down in front of him. He landed on his feet, bouncing to all fours but chipping a bone in one hand before rising. He picked up the carry-on bag and turned to his wife. (They had borrowed the bag from one of their daughters. In a crisis it is not uncommon to lock onto a simple action such as being protective of a borrowed piece of luggage.) Sickeningly, he saw first one person, then a second person, land on his wife as they jumped off the wing.

"I don't think they could have seen Isabel," Monda later suggested. He did not want to believe that people would deliberately jump on top of her to break their own falls. Unable to move, Isabel sustained further injuries because of the bodies landing on her. Four vertebrae in her back were cracked, and the broken foot became a crushed foot.

Monda waded into the pile of people and pushed them aside to get to his wife. "Get up!" he encouraged. "We've got to get away!"

"I can't," she answered through her pain. "My leg's broken."

"Well then, lean on me and I'll pull you," he insisted.

"I can't do that, either," she replied. "My arm's broken."

Monda looked around just as a man hurried up. Monda said later he believed the man was a local resident who lived next to the airport. The man spoke no English, but through gestures Monda indicated quickly that they should pull Mrs. Monda away from the plane. The man nodded rapidly. The two pulled Mrs. Monda all the way to near the third taxiway turnoff, C-3, the one the controller had told the Pan Am crew to take. Then both men returned to the plane to see if they could help anyone else.

How that man got to the plane so quickly is not clear. It's possible that he was another survivor who had gotten out at about the same time as the Mondas and was, as some other people were, simply shocked into muteness. Such a reaction can happen in a tragedy. The air traffic controller who last spoke with a Pacific Southwest Airlines flight that crashed in San Diego in 1978 was mute for three days. So the man helping Monda may have been another survivor – possibly Juan Murillo, the Pan American agent who had been deadheading in the cockpit.

As the perception of danger increased, and initial shocked inaction began wearing off, so did the haste of the remaining passengers in the economy section of the plane. Several minutes had now gone by, and flames were ripping through the rear of the fuselage. Within another minute or so, the flames and the fumes they released would take the lives of numerous passengers in the rear of the plane.

In many air crashes, the safest place to be sitting is the rear of the plane, for one obvious reason. Crashes often involve a plane falling out of the sky back to the ground; in such a situation, the front of the plane hits first, absorbing much of the impact.

The Tenerife crash was an exception. The worst place on the Pan Am plane to be sitting was in the rear. The passenger section on this particular 747 was divided in half, between Rows 30 and 31; the farthest back anyone who managed to survive was sitting was about Row 40. Even farther back, behind a section of galleys in Rows 41 through 56, were those in the last section – passengers who had asked for, and gotten, seats in the plane's smoking section.[10] They are the anonymous victims of the crash, because no one sitting near them survived to recall last actions, last words, last thoughts. There may have been jokes among these people during the flight from the United States about their location: lighthearted kidding about having less-desirable seats to be able to smoke a cigarette. Perhaps, after the crash, there was very little awareness of what was happening. The left-side landing gear and rear sections of the KLM jet's fuselage crashed through the right side of the rear of the Pan Am plane, on an upward slant, directly through the passenger seating area. The explosive collision with the KLM plane surely killed most of those passengers instantly. The impact was, in fact, so great that several sections of the Pan Am fuselage were found near the KLM fuselage several hundred meters down the runway. Fires broke

---

[10] Smoking was permitted on international flights until the 1990s.

123

out rapidly, and the toxic fumes would have quickly brought unconsciousness to anyone who hadn't been killed by the impact.

But in front of the row of galley bulkheads, it was different. The middle two sections of the plane run from Row 20 to Row 40, which was a safer area on this day. A fairly large group of passengers successfully evacuated the first-class section, but in terms of numbers, more got out from this part of the economy section.

The Mondas, in 32-A and 32-B, were among the first out of the economy section. A few passengers later came Bennett and Madeline Reynolds, who had been sitting just a few seats away who used the same window hole. They had struggled just to get to the opening. Mrs. Reynolds, in 32-C, was among those who initially had been unable to unbuckle her seat belt. Her husband reached from behind her to do it, freeing her, and then urged her to move to the hole that Monda was now following his wife out of. Mrs. Reynolds stood up just as an explosion shook the plane, and she was knocked flat on her back in the aisle. Others now pushed past them to get to the Mondas' window hole. Again, Bennett Reynolds helped his wife up, and they followed other passengers through the hole and onto the wing.

At this point, Monda was walking down the wing and away from the fuselage, instead of getting off the wing right away, as his wife had done. But others, who were in between Monda and the Reynoldses during the evacuation, jumped off the wing as soon as they could. Several of these people were the ones who inadvertently landed on Mrs. Monda. Only moments before, she had survived the collision in better shape than almost any other passenger on the plane, and now she was badly injured.

The Reynoldses also walked down the wing, away from the fuselage, before easing themselves off the back edge. But both of them also landed badly, Reynolds breaking a bone in his heel and his wife suffering a broken ankle, cracking both hips, and chipping a bone in her right hip. Along with almost everyone else on the plane, each was cut by flying metal.

Reynolds, 59, and his wife, 61, were unable to rise to their feet. They crawled together, away from the wreckage. "If we're going to go, we'll go together," Reynolds told his wife. As they crawled, they saw a dazed fellow passenger standing nearby.

"Could you help us, please?" Reynolds pleaded.

"I'm sorry," the man answered politely, "but I can't." He held up his hands, and the Reynoldses were both shocked to see that his fingers had been severely burned down to the knuckles.

Paul and Floy Heck, in 34-D and 34-E, got out shortly after the Mondas, and through the same gap in the fuselage left by the missing window. Mr. Heck, a careful passenger, had earlier pointed out the emergency exit to his wife, an exit that never opened. But they were able to follow the people who were jumping through the hole used by the Mondas. That opening was quite close to the emergency exit. Heck would later say that the safety card in the seatback that he studied before takeoff did help save him and his wife. Their success was an important example of the value of mental preparation.

Floy Heck was later quoted in media reports as saying she had noticed dozens of people who were sitting and apparently waiting for instructions.

"They just didn't move," she told the Long Beach *Press-Telegram* shortly after the crash. "I believe at least another one hundred could have been saved, but they were sitting there just transfixed."

Beth Moore got out of that exit, also, and her experience paralleled that of Mrs. Monda. When the collision happened, she was just sitting up after having made some adjustments in her carry-on bag. That may have saved her an injury, because her husband, Walter, was struck on the head by debris and hurt badly. She looked at him and was shocked to see blood, yet he managed to rise and point out to her what to do.

"Beth, go out that hole," he stated, ever the commander. She looked past his arm to the hole the Mondas were climbing through. She was two rows behind that hole and managed to climb over the seats toward it, purse slung over her shoulder. Along with many other women on board, Mrs. Moore was shoeless.

Because Admiral Moore had had the presence of mind to point out the nearest exit, Mrs. Moore assumed that he was physically capable of following her. Perhaps he was, and stayed behind to direct others out.

Mrs. Moore never saw her husband again.

She didn't know that outcome, of course, as she climbed out the hole. As she stood on the wing, she was momentarily completely alone. The wing was slippery because she was shoeless, so she had difficulty maintaining her balance. She could see smoke shooting up about 50 feet farther down the wing, under which a fire was now raging.

Unsteadily, she edged to the front of the wing, about six feet away from the fuselage. "I have to get off and away," she said to herself, and then, as if stepping off a curb, she simply walked into space, off the front edge of the wing, plummeting straight down to the ground. She landed horribly, her right foot and right leg taking most of the impact. That leg immediately collapsed beneath her, with the femur shattered and the foot bones broken. One vertebra, the eighth, was cracked in the landing. Her hip joint was damaged and her pubic bone was knocked out of position.

Mrs. Monda lay on the ground under the back part of the wing, while Mrs. Moore lay near the fuselage under the front part of the wing. Both women were hurt so badly that they were unable to move.

"I was standing on the wing in nylon stockinged feet," Mrs. Moore later recalled. "I had my purse on my arm. It was very slippery, the wing was. And the plane was burning. I was out there alone. And I don't think I did this out of bravery. I don't think I had a choice. I simply had to jump off that wing."[11]

Mrs. Moore had lain there for perhaps 10 seconds when there was a shockingly painful blow to her right shin and foot. As with Mrs. Monda, someone had just landed on her.

She was able to turn her head slightly and saw that it was another woman. "Help me, please!" Mrs. Moore yelled, but the woman ran away. She began calling for help at the top of her lungs but was rewarded for her efforts by having two more women land on her. From the wing above, it may not have been possible to hear Mrs. Moore's cries for help. From that height, she may have appeared simply as a body that could be used to help someone else. And yet…it was also possible those other passengers were fully aware that Mrs. Moore needed help, but their own priorities

---

[11] This information, and that concerning the Mondas, was taken from telephone interviews with several survivors.

had taken over and there was only one life they were interested in saving: their own. The danger had become too great for them to think about anyone else.

Mrs. Moore began to think that no one would help her. Her pain was horrible but not enough to make her lose consciousness. The instep on her right foot was now shattered, and her other injuries were aggravated by the blows and the weight of the people who had landed on her. Slowly, ever so painfully, a few inches at a time, she dragged herself away from the fuselage, as it burned more ferociously. Then, like a godsend, the face of a pretty young woman appeared over Mrs. Moore. "Don't worry," the woman said. "I won't leave you." It was Dorothy Kelly, one of the flight's pursers.

In 32-D, 32-E, 32-F, and 32-G, just behind the lavatories in the middle seat section, were four more friends from the Leisure World retirement community: Walter and Grace McGowan, 77 and 75 years old, respectively, and Herbert and Lura Waldrip, 71 and 67 years old – among the oldest couples on the plane.

Mrs. McGowan sustained the most peculiar injury in the crash. When the collision took place, the movie screen that was hanging almost directly over her head tumbled down from its ceiling storage compartment and broke a bone in her foot.[12] A metal object struck Waldrip on his head and broke his glasses. The four of them then struggled over to the left edge of the fuselage. When Mrs. McGowan hesitated, she was pushed out onto the wing by a crush of people behind her. When she moved to the edge of the wing, she hesitated, and again the flood of people escaping from the plane pushed her over the edge, breaking her other foot in the fall, as well as a thumb.

Her husband was also having a difficult time: when he climbed out of the cabin onto the wing, his pants got stuck on a ragged piece of metal protruding from the wing. McGowan was momentarily helpless and couldn't free himself, but then Waldrip, right behind him, unsnagged his friend's clothing. When both men jumped, they landed much better than their wives and suffered no broken bones – but both had burns from the metal of

---

[12] In those days of flying, films were shown on a few small movie screens that hung in front of different sections of the passenger cabin. No airlines yet offered individual screens for each passenger.

the wing, which was heating up rapidly from the fires underneath it. Lura Waldrip also landed heavily, breaking her left leg and spraining an ankle.

When McGowan reached the ground and looked around for his wife, he began gasping for breath. A sufferer of angina episodes, he felt he was having another one. But with the aid of his friends, he was able to walk over to the nearby grass field adjoining the runway, where he sat down and swallowed three nitroglycerine tablets that he carried in a pocket. They helped.

All the passengers who were among the latter group to get out of the plane suffered burns among their injuries. Ethel Simon, the woman who'd had a leg cramp during the flight, also climbed out the Mondas' escape portal. After jumping off the wing and spraining an ankle, she couldn't find her husband and wanted to return to the plane, but one of the surviving flight attendants held her back. As she stood looking at the plane, she saw it "aglow" with fire and sparks, she would later tell government investigators, in one of the most descriptive accounts of the incident by a passenger. "There was panic and screaming," she added.

After the collision, Erma Schlecht recalled being as stunned as many other passengers. But then another thought moved quickly into her consciousness. "Don't just sit there...do something!" she told herself. Traveling alone (she was a widow), she climbed out of her seat and got moving.[13]

Jean Brown, the travel agent sitting in 37-C, had an identical realization. After the collision, she said later, she looked around at the injured and dying. "Well, this is the way to die," she announced to herself, "in an airplane crash." She sat passively for several moments, as did many others, before she suddenly realized, "We can get out of here!"

This far back in the plane, the left side of the fuselage had peeled away, creating almost a ledge alongside some of the seats. Mrs. Brown turned to the couple sitting between her and the outside of the plane, Mike and Dahlia Jones, and said sharply, "Unfasten your seat belts. We've got to get out of here!" The insistent manner in which she spoke apparently snapped them out of their dazed state. All three rose, the Joneses first climbing over

[13] Mrs. Schlecht's comments were made on a PBS documentary, "The Deadliest Plane Crash," which appeared on the *Nova* television series in 2007.

the broken fuselage onto the wing and then helping Mrs. Brown.[14] Mrs. Brown saw no one follow her, and they became among the last passengers to get out of the plane.

Fires were now licking through most of the cabin, and the plane's metal had crumpled and collapsed in many places, exposing jagged edges. The Joneses immediately went to the front edge of the wing, in between the fuselage and the inboard engine, but were met with extreme heat and flames. They jumped anyway. Both would die at local hospitals within hours.

Mrs. Brown, however, turned toward the back edge of the wing, a seemingly small decision that saved her life. She started to make her way to the rear edge, but her foot got caught in an open section of metal and several anxious moments passed before she freed herself. Unlike the Joneses, she decided to walk farther down the wing, away from the fuselage. The flames were less intense past the first engine, and from there Mrs. Brown jumped off the wing's back edge. She leaped, missing most of the heat, but scorching her legs severely. On landing, her body collapsed and she, too, at first was unable to rise. Laboriously, she slowly pulled herself to her feet and limped away from the wreckage. On her return to the United States, she would endure two months in the Brooke Army Medical Center burn hospital in San Antonio – but she survived.

There were others even farther back in the plane who managed to escape: Larry and Phyllis Walker in 40-A and 40-B, Marian Andersen in 40-C, and Charles Pinkstaff, in 43-A. The back of the plane was a junkyard filled with fumes and smoke, yet somehow all fought their way to gaps on the left side of the fuselage, near the one used by Mrs. Brown and the Joneses.

"I saw only dead people," Larry Walker would report later. He and his wife both felt that it took at least five minutes to get out of the plane. Both also were burned badly, and Mrs. Walker hurt her head when it flew forward and struck the back of Seat 39-A during the collision.

There was a third escape route for the passengers sitting in front of the center lavatories, and passengers David Alexander and Roy Tanemura

---

[14] "Mike and Dahlia Jones" are pseudonyms.

found it: through the roof. Alexander was responsible for helping save other passengers because they saw him climbing up and out. Before then, they hadn't been sure what to do. These included Albert and Florence Trumbull, sitting in the same row as Alexander. Alexander was in 30-C, and the Trumbulls were in 30-F and 30-G, on the right side of the aircraft.

For months after the accident, Alexander could not remember what had happened in the initial moments after the crash. He was able to reconstruct the events only after painful and difficult concentration: the Ronders on his left had immediately disappeared, falling through the floor into the cargo compartment after the collapsing overhead compartments tumbled onto them.

"I'm going to die," Alexander said to himself. Then, as with Mrs. Brown, another thought moved into the center of his consciousness: "No, I'm not," he thought.[15]

With his camera still strapped around his neck, Alexander stood up. He noticed that part of the plane's roof had ripped open almost directly overhead. That could be a way out, he thought, quite sensibly. He worked his way onto the top of his seatback and climbed through the roof of the plane. The ceiling in a 747's cabin is eight feet high, thus the climb was not easy. Additionally, his glasses had been knocked off during the collision, so he couldn't see well. Alexander nevertheless made it onto the roof and slipped down the side of the fuselage, as if on a playground slide, onto the left wing. With flames and smoke around him, he stood momentarily. Smoke and fog were now swirling around him, but he was able to see a woman lying on the wing. He did not know who she was. He moved the woman off of the wing, in case she was still alive, and then jumped down. Unable to see the woman through the plumes of smoke, he turned and ran away from the fuselage. He ran about 75 yards, then turned around, breathing hard, stunned, dazed, shocked, as the orange flames and black smoke billowed into the sky and explosions shattered the metal, sending more showers of metal fragments into the air.[16]

---

[15] This information is based on interviews with Mr. Alexander.

[16] "It was like the Hindenburg blowing up," Floy Heck told a newspaper. Her reference was to the 1937 explosion of the German dirigible as it attempted to dock in New Jersey.

Photo courtesy of David Alexander

This photo of the burning Pan Am jet, taken by survivor David Alexander after he'd escaped from the plane, is probably the first photo taken after the collision.

It was then that he realized he still had his camera around his neck. There was surely no chance of going back. He raised the camera and took five pictures of the burning plane as some of the remaining survivors tried to get away from it. His pictures were the first taken of the disaster that was now unfolding.

Many months later, Alexander talked with Albert and Florence Trumbull, who had been sitting in 30-F and 30-G. They told him that seeing him leave the plane had helped them realize that they had to respond and get out, too.

Florence Trumbull had been bent over, putting some money in her tote bag, when the collision happened. She threw her arms over her head for protection and remained crouched. When she sat up, she and her husband looked around. Those who remained in their seats around them seemed calm, too calm. "It was like catching a deer in your headlights," Trumbull would later say: many passengers simply sat wide-eyed, immobile, uncomprehending.[17]

---

[17] This "negative panic," or behavioral inaction, is explained by Dan Johnson and others in the following chapter.

Then they looked to their left. The Ellerbrocks, who had been sitting in the seats next to them, were gone. And Alexander was already climbing up on his seat to get through a hole in the cabin roof. They rose and moved to the left side of the plane, dodging live electrical wires that were flashing and popping through the cabin. Trumbull felt one brush across his arm; it burned him.

When Mrs. Trumbull made her way onto the wing, she saw a man gesturing below for her to jump into his arms to break her fall. She did so, but at age 70, her body was not able to withstand even the partial fall, and she broke a thigh bone.

The Ellerbrocks, in 30-D and 30-E just in front of the lavatories, had responded quickly after the impact. Fragments of the ceiling had fallen during the collision of the two planes, striking Byron on the left side of his forehead and his left eye, opening cuts. "For God's sake, get out!" Grace Ellerbrock later remembered yelling at her husband, realizing they had to evacuate the plane.

Ellerbrock pulled his handkerchief out of his pocket to hold in front of his nose and mouth, and he and his wife moved to leave the plane but immediately got separated. Mrs. Ellerbrock somehow made her way through the same hole in the fuselage others had used, while her husband climbed up and out, following David Alexander's route. Then he toppled from the top of the plane down to the left wing, and then again to the ground – a tumbling fall, in two stages, of more than 30 feet. The fall smashed his pelvis, an extraordinarily painful injury that sent him into shock and left him in a sitting position against part of the plane's fuselage. He was saved from vertebrae damage, he would later say, by the fact that he was wearing a corset for sacroiliac discomfort.

Mrs. Ellerbrock had also gotten to the ground by then and was ready to move away, only to turn and see her husband, bleeding profusely and sitting near the plane. Herself a mass of cuts, she ran to him and urged him up, but with his injury he was unable to move.

"You push and I'll pull," she insisted, and so they set off, he working his legs and she (at five feet, four inches and 130 pounds, compared to her husband's six feet, two inches and 200 pounds) pulling under his arms. In another situation, it would have looked like a game to be played at a picnic. But this was a race for life.

Others in their section of seats made their way out of the roof hole Alexander had used: Norman Williams, Mario Tyzbir and Roy Tanemura.

Tyzbir, 61, sitting in 26-B with his wife next to him, turned around after the collision to see Alexander climbing up and out of the plane. Tyzbir hesitated. In front of him he saw only fire and smoke. Around him were injured people. Up seemed to be the only place to go. Tyzbir unsnapped both his and his wife's seat belts, then they both stepped over the motionless man sitting next to Tyzbir on the aisle, in 26-C. A major explosion shook the cabin as the two climbed onto the backs of their seats, trying to reach the roof. Tyzbir swung himself up onto the wrecked roof, steadied himself by lying flat on a less-mangled section of the plane, and then reached back for his wife and grabbed her hand. He had just begun pulling when another explosion shook the plane, and Mrs. Tyzbir fell backward into the cabin. Tyzbir tumbled off the roof and all the way down to the ground, fracturing a vertebra, bruising and cutting himself. He began crawling away from the plane on his hands and knees.

The horror and tragedy of Tyzbir losing his wife was matched by what happened to Roy Tanemura and his wife, in 29-F and 29-G.[18] The impact of the collision had loosened some seats from their floor tracks,[19] and people around them were slumped down and unmoving. Behind them, the Ellerbrocks were gone already, and the Trumbulls were beginning to make their exit when the Tanemuras began to respond.

They unbuckled themselves and managed to get into the right-hand aisle, where Mrs. Tanemura was the first to see the possibility of climbing up and out. She may have seen David Alexander, who had been sitting in the row in back of them, doing exactly that.

"Climb up there and pull me up," she said to her husband, gesturing upward. Tanemura, not a tall man, immediately attempted to do so. He got a foothold by using a magazine rack on the lavatory wall as a makeshift

---

[18] This information is from an interview with Mr. Tanemura.
[19] Passenger jets are now manufactured with higher standards of seat stability than they were in the 1970s.

ladder and, with difficulty, was able to scramble up and onto the roof. Flames and heavy smoke were now filling the cabin, and he gasped for breath when he made it to the top of the plane. Then he turned around and reached back down to grab his wife's hand – and in a moment that seemed to be taking place in slow motion, he watched in horror as his wife succumbed to the fumes and smoke, falling slowly backward to the floor and disappearing into the smoke.

Tanemura hesitated, unable to decide whether to go back down. He then realized that he was not physically able to get back down and combine the pulling and pushing required to get her up to the roof. He looked over at the still-closed emergency door, in front of which a crowd of people was now standing – but some were already crumpling to the floor, as had his wife. At the front of the line was his friend Ted Freeman.[20]

"Ted! Ted! Freeman! *Freeman!*" Tanemura screamed. Mr. Freeman never even looked up, and the nightmare tableau of the passengers waiting for an emergency door that would never open would be Tanemura's last image of his friend. He became convinced that Freeman was in shock.

Tanemura stood for another few moments, a solitary figure standing almost in defiance on top of a burning 747 jumbo jet. Then he turned and, as Alexander had done, slid down the fuselage to the left wing. Now he wanted only to get away. Unlike everyone else, he ran all the way down the wing, past the burning engines, in the process singeing the back of his sport coat. He ran to the very end of the wing, then flung himself off, in the fall breaking an ankle and a wrist as he tumbled onto the runway. His glasses and watch flew off, but he ignored them and began crawling away. He crawled about 50 yards from the end of the wing before finally, painfully, standing and turning around to face the wreckage of the plane, now burning like an oil refinery. He knew then, with a horrified certainty, that his wife was gone.

[20] The name was changed as a courtesy.

CHAPTER 14

*P*anic – *"a sudden sensation of fear, which is so strong as to dominate or prevent reason and logical thinking, replacing it with overwhelming feelings of anxiety and frantic agitation consistent with an animalistic fight-or-flight reaction…"* The word derives from the Greek *"panikon"* (sudden fear), referring to the woods god, Pan. When humans would walk through a lonely place, Pan would sometimes frighten them with a loud yell that would generate fear, hyperventilation and a stampede.[1]

In the 1970s, the public's understanding of crisis behavior put every-one into one of two categories: those who can keep their wits about them and behave rationally, with purpose and courage, and those who panic and act irrationally. Fight or flight, essentially.

There was little panic in the Pan Am plane on the runway at Tenerife.

In fact, the absence of panic is the case in many emergencies, not just aircraft evacuations. Among all kinds of disasters, those that involve fire can frighten the most – like horses in a stable, humans will stampede to avoid fire.

But "panicking," in the sense of having a sudden, overwhelming fear that produces irrational or hysterical behavior, is not as prevalent as we might suspect. There is a third type of behavior, more prevalent than panic or heroism: it's the inability to respond at all.

---

[1] "Panic," Wikipedia.com.

"A relatively high incidence of inaction and a low incidence of panic have been noted in disaster situations," psychologist Dan Johnson wrote after the Tenerife accident. "Perhaps the most common cause of death in airplane accidents (other than the trauma of the crash itself) is that people don't get up and move."[2]

In the 1970s and 1980s, Johnson was the president of The Interaction Company, a research firm that produced emergency information safety cards for some airlines, including Pan American. He and associate Beau Altman extensively studied crashes and how people behave in emergencies. Both were former employees of McDonnell Douglas Corporation.

Instead of the two choices of fight or flight, there are three possible actions when an individual faces a confrontation of some sort, Johnson explained: the individual can attack the agent of harm, avoid the confrontation, or not act at all. This third response has become known as "behavioral inaction," "negative panic," or, simply, "freezing."

John Leach in Great Britain has spent many years studying human behavior in various emergency situations, focusing on aviation. He has reported that up to 75 percent of humans in an emergency will have a "stunned and bewildered" response. Another 10 to 15 percent will be "calm, cool and collected," while the remaining 10 to 15 percent will be in full panic: "uncontrolled and irrational."[3]

Studies of actual plane crash evacuations by the Civil Aerospace Medical Institute, an arm of the Federal Aviation Administration, indicate that as many as 85 percent of the passengers in those crashes exhibit at least some components of what the agency called "disaster syndrome": stunned, docile, bewildered or unresponsive behavior, any of which interfere with the individual's ability to function.[4]

Charles Catanese is a California psychologist who wrote his doctoral thesis on the emotional effects of the Tenerife crash on the Pan Am survivors. He suggested that a depression might set in during an extreme crisis.

[2] *Just In Case: A Passenger's Guide to Airplane Safety and Survival*, Plenum Press, 1984, was useful in the preparation of this book. Johnson was also interviewed by Jon Ziomek.
[3] In 2018, Prof. Leach was a Senior Research Fellow in survival psychology at the University of Portsmouth. He supplied Jon Ziomek with copies of his research.
[4] Formerly the Civil Aeromedical Institute.

The inability to face reality, the lack of emotion and response, the docility – all of these can be seen as symptoms of a depressed state.

In his thesis, Catanese quoted behaviorists Kurt and Gladys Lang: "A disaster that is completely unanticipated, unprecedented and undiscriminating will create the greatest amount of disorganization and therefore poses the greatest threat to morale."

Dan Johnson has this example: In April 1952, a commercial airliner had to make an emergency ditching in the Atlantic Ocean near San Juan, Puerto Rico. The passengers were not told beforehand what was going to happen, nor were they briefed on the use of their life jackets. In those days, such a briefing was not mandatory.

After the plane had landed on the water, the flight attendants then shouted to the passengers where the jackets were, and to put them on immediately. There was confusion among the passengers, and only some of them responded to the attendants' commands.

The second officer then came into the cabin from the cockpit with a life raft, which he launched into the water through one of the overwing exits. The captain went to the main cabin door and opened it, yelling to passengers to leave the plane immediately. No one obeyed him. He then began forcibly shoving people out the door and was able to get a few out and into the water before a large wave knocked him into the ocean.

Of the 69 people aboard the aircraft, 52 drowned, all passengers. Perhaps some had been hurt in the rough landing and were not able to respond. But many simply remained immobile.

Johnson also cited a 1970 emergency evacuation of a wide-bodied jet while it was still on the ground. During the incident, the reason for the evacuation – a fire warning – turned out to be a false alarm. But it was impossible to halt the evacuation in the middle of the process, so the passengers were allowed to keep leaving the aircraft according to the crew's instructions.

However, one crew member, who had learned that the danger did not actually exist, became an objective observer, watching individual responses among the passengers. He saw several passengers sitting passively in their seats instead of leaving the plane. And one woman was in a "rigid, trance-like state," lying on her side in one of the main cabin aisles. When she was lifted, she maintained her rigidity, like a department store mannequin.

Still another example: After an emergency landing of another airliner, a woman passenger unfastened her seat belt and stepped into the aisle while the plane was still moving rapidly down the runway. There was a fire in the plane's cabin, but she was able to make her way to a window exit, in front of which sat an unmoving man who appeared to be in a state of shock. She moved him away, opened the window exit, and then dove through the window onto the wing.

The man who had been sitting next to the window also escaped and later reported that he had no idea how the exit window had been opened. He did, however, remember seeing a woman lying on the wing.

Apparently, the man suffered a breakdown in perception of external stimuli for a few moments and never saw or felt the woman push him aside, Johnson theorized.

That's behavioral inaction – freezing.

Joseph LeDoux, director of New York University's Emotional Brain Institute, has noted that this freezing behavior has even been recorded on video. Following the Olympic Park bombing during the 1996 Summer Olympics in Atlanta, a nearby security camera showed that "many people froze," LeDoux reported in a December 2015 *New York Times* op-ed article. "Then, some began to try to escape, while others were slower on the uptake. This variation in response is typical. Sometimes freezing is brief and sometimes it persists."[5]

No one wants to think they'd act in such a helpless way. These people were simply unable to respond to an emergency that threatened their lives.

"The trio of freeze, flight and fight are fairly universal behavioral defensive reactions in mammals and other vertebrate species," LeDoux noted in his book *Anxious: Using the Brain to Understand and Treat Fear and Anxiety.*[6] "Given the freezing, fleeing, and fighting innate response programs that

---

[5] Joseph LeDoux, "'Run, Hide, Fight' Is Not How Our Brains Work," *New York Times*, December 20, 2015.
[6] Penguin Random House, 2015.

are hardwired into brain circuits, the response selection problem can be reduced to a question of circuit activation.

"Threats activate defensive survival circuits, and this lowers the threshold for the expression of each of the defensive responses. Freezing has the lowest threshold and so is activated first." But responses can change quickly, he said: freezing can give way to fleeing or fighting.

Researchers, safety officials, and passengers will surely all agree that good crisis behavior includes being calm and having clarity of vision in problem-solving.

But our brains don't make this easy. John Leach and others have noted that in a sudden crisis, our brains generate cortisol, which slows down rational thinking.

What can help us: taking a few moments to consider emergency response possibilities. This theme – the value of preparing for the possibility of an emergency by practicing one's response – is repeated throughout the research in this field.

Denial of an emergency situation "can be overcome if the person asks himself or herself the question: 'What is my first response?'" Leach has written. "This is a simple but effective question that triggers the supervisory system to organize the relevant cognitive components to provide an answer and in so doing also establishes a psychological state of preparedness for an emergency."[7]

And in *The Unthinkable,* writer Amanda Ripley noted, "The best way to negotiate stress is through repeated, realistic training…Confidence comes from doing."

In an airplane, the simple act of *looking at the safety card* is a form of this rehearsing. Paying attention to the flight attendants and the safety video during the safety talk are other ways to rehearse. This reviewing of information creates a path in the brain that we can follow, if the need arises.

"Even if this cut only a few seconds off our freezing, it might make the difference between life and death," LeDoux noted in his *New York Times* article.

---

[7] From Chapter 3, "Psychological Factors in Underwater Egress and Survival," by John Leach, in *Handbook of Offshore Helicopter Transport Safety,* by John Taber, Woodhead Publishing, 2015. An abstract can be found here: https://www.sciencedirect.com/science/article/pii/B9781782421870000031.

A 2007 presentation by FAA safety experts noted that improving cabin familiarity for passengers "improves safety understanding." However, the title of the slide presentation in which this comment was made was "Passenger Safety Awareness Reprise 2007: Still Ignorant After All These Years."[8] In other words, despite government and some industry efforts, many passengers remain unwilling to absorb the information that might save their lives. The FAA report said a high percentage of all passengers, when asked shortly after their flight, can't recall details from the safety card, such as the necessity to put on one's own oxygen mask before helping companion travelers.

The study on which this presentation was based grouped passengers according to their attention to safety: they were either paying attention to the flight attendants and scanning the safety card, or they weren't paying attention. Most people are in the latter group. Many in that group are young men who have flown regularly, so there may be an inherent level of existing knowledge.

Interestingly, the presentation went on, "Half of those who usually don't pay attention to flight safety briefings and a majority of those already paying attention would pay even more attention to safety briefings if they saw other passengers paying attention." The same comment was offered about reading the safety cards in the seatbacks.

"There is a need for increased efforts to improve passenger attention to safety presentations," the report said.

In 1972, Johnson tried to create a stress situation in the laboratory that would be similar to what is experienced by passengers in an aircraft emergency. Obviously, he couldn't crash a plane for his test. Rather, he set up a situation in which the test individuals might feel genuinely threatened. This is what he did:

Subjects were put in front of a console of switches that vaguely resembled those found in an airplane cockpit. They were given instructions on a television monitor about pushing some of the switches in specific sequences. Then, while they were repeating the instructions into a microphone, their

---

[8] This report is available online as a PowerPoint presentation at: http://www.fire.tc.faa.gov/2007 conference/files/evacuation/wedam/corbettpasssafetyaware/corbettpasssafetyawarepres.pdf

own voices were played back to them 0.16 seconds later as a way of deliberately confusing them.

Additionally, some of the subjects were told that if they didn't perform the right actions with the switches, they would be given a painful electric shock. This was not actually done – only the threat of the shock was given. The subjects believed it would happen.

Johnson said this situation would be psychologically similar to that of airline passengers in an emergency. It induced confusion, it called for novel responses by the subjects, and there would be physical punishment for incorrect behavior. In an airplane emergency, confusion certainly exists, passengers are called upon to act in ways they may be totally unfamiliar with, and certainly there is a threat of injury (or worse) if they don't act properly.

Johnson used 33 men and 31 women for the test, evenly distributed in age, ranging from 20 to 65 years old.

"Overall, twenty-nine of the sixty-four subjects (45 percent) displayed inaction at least once," Johnson reported. "Six of the subjects showed inaction twice, while three others showed it three times."

Intriguingly, there was no correlation between the threat of physical harm and the inability to push the proper switches. Those who were threatened with electric shocks were just as liable to "freeze" as those who were not so threatened.

Psychiatrist John Duffy, who extensively studied aviation and aviation crash victims in the 1970s and 1980s, has suggested that some people are predisposed toward having a more passive reaction to a crisis than others.[9] In their attitude toward life, they feel that the world acts upon them, as opposed to the other way around.

"There are different kinds of personalities, some being more dependent on others," agreed Dan Johnson. "Some persons are more information-seeking than others, and some prefer not even to think about this kind of unpleasant reality."

---

[9] Dr. Duffy became an FAA consultant and college instructor, and also served as an assistant surgeon general of the United States.

Johnson called this dichotomy "external or internal focus of control. The person with external control thinks that fate acts upon him, whereas the person with internal control thinks that control of his or her fate is located inside himself or herself."

Many psychologists have noted that people with some knowledge of, or background experience in, crisis behavior would be expected to show less "maladaptive behavior" – pilots, for example.

A year and a half after their experience on Tenerife, Caroline and Warren Hopkins met a Hartselle, Alabama, businessman named Don Foster. Foster, a private pilot, was on board a Southern Airways DC-9 flight just eight days after the Tenerife crash, in April 1977. His plane was caught in a severe thunderstorm, with hailstones as large as grapefruit smashing against the plane. The cockpit windshield was cracked, and both jet engines malfunctioned.

As he looked out the window from his seat near the rear of the plane, Foster was among the first to notice the engines were not functioning. A cautious flyer, Foster told the Hopkinses that he always sat in the third seat from the rear on DC-9s because the rear of the plane sustains the least amount of impact if there is a crash-landing, and the third seat from the rear in a DC-9 is the last seat that still has a window view of the engines. Airlines and aircraft manufacturers see the rear of a plane as usually safer – that's where they store the flight data and cockpit voice recorders. Those recorders are used by safety investigators to determine the mechanical activities on a flight that has trouble and are always an important part of crash investigations.

On his flight, remaining remarkably calm, Foster rose from his seat and took a pillow and his leather coat from the overhead storage rack. He wrapped the coat around his head as protection from the expected fire after the crash-landing, which he was already anticipating. He used the pillow as a cushion in his lap. Then he put himself in the "brace position," as the airlines call it: folding his arms across the top of the seatback in front of him, putting his feet next to the bottom edges of the seat in front of him, and then cradling his head in his arms.

There was no "life passing before his eyes" moment, just a total calmness that overcame him and kept him physically loose, Foster would later tell the Hopkinses.[10] He felt strongly that he might die, yet he had the presence of mind to prepare himself for the crash, thereby increasing his chances of living. There was no hysteria, no frozen fear, no behavioral inaction.

The plane did indeed crash-land on a rural highway, then smashed into some buildings before coming to a stop. Foster sustained a broken neck – but he lived. Those in the front section of the plane were killed.

Foster's background as a private pilot increased his understanding of the situation. That higher awareness of what do do surely contributed to keeping him calm – and alive.

In a 1979 study, the Civil Aeromedical Institute found that in addition to private pilots, other good risks in an emergency include athletes and soldiers.[11] Athletes are, of course, trained to react quickly. And soldiers, or former soldiers, would be able to respond because of their own experience in tense or life-threatening situations.

Several men on board the Pan Am plane had past military experience, and that may have helped them react. Warren Hopkins had served in the Pacific during World War II; Tony Monda had been an Army rifleman, fighting through Western Europe; Walter Moore had served in the Navy in the war's Pacific Theater; Albert Trumbull had risen to the rank of colonel while with Army engineers in Germany. Additionally, Jack Ridout and Bo Brusco were private pilots.

Pilots, athletes, and soldiers – most of the people in those categories in 1977 were men. Women were not considered good risks in crisis situations, along with – no surprise – the elderly. According to the Civil Aerospace Medical Institute, an elderly person can move only about half as fast as a young person.

So survival risks seem to be tilted in favor of young males, and statistics of that era bore this out. The previously mentioned Civil Aeromedical Institute study of aircraft emergency evacuations found that in a 1965 Salt

---

[10] Don Foster was also interviewed by Jon Ziomek.
[11] D.W. Pollard, J.A. Anderson, R.J. Melton, "Injuries in air transport emergency evacuations," Civil Aeromedical Institute, 1979.

Lake City crash, 13 of the 16 females aboard a burning Boeing 727 did not make it out of the plane, while 48 of the 66 males aboard did successfully evacuate. In a 1964 fire in Rome aboard a Boeing 707, the average age of the survivors was 30, and that of those who perished was 36 and a half.

As Pollard and his colleagues put it, "In our culture it is more socially acceptable for females to be passive and males to be aggressive."

At least, this was true in the 1970s.

But fatalities may have been even worse in that era because of a passivity about the flying process that was nurtured by the airline industry, which behavior experts say can turn into maladaptive behavior.

Psychiatrist John Duffy has noted that as air travel increased significantly in that time period, many airline passengers felt "protected" by the crew of an airliner, which may yet be true today. Few passengers who fly often actually expect an accident to happen. And flying certainly is statistically safe.

Thus, in the rare occurrence of an accident, the loss of those friendly nurturers – the crew – could contribute to confusion and even helplessness among passengers.

There's one more group to discuss in terms of surviving an air crash: the flight crews themselves.

"They've been taught what to do," said Dan Johnson. "They may not really expect to have been through an emergency in the past, but they respond very well. They don't panic, [they] don't run away. They stay at the door and they help people to the best of their ability."

On the other hand, he continued, "passengers are not trained or educated as to what to do. When the [emergency] situation develops, they are thinking at a very low level, cognitively. If you've ever been in a stress situation or seen people in an unexpected stress situation, they do the dumbest things. They don't really look at all the options available to them in a calm manner. The flight attendants have been trained and don't have to try to think out a good course of action. So the flight attendants [and the cockpit crews] respond better than the passengers."

Confirming one of Johnson's points, the previously mentioned CAI study noticed a "semi-rational, low level of rational thinking" by passengers who are under extreme stress but are still trying to sort out proper behavior for the situation.

In one of the crashes studied by the CAI, a 1961 United Airlines crash in Denver, a man who led his wife and daughter into the center aisle of the burning plane walked a few rows back and then had his family duck down with him behind a row of seats. The man was trying to escape the flames. In the interior of a plane, the idea of escaping a fire by moving only a few rows away could be considered an example of a "low level of rational thinking." But it was as good as the man could do at the time. Fortunately, the man and his family eventually made their way out of the aircraft.

In his doctoral thesis, Charles Catanese explained that anxiety increases in a crisis, along with confusion. The more confused someone is about their situation, the more anxious they become – until their anxiety is overwhelming and they can't function well enough to save themselves.

"Our behavior is planned, initiated, monitored, and modulated through our cognitive system," John Leach wrote. "We respond to the model we have created of the surrounding environment and not directly to the environment itself.

"For the most part this cognitive model is sufficiently accurate and robust, but occasions can arise during which the external world changes so suddenly that our cognitive model lags behind the new reality. It takes time to create a fresh representative model of the new environment and it is our behavior during this period that often determines whether or not we survive."[12]

Federal Aviation Administration certification rules require that an aircraft manufacturer be able to demonstrate that its fully loaded planes can be evacuated in 90 seconds or less.

That sounds impressively safe. What could happen in 90 seconds? But it presumes several factors: that the aisles are reasonably clear, that there is no "maladaptive behavior" among some of the passengers that could interfere with other passengers, and, most important, that the passengers know what they're supposed to do in an emergency.

---

[12] John Leach, "Psychological Factors in Underwater Egress and Survival," cited earlier.

That last point is a problem. Dan Johnson's research from the 1980s suggested that only 15 percent of the passengers on board a commercial airliner either watch the safety demonstration or actually read the emergency information card.

As has been said earlier, in the early decades of jet travel, the airlines did not make much of an effort to convince passengers that this part of the flight is important (with the notable exception of many flight attendants), so perhaps it's not surprising that so few passengers paid attention.

This indifference has only gotten worse because of the distraction of mobile phones and tablets. Officials with the flight attendants' union, the Association of Flight Attendants, have lobbied the FAA for years to tighten the rules about mobile electronics because of their concern about ignorant or oblivious passengers.

Johnson has said airline passengers must take the responsibility if they choose not to watch the briefings. One of the key points in his *Just In Case* book is this: "The safety equipment on commercial airliners is designed to be easily used, for the most part, *by the passenger who has made the effort to learn a little about it.*"[13]

But Johnson and his then-colleague Beau Altman also wrote, "The information is usually put forth in such a bland, uninformative manner on the card, and the live briefings are usually so monotonously routine and restricted, that passengers are not motivated to think seriously about flight safety.

"Passenger education is a major factor in overcoming behavioral inaction. When an emergency occurs, those passengers who know what to do are less likely to exhibit maladaptive behavior than those noneducated in safety procedures. *Training increases the probability of survival.*"[14]

John Duffy, the FAA psychiatrist, agreed. "The more time people have to prepare for the eventuality [of a crash], the better they are able to cope with the situation," he said.

Johnson pointed out that none of the subjects in his experiment were given any leadership or training. Those with no leadership or training in

---

[13] Author's emphasis.
[14] Author's emphasis.

their background "performed significantly worse than the groups with experience or leadership," he summarized.

"One could conclude that there may be less maladaptive behavior, with or without perception of threat or confusion, if the passenger knows or is told what to do.

"The prime factor associated with the incidence of maladaptive behavior is probably knowledge of correct actions to take, provided by leadership or training."

That supports a conclusion by C. E. Yost in a 1967 study done for Pan American World Airways – one of the earliest ever done – on emergency jet evacuations. One of Yost's conclusions was that "providing more explicit briefings could increase the probability of passenger escape in a survivable accident." More than half a century later, safety officials say the same thing.

Here is what a passenger said after the December 1978 crash-landing of a jet in Portland, Oregon: "They really briefed us well. Otherwise, I wouldn't have known what to do."

And in the aforementioned 1961 emergency evacuation of a United Airlines DC-8 in Denver, "Vocal and physical assistance by crewmembers was a strong source of reassurance" for the passengers, according to the Civil Aeromedical Institute report.

Flight crew members can also keep an evacuation orderly. Imagine the difficulty of getting out of a cabin when there's no direction, no sense of order. Some people will be fast; others will be slow. Some will insist on picking up their carry-on bags. Faster, more agile passengers will push the slower ones in front of them and create traffic jams in the aisles, creating what's known as the "faster is slower" effect if the flight attendants don't keep the passengers moving evenly between available exits. So there is significant value to a close relationship between crews and passengers.

After an October 2016 emergency evacuation of an American Airlines flight at O'Hare Airport in Chicago, the NTSB accident report noted that some passengers jumped out of their seats before the jet had come to a stop, ignoring commands from the crew. Others insisted on bringing their carry-on baggage during the evacuation, despite urgings to the contrary from the crew.

All of which indicates the need for better information distributing – and better listening by passengers. All passengers can remember being told to keep their hand luggage tucked under the seat, or to keep their seatbacks fully upright until after takeoff, but how many have ever stopped to ask why? The reason for these rules is crucial: the Federal Aviation Administration requires them in order to help speed up a plane's evacuation, should one be necessary. No one should be trapped with their foot under a piece of carry-on luggage, or be unable to step quickly into the aisle because a tray table hadn't been folded up, or because the seat in front of them had already been tilted back. Ensuring a smoother evacuation is an important reason for those rules about carry-on luggage or keeping seatbacks upright, but too many passengers think these are just airline rules because the reason for them hasn't been explained.

Basic psychology says it's easier to obey a rule if the reason for that rule is clear. "If people are given a reason why they should or should not perfom an act, a greater increase in understanding would be expected," said Johnson.

"If some anticipated incident is not explained truthfully to the passengers, their imagination will conjure up a situation that may seem even more dangerous than it really is," he continued. "By not informing the passengers of the true situation, perhaps in the mistaken belief they would be more frightened if given concrete information, the crew members could actually be setting the stage for panic."

One pilot said he was in favor of increasing safety measures aboard airplanes but balked at the idea of giving more information to passengers.

"There's no training of this to passengers because it might scare the hell out of them," he said.

True, there might be an initial queasiness about actually trying on a life jacket aboard an airplane, or being forced to watch a movie of a simulated evacuation. But what is the alternative? Some, perhaps many passengers would prefer to have a thorough knowledge of emergency procedures. Even if they don't need the information – and the odds are that they won't – the security of having such knowledge could increase passenger confidence about flying, in addition to strengthening their response capabilities if a rare emergency response is required.

After all, even ocean liners have lifeboat drills.

Amanda Ripley has discussed this in her book *The Unthinkable*. When rules are not explained fully to passengers, the result is a self-proving rule. Some crew members think of passengers as not being able to handle much information about safety, and information is withheld that would help passengers understand the *why* of a rule, such as the carry-on luggage rule. That ignorance can result in less adaptive behavior, which then convinces crew members that their first appraisal of passengers was correct – passengers really are less able to accept the safety information.[15]

After a US Airways 1549 emergency landing into the Hudson River in 2009, many of the passengers – understandably – had trouble getting on an airplane again. One passenger who did return successfully to flying was quoted as saying that when he travels now, he makes a point of talking to the crew. The passenger, Dave Sanderson, said he "also learns about the plane, including the exit strategy and what kind of doors it has."[16]

In a 1970 Federal Aviation Administration study, Dr. Clyde Snow and two colleagues, John J. Carroll and Mackie A. Allgood, studied three air crashes and the evacuations that followed:

- ▶ A United Airlines DC-8 that crash-landed at Denver's Stapleton Airfield, killing 17 passengers and leaving 97 survivors;
- ▶ A United Airlines 727 that crashed at Salt Lake City, killing 43 out of 85 passengers; and
- ▶ A Trans World Airlines 707 that ran into a truck while attempting to take off in Rome, Italy, killing 45 out of 62 passengers.

The crashes took place during the 1960s. They represented a mix of severity. The Denver crash had comparatively few injuries and a comparatively calm and orderly evacuation; the Salt Lake City crash was of a middle-range of intensity and fatalities; and the Rome disaster saw fire and explosions disrupt the evacuation process, severely limiting the number of those who safely got out of the plane. For their study, Snow and his colleagues studied body locations in the jets.

[15] Ms. Ripley discusses this at length in "Risk," Chapter 2 of *The Unthinkable*.
[16] "Survivors grapple with flying again," an Associated Press article in the *Chicago Tribune*, April 26, 2018.

The "survivability" of those accidents was found to be dependent on three factors: location of seat, age of passenger, and gender.

The first factor was the distance a person sat from an emergency exit, which seems logical. The farther away a passenger was from a usable exit, the harder it was to reach because of the amount of available time after the crash to get out. A computation in the Snow study showed that those who survived had to go an average of half as many rows to get to the nearest exit as those who died. For first-class passengers, the seat-to-exit distance was less than four rows (about two and a half rows), and for economy-class passengers, the seat-to-exit distance was about four rows for the surviving passengers and seven to nine rows for the fatalities.

Intriguingly, they found that several passengers gave up their initial proximity to an exit in order to use, or try to use, an exit farther away. This may have been because those passengers hadn't looked around and identified nearby exits in front and back of them. In a moment of crisis, they acted in what seemed like a logical way – they tried to get out the same way they got in.

The Snow report also was an early study demonstrating that some people act irrationally in a crisis.

In one example in the Salt Lake City crash, a man dropped to his hands and knees in the center aisle after the plane had skidded to a stop. He was keeping himself low to avoid smoke in the cabin. That was sensible. However, he then crawled through the legs of those standing in the aisle and kept going all the way forward into the cockpit, in the process passing right by the open front door of the aircraft. He tried to kick out a window in the cockpit – unsuccessfully – then got back down on his hands and knees, and crawled back into the passenger cabin, again passing by the opened door. A crew member finally saw the man and only just in time pulled him out of the burning wreckage.

Other people *never noticed that they were sitting adjacent to window exits* and instead tried to make their way up the aisles to a door. In the Salt Lake City crash, several bodies were found just forward of the rear galley door, which had been opened by a flight attendant shortly after the plane had come to rest. But by then, most people were crowding forward in the aisle and never bothered to look backward to see that a door was open and available only a few feet in the other direction.[17]

These are examples of the tunnel vision that can affect a person in a crisis. Individuals become locked into specific behavior that, to them, seems rational (for example, "I'm going to get out through the door I used to enter the plane"), but in fact is detrimental to their ability to get away from the wreckage. During the Denver crash, the bodies of a woman and her child were found huddled behind a seat, an action taken because of a desire to hide from the flames raging through the cabin.

These findings were generally confirmed in a 2002 study by Ching-Jui Chang and Hae Chang Gea of Rutgers University's mechanical and aerospace engineering department. Their work was explained in a 2007 FAA presentation by Garret "Mac" MacLean of the FAA's Civil Aerospace Medical Institute.[18]

Chang and Gea's research showed that flight crews must *actively* direct passengers evenly among the cabin exits to achieve the most efficient emergency evacuation, MacLean said. This is because anything in the aisle (luggage, pillows, blankets) will delay evacuation. Also, low illumination can confuse passengers; passengers tend to move in one direction unless directed otherwise; heavier people and older people are slower and can block faster passengers, and so on.

Interestingly, the Rutgers researchers also noted that overwing exits can be used as quickly as a door exit, but fewer passengers use them in emergencies. A portion of all airline passengers, when asked just after the conclusion of a flight, said they hadn't noticed their plane had overwing exits.

In the Tenerife crash, Roy Tanemura's friend Ted Freeman was patiently standing in front of the closed and locked emergency door in the Pan Am plane when Tanemura last saw him. That the door had become useless was not a realization Freeman had; in the crisis, his mind had taken him as far as it would go just then – that he would get out of an emergency door, and

---

[17] This crash took place before the "In some cases, your nearest exit may be behind you" warning was added to pre-flight safety briefings. In fact, this study is one of the reasons for the instigation of that warning.

[18] Slide show and presentation by "Mac" Maclean, program director, FAA Civil Aerospace Medical Institute.

the process of improvising an escape would not be necessary. Perhaps logical, but not successful.

Many people in these crashes thought only of saving themselves or members of their families. In less-threatening situations, people become more generous in their thinking – making sure, for example, that women and children are getting off or out. As the degree of threat to self goes up, altruism drops. In one sad exception to this in the Tenerife crash, a man in first class aboard the Pan Am plane – Jack Daniel, sitting one row behind the exit door used by Warren Hopkins – was in the middle of evacuating the plane with his wife and daughter when he heard an acquaintance cry for help. He turned back. The result was that he never got out of the aircraft.

Once out of the plane, with the most immediate threat to life removed (that of being trapped inside), many passengers become more at ease and are once more willing to offer help to those who seem to be in need.

Age and gender are the two other factors that most influence one's chances of survival in a plane crash, according to the Snow report.

In the Denver crash, which was the least severe of the three incidents noted, the mortality rate between males and females was about even. But at Salt Lake City and Rome, only 18 percent of the women survived, compared to 54 percent of the men. Only a few of the women aboard had children to take care of, so that could not have been a major factor in the different percentages.

The survival rate at Tenerife was dismally low, but the gender comparison still holds up: 17 percent of the females survived, compared to 23 percent of the males.

Again, there are several reasons for these numbers. In moments of extreme crisis such as represented in these accidents, many women in the 1960s and 1970s had not been socialized to be the fast-acting partner. The innate ability surely exists. A perfect example: Grace Ellerbrock in the Tenerife crash yelling at her husband and seatmates to shock them into action, and then thinking clearly enough to help her husband get away from the burning plane.

But social expectations and training are difficult to change in a few pressure-filled moments. For many decades, women assumed a more passive role in society; those few seconds of hesitation were repeated through not just the crashes studied by Snow and his colleagues, but in the Pan Am plane on Tenerife. Joani Feathers, a former police officer, did not respond as quickly as her friend, Jack Ridout. Warren Hopkins snapped his wife into action with his command, "Let's go!" Jordan Tartikoff had to insist to his wife that they leave the plane. Bo Brusco helped his wife out of the planet. Walter Moore told his wife, Beth, which exit to take. Tony Monda steered his wife out the window exit near them.

There are other differences between the sexes that may account for the survival rate. Women are, on the average, smaller than men. In the 1970s, they had an average weight of 142 pounds compared to 168 pounds for males, according to Snow's study.[19] As Snow put it: "Such a size disadvantage, along with its correlates in both absolute and relative strength, would be expected to operate strongly against females in evacuation in which active competition for exits occur."

In other words, if there is any kind of physical exertion, such as climbing over broken seats or jostling with other passengers in order to reach an exit, women are at a disadvantage.

None of the survivors of the Tenerife crash who were interviewed said this kind of competition went on. That's good, although it's possible that no one remembered such a struggle because of the tunnel vision experience – one simply did what one had to do to get out of the plane, not noticing if someone else was getting shoved out of the way.

Physical competition for an exit has been documented in other crashes. In the Salt Lake City evacuation, one flight attendant apparently was not opening a door fast enough for a male passenger who was waiting just behind her. So he knocked her out of the way and then flung himself out the opening.

Physical strength itself is a factor. At Tenerife, at least four men – David Alexander, Norman Williams, Byron Ellerbrock, and Roy Tanemura, and

---

[19] Those averages have climbed steadily. In 2014, the average American woman weighed 168.5 pounds, as much as the average American man in the 1970s. The average man's weight was up 16 percent to 195 pounds, according to the U.S. Centers for Disease Control. This doesn't help, either, because those weight gains weren't all muscle.

perhaps others – escaped by climbing up through the roof and then down the fuselage to the left wing. No woman apparently was able to do that, probably because of a lack of physical strength, plus the additional problem of more restrictive clothing.

The last factor in the Snow study was age. In the Denver, Salt Lake City, and Rome crashes, 13 out of 24 children on board were killed, thus making them the most vulnerable age group in an emergency situation.

However, there were no babies or very young children on the Pan Am plane at Tenerife. The passengers were predominantly older, as Warren Hopkins had pointed out to his wife at JFK Airport when they boarded the Pan Am plane.

The overall incidence of death reported by Snow and his colleagues in the three crashes they studied was 54 percent among children, 39 percent in young adults (16 to 55 years), and 35 percent for adults older than 55. These statistics are inconclusive about adults in general, but younger males seem to have had an advantage. This isn't surprising – older people would be expected to be slower-moving.

Using only injury statistics, and not death, it was shown by Snow, Carroll, and Allgood that children, females, and old males had a higher injury rate than younger males.

Snow and his team checked their numbers by subjecting volunteers to tests that simulated an emergency evacuation from a jet airplane. The actual reason for the test was to compare the effectiveness of existing single-door window exits with a new double-door exit.

Two hundred and eighty volunteers were used for the experiments, with an age breakdown ranging from small children to those above retirement age. The groups evacuated a wooden mockup of a jet airplane in a simulated emergency that was monitored and controlled by professional flight attendants and flight crew.

What happened in the tests is not what happens in a real emergency because the result was an orderly, calm evacuation. An equal number of men and women and children, with no differences for age, deplaned at approximately the same time. There was demonstrable concern for others and no selfishness or panic.

"In contrast," the Snow report noted, "at Salt Lake City when 55 percent of the adult males had escaped, only 25 percent of the adult females and none of the children were outside the aircraft. At Rome, about 85 percent of the adult males [including those who died outside] were outside of the aircraft…but only 40 percent of the adult females and one-third of the children had deplaned at this time."

Only in the Denver crash did passenger behavior resemble the controlled test. In that crash, there was enough time for most of the passengers to deplane calmly through the exit doors before the fire swept through the aircraft.

Missing in the test, Snow readily acknowledged, was the "confusion and chaos produced through many passengers choosing more distant exits" than the one nearest to their seat. The tests, after all, assumed that everyone in the plane understood where the nearest exit was and knew how to get there.[20] But the likelihood of that happening or being the case in any 21st-century commercial airline flight is not good.

"The findings that females, the elderly, and children face greater survival risks is not unexpected and is probably not a peculiarity of aircraft disaster," the Snow report summarized. "'Women and children first' is a cry that, down through the ages, had undoubtedly been more often uttered than honored, and in shipwrecks, fires and natural disasters these more vulnerable individuals have probably contributed disproportionately to the toll of victims.

"Yet the statistical evidence demonstrates that chances of survival are to some extent affected by as yet ill-understood bio-behavioral factors." For example, the report continued, do adult females have lower survival rates

---

[20] Compare this idealized evacuation scenario with the Dan Johnson statistic presented earlier: in the 1970s, as few as 15 percent of the passengers on board actually watched the flight attendants deliver the safety briefing. The remainder chatted, continued reading, or stared into space. That statistic has not improved in 40 years, thanks in part to more electronic distractions such as mobile phones and tablets, and continued passenger fear and/or indifference. This partially explains why some passengers pick a more distant exit during the stress of evacuations – they simply weren't familiar with the layout of the cabin. As noted earlier in this book, the Association of Flight Attendants was adamantly against the relaxation of existing FAA rules about using mobile phones and tablets during a flight because of the concern by its members and leaders that passengers would become even less attentive than they already are. That union's lobbying efforts have not been successful.

"merely because they are smaller and less strong than competing males, because they wear more flammable attire, or because they react differently in crisis situations? If the [last] hypothesis is found to be true, are the sexual differences in behavior due to less passenger experience and lack of familiarity with the aircraft or to deeper psychosocial and cultural factors?"

In all three crashes studied, the Snow report concluded, "the distance between initial seat location and the nearest usable exit tended to be greater among fatalities than survivors. This leads to the conclusion that it is better to sit closer to an exit than farther away.

"Of more significance, however, is the fact that many passengers sacrificed an initial advantage by attempting to escape from more distant exits and thereby became fatalities. While some decisions may have been 'rational' – that is, made because nearby exits appeared to be blocked, crowded, or otherwise inaccessible – evidence indicates that many were based on lack of familiarity with exit configurations or through panic.

"Such findings suggest that more intensive preflight briefings on exit use and location are important. They also reflect the necessity of positive and direct crew assistance through the actual evacuation."

The report concluded with the same suggestion reached by The Interaction Company's Dan Johnson and his colleague, Beau Altman, in their 1970s work and repeated in later studies: passenger education is crucial. Nothing has changed except for the addition to the files of more air disasters – including the one at Tenerife.

In the years since the Tenerife disaster, too many among the general public have continued to demonstrate a lack of awareness of safety procedures. This has been seen in later air crash evacuations and has crossed into other disasters – fires, floods, tornadoes, and earthquakes. (How many of us still think the safest place during an earthquake is a doorway? That's wrong.)[21]

Exposure therapy calls for overcoming avoidance of what makes a person fearful – face your fear, the thinking goes, and figure out the best response. This conditions the brain and can increase the likelihood of a

---

[21] Get out of the kitchen and away from bookcases and windows. Get under a table or against an interior wall.

good response in an emergency. "The basic idea underlying exposure therapy is that facing your fears will condition you, via extinction, to be less responsive" to the most frightening parts of the situation, Joseph LeDoux said in his 2015 book *Anxious*.[22]

"Individuals under-perceive risk," said Dennis Mileti, director emeritus of the University of Colorado's Natural Hazards Center.[23] "The public totally discounts low-probability, high-consequence events" such as an emergency jet evacuation, he said. "The individual says, 'It's not going to be this plane, this bus, this time.'"

One of the saddest examples was the reaction of workers inside the World Trade Center towers during the September 11, 2001, terrorist attacks. A 2005 *Time* magazine article reported that interviews with some of the survivors revealed a dismaying amount of the behavioral inaction explained earlier in this chapter by Dan Johnson and John Duffy. More people could have survived the collapse of the World Trade Center towers if they'd acted more quickly after the jets crashed into them.[24]

The most successful evacuation on September 11 was carried out by the Morgan Stanley brokerage, and it was led by the company's chief of security, Rick Rescorla. For years before that horrible day, Rescorla had carried out practice drills at the company's World Trade Center offices. After the planes crashed into the two towers, 2,687 Morgan Stanley employees evacuated their offices safely – almost every Morgan Stanley employee except for Mr. Rescorla and 12 others. He had stayed behind to check for stragglers.

"Knowing where to go was the important thing," one of Morgan Stanley's employees, Bill McMahon, said later. "Because your brain – at least mine – shuts down in a disaster. One thing you don't want to have to do is think in a disaster."[25]

---

[22] LeDoux, *Anxious*, 263.
[23] Quoted in Ripley, *The Unthinkable*.
[24] Ripley, "How to Get Out Alive."
[25] Ripley, *The Unthinkable*, 208.

CHAPTER 15

Psychologist Dan Johnson's conclusion about behavioral inaction, also known as negative panic or freezing, is that it is "the most maladaptive of behaviors in situations which require a series of quick, correct, avoidance responses to assure survival."

An intriguing aspect of this negative panic is that it apparently strikes in degrees. "This variation in response is typical," according to Joseph LeDoux. "Sometimes freezing is brief and sometimes it persists. This can reflect the particular situation you are in, but also your individual predisposition."

Writing in the December 20, 2015, *New York Times*, LeDoux noted, "Some people naturally have the ability to think through a stressful situation, or to even be motivated by it, and will more readily run, hide or fight as required. But for others, additional help is needed."

LeDoux has created this this response in laboratory rats. Outside of the laboratory, though, there is plenty of evidence for this freezing response in other crashes, not just at Tenerife.

At Tenerife, Roy Tanemura witnessed his friend Ted Freeman standing calmly in front of the plane's emergency door. Mr. Freeman had been able to respond to the initial shock of the collision, but, as the emergency door remained closed, had not been able to construct a series of actions that would have gotten either him or his wife out of the plane. Tanemura said later that he was convinced Freeman had probably been struck on the head by flying debris and was not capable of fully processing the situation.

Caroline Hopkins distinctly remembered three people standing in the aisle next to her husband's seat after the KLM-Pan Am collision – they were waiting, she believed, for stronger clues on how to behave and what to do. She herself needed no further encouragement than the strong words from her husband.

There were other important examples of this on Tenerife, which – fortunately – ended properly for those who had them: passengers David Alexander, Jean Brown, and Erma Schlecht. After the initial impact, Alexander and Brown had the same reaction:

"I'm going to die."

Yet, after several seconds or perhaps many seconds, both worked through that thought to a new realization: "I don't have to die. I'm going to get out of here!"

For Alexander, the next step was simpler than for others: his exit route was directly over his head, so he climbed on top of his seat and got out.

Mrs. Brown's escape was not as simple. She sat in 37-C, on the aisle on the left-hand side of the plane, two rows behind the rear edge of the left wing. After the collision and her initial shock, Mrs. Brown then turned to the couple next to her and said sharply, "We've got to get out of here!"

Her command apparently snapped through the couple's own state of immobility, and they responded. All three rose and joined others who were pushing their way out onto the wing on the left. Following the couple, Mrs. Brown became possibly the last survivor to get out of the Pan American plane.

Why were others unable to come to that awareness?

Albert Trumbull distinctly recalled the faces of those still in their seats as he and his wife made their way out of the plane. Those faces were, he later said, like "catching a deer in your headlights," a glassy-eyed stare into the distance. Many of those people were injured, possibly even dead. But others were not. Judging from what many of the passengers themselves later said, there may have been more than 100 people alive and mobile aboard the Pan Am plane after the collision. Many of those may have been unable to leave because of their distance from a usable exit and the influence of smoke and fumes. But others could have, and they just didn't.

As explained in the previous chapter, psychologist Dan Johnson has tested the occurrence of behavioral inaction in the laboratory. Twice as many females as males demonstrated such behavioral inaction when faced with situations they were unfamiliar with. This may have partially reflected the existing 1970s culture, in which women were seen as more passive than men.[1] The inaction occurred regardless of the severity of threat to participants in Johnson's experiments, even including possible electric shocks.

Johnson and his colleague at The Interaction Company, Beau Altman, were convinced that behavioral inaction is different from psychological shock, in which a person would be oblivious to the internal and external environment and display a stupor-like behavior. They believe that negative panic is a behavior that hits people who are unable to respond to danger in their environment.

"Every human being has his or her point of emotional vulnerability," added psychiatrist John Duffy, a former FAA consultant and assistant U.S. surgeon general. "From a psychological point of view, we share a certain commonality in basic emotions like love and fear. Built on top of these emotions are the factors that go into determining what kind of people we are. But a profound event can reach into parts of our unconscious that we have really rather successfully kept under wraps, possibly an area of success and accomplishment that overlies some real kind of inadequacy.

"Perhaps for healthy people that breakpoint wouldn't be reached without an awful lot of stress. There are other people who are very vulnerable, and just a small degree of stress can precipitate an emotional decompensation, a total collapse."

Possibly that happened to a number of people aboard Pan American Flight 1736. Their own decompensation – giving in to passive impulses that resulted in their loss of life – came with the sudden and terrible combination of circumstances: the collision, the fires, and severe pressure to master a deeply confusing and stressful situation.

Maintaining calm in the face of danger can represent one of several behavior patterns. It could be actual bravery, for example – overcoming

---

[1] The feminist movement was only just achieving social prominence during this decade, and mainly among younger women.

the fears of the situation to maintain a logical grip on one's behavior. It also, however, could represent denial of reality, such as exemplified by those people who fell victim to behavioral inaction.

Denial is, in fact, "our most important and most powerful psychological mechanism," Duffy noted. "It's the one we bring into bear the quickest."

"Denial can reduce anxiety but it also reduces the likelihood of survival," researcher John Leach has noted.[2]

In most stressful situations – pressures at the job, irritations with the children, a lost ticket at the dry cleaners, a rude clerk at the supermarket – one's life is not on the line, of course.

Therefore, Duffy continued, "denial is clearly the best" mechanism (among others such as sublimation, reaction formation, and repression). People can cope with the occasional minor hassles of their daily lives by just denying the existence of a problem.

Denial is not, however, the most helpful response over the long term "because really what it does is robs one of a conscious awareness," Duffy continued. "We might go about with the belief that we've solved the matter," when in fact the problem lies just underneath the surface. So we kick the dog when we get home from work, or yell at the kids, and let out our tension."

And especially when life or death is involved, we can't wait until later to let out our frustrations. Denial becomes the worst, not the best, reaction.

Bravery itself is an ethereal quality. It is what society expects of us all in these situations, Duffy said. "Altruism is society's demand upon a survivor." But in truth, some people "will abandon their spouse in trying to save their own skin. That in itself is a great source of extreme guilt, and emotional decompensation. That is, the individual did not meet the expectation of heroism. It's expected of all victims, unless they are literally maimed. If they're mobile and operating, they are expected to behave in that heroic fashion.

"I think it's an historic and cultural process. It starts out in childhood. We learn about heroes; we learn about sacrifice, the Boy Scouts, awards, this sort of thing.

---

[2] This quote is from "Psychological Factors in Underwater Egress and Survival," by John Leach, cited earlier.

"Everyone has seen this in their local newspaper from time to time: two teenage boys are fishing near the dam and the one boy loses his footing and falls in. The other boy jumps in after him, and they both drown.

"You have in adolescence the conviction that in danger, we must be brave. It's not that there's anything wrong with being brave, it's just that we're using the wrong term. In my judgment, what we really need is thoughtfulness. In other words, it's not important to be brave, but it is important to be judgmental, to make important decisions in a crisis. There is no point in trying to return to a burning plane if it's engulfed in flames. There's no point in jumping into the water to save someone who is caught up in a whirlpool when it's clear that you as the potential rescuer will be lost in the process. So it's a quality of judgment that is needed rather than bravery."

There were at least two passengers who came out of the Tenerife crash hailed as heroes by the media, not counting the surviving crew members (all of whom were decorated by the U.S. Department of Transportation for their actions that day). One was Jack Ridout, who, in early media reports, was given credit for saving the lives of several people from the first-class section by urging them out of the opening that Warren Hopkins first used. San Diego newspapers ran articles for several days talking about how Ridout was a real "take charge" person who had already saved several lives earlier in his own life.

A 2015 op-ed article in the *New York Times* noted that many people who act heroically later say that they acted on instinct, or without thinking about consequences.[3] People can be trained to act selflessly, such as soldiers. Co-author David Rand noted in an interview that a civilian may decide to put others first if the first person sees great potential harm to the other person by *not* acting. Similarly, civilians on the Pan Am flight such as Jack Ridout already had experience with the value of putting others first.

The media reports exemplified how our society does indeed reward the hero and give him or her special status. Ridout saved Joani Feathers by helping her out of her seat and pushing her to the exit, and his own

[3] Erez Yoeli and David Rand, "The Trick to Acting Heroically," August 20, 2015.

background may have inspired him to help others find their way out of the Pan Am jet. Ridout's impressive cool-headedness in those horror-filled moments provided the media with a hero.

Being a hero is presented by the media as a noble form of behavior that many of us hope for ourselves.

But this is a macho kind of ethic that Duffy said he does not care for. He spoke of treating a flood survivor who had delayed getting professional counseling for years. Finally, the survivor admitted he'd been troubled by feelings of insecurity and bad dreams since the catastrophe. Duffy asked him why he hadn't come in for help sooner, and the man replied that he didn't think it was manly to do so.

Another Tenerife Pan Am hero passenger was Grace Ellerbrock. She was the passenger who had insisted to her husband back in Los Angeles that they change seats with another couple so they could get the inside seats they wanted. Later, after the collision had taken place, she shook him into awareness by shouting, "For God's sake, get out!" And when both finally did make it out of the plane, she helped drag her injured husband away from the wreckage, although he outweighed her by nearly 70 pounds.

Mrs. Ellerbrock's clear-headed actions in maintaining a focus about how to proceed in the emergency was obvious. *Family Circle* magazine published an article on her Tenerife experience, from which this information is taken.

Another example of exceptional behavior was Dorothy Kelly, one of the senior flight attendants. A year after the incident, she and the other surviving crew members were given the Department of Transportation's Safety Award, the agency's highest award for bravery. Kelly was cited for her action after the impact in helping several survivors get away from the burning Pan Am plane, including its captain, Victor Grubbs.

In 1972, a Delta Airlines Convair CV-880 jet collided with a North Central DC-9 at O'Hare International Airport in Chicago. No one was seriously hurt on the Delta jet, but some crew members left their stations during the emergency evacuation and got out of the plane before all of passengers had been evacuated. That brought them a reprimand from the National Transportation Safety Board. They were following instincts that were logical but were not in keeping with what we expect of those in authority.

Internal denial of danger may be an important facet of behavioral inaction experienced by some in the Tenerife disaster and other plane crashes – and, for that matter, similar emergencies, according to psychologist Dan Johnson. Perhaps people have fatalism about flying, he suggested, because of a misunderstanding that flying is more dangerous than it actually is.

There's a passivity to this condition that may contribute to negative panic. "Something or someone will intervene for us because I'm not sure what to do," would be the thinking. Several of those who survived the Tenerife disaster acknowledged this. Mrs. Tartikoff was insistent that someone in the crew would tell the passengers what had happened and what everyone was to do. She later told survivor David Alexander that she had to be forcibly removed from the plane by her husband. Mrs. Margaret Ellingham, mother of Penny Quade and June Ellingham, had the same response. She sat several seats in front of Mrs. Tartikoff in first class, on the right-hand side of the plane, and refused to respond to what her daughters were pleading with her to do: get up and get out.

"The stewardesses are going to come," she told them, shaking her head. When she was finally convinced to at least rise, the women began dragging her toward the exit, at which point the floor collapsed and she was lost into the interior of the plane.

And there was the "deer in your headlights" observation by passenger Albert Trumbull.

John Duffy spent much time analyzing this phenomenon in the 1970s and 1980s. He has a theory about why some people are more passive than others in such moments of crisis, which states basically that they are more passive people to begin with.

There are individuals, Duffy explained, who feel that the world acts upon them, who expect the actions of others around them to influence their own lives beyond their own ability. Perhaps a majority of the world is this way. Another group, the other side of the coin, comprises action-oriented individuals who believe they act upon the world.

Duffy's point is that the second group will be better represented among the survivors of a crash than the first group. That held true in the Tenerife crash: Warren Hopkins leading his wife out, Jack Ridout helping Joani Feathers, Grace Ellerbrock insisting that she and her husband switch seats in order to get their desired cabin position, Paul Heck pointing out the emergency exit to his wife, Walter Moore directing his wife out, Erma Schlecht's and Jean Brown's and David Alexander's independent but identical realizations after the collision that they would not sit and die, they would *live*.

When people with this type of personality board an airplane, Duffy said, they look around to see where they are and where the emergency exits are. They read the safety card in the seatback pocket; they listen to the safety briefing or watch the safety video. They say to their spouses, "Dear, we're in this seat; the closest exit is right there, onto the wing." And they know how to open an overwing exit because they've read the instructions. (Overwing exits are the only exits that will almost certainly not be opened by flight attendants, whose responsibility is to guard the doors at the front and rear of the plane.)

Other writers agree on this. "Fear…makes paralysis stronger," Amanda Ripley wrote in *The Unthinkable*. "So it makes sense that if we can reduce our own fear and adrenaline, even a little bit, we might be able to override paralysis when we need to.

"The brain functions better when it is familiar with a problem. Everyone can manufacture self-esteem through training and experience… confidence comes from doing."

Those in Duffy's first group are more passive about travel. "It's like a little denial," Duffy commented. "They don't necessarily give up, but when they enter the aircraft and sit down, they kind of turn themselves over to the aircraft crew, and it's a very passive kind of thing. And unless they're in an accident and they are motivated by the crew members, they won't move."

Johnson agreed with Duffy's notion about passive and aggressive individuals. "There are different kinds of personalities, and some are more dependent on others," Johnson said. "Some are more information-seeking than others, and some prefer not to even think about this kind of unpleasant reality."

Johnson described the dichotomy of passive-aggressive people. They have an "'internal' or 'external' focus of control. The person with internal control thinks that control of his or her fate is internally located inside himself or herself. Externally controlled people think that fate acts upon them. A successful businessman would be one who is probably more internally controlled than others."

He summarized: "Probably the most common cause of death in airplane accidents [other than from the impact] is because people don't get out and move, versus panic. A person may panic and run from the situation," which is better than no mobility at all. "There are just too many cases where people sit inside the plane, Tenerife being one example."

One is reminded at this point of that era's airline television commercials, which insisted that they were going to try very hard to spoil their passengers.

As safe as the industry is, there are accidents, and it doesn't seem outrageous to say that there always will be. Johnson has explored the reasons why some people give up so much control when they get on a plane. He suggested it could be for one of many reasons: the contributing factor of the airlines' own marketing, a belief in one's immortality and that an accident simply won't happen to them, a belief that the air crew will take care of them, a belief that if an accident did happen they would find out right then, immediately, what they were supposed to do – which connects to the misunderstanding that they think they will have many minutes to determine a plan of action, even though the actual amount of time in such emergency evacuations is usually just a few moments.

Johnson also suggested the possibility that passengers "may not want to let on that they are naïve as flyers," so they won't pay much attention to the flight attendants or to the safety cards because other people aren't, either. "It's kind of nice to be sophisticated and a jetsetter," Johnson said.

Also, a passenger may think he or she already knows everything because they have indeed watched the flight attendant go through the briefing and think that's all there is to it. In fact, some flight attendants don't even point at the emergency doors during that briefing. In the 1970s, for example, some only referred to the doors in their safety speech, while others made that feminine wave in the doors' general direction.

Suzanne Donovan, one of the surviving flight attendants on Pan Am 1736, said she spent years after the Tenerife accident telling her friends, "Make sure you know where your exit is. Make sure you know how to get out of the airplane."[4]

Flight attendants usually react well in such situations because of their training, which is why the previously mentioned example of the crew in the O'Hare crash was so unusual.

"They've been taught what to do," Duffy said. "They may not really expect or have been through an emergency like this in the past, but they respond very well. They stay at the door, and they help people to the best of their ability."

On the other hand, he continued, "passengers are not trained or educated as to what to do. [If a crisis] situation develops, they are thinking at a very low level, cognitively. If you've ever been in a stress situation or seen people in an unexpected stress situation, [some of them] do the dumbest things.

"To them it may appear logical, but they aren't thinking well. They don't really look at all the options available to them in a calm manner."

The erratic behavior passengers exhibit could be seen at Tenerife in such examples as passengers huddling in front of an unopened emergency door, unable to come to grips with the fact that the door wasn't going to open; passengers huddled in between seats, as if that would protect them from the fires in the cabin; and passengers carrying out some mundane task, such as picking up a carry-on bag or a purse.

But what did happen to the Pan Am crew at Tenerife?

Nine flight attendants, including one purser, were killed: Mari Asai, Francoise de Beaulieu, Christine Ekelund, Luisa Flood, Sachiko Hirano, Miguel Torrech Pere, Marilyn Luker, Carol Thomas, Aysel Sarp Buck.

Four survived: Dorothy Kelly, the first-class section purser; Joan Jackson of Nashville, Tennessee; Suzanne Donovan of Harrisburg, Pennsylvania;

---

[4] She was interviewed for "The Deadliest Plane Crash," a 2007 PBS *Nova* documentary.

and Carla Johnson of New York, New York. All four suffered minor injuries while trying to help passengers, and all were honored by the Department of Transportation for their actions.

All three crew members in the cockpit survived, as did the two men who were riding as extra passengers. Here is the chronology of the crew members' struggles, as they themselves explained in the final crash report of the National Transportation Safety Board:

When the cockpit crew saw the KLM jet looming in front of them, all instinctively ducked, just as Florence Trumbull had done back in her economy-class seat as she looked out the window. Second Officer George Warns threw his hands over his head protectively. After the impact and everyone had regained their senses, it was clear they had to leave the plane immediately.

Warns stood up and checked the emergency exit just in back of the entrance to the 747's cockpit. "It was all chewed up," he later reported. So there was no chance to leave that way.

Captain Grubbs moved past Warns and made his way into the lounge area. As the captain stepped back, he saw a woman lying on the floor of the lounge, on the only part of the floor that remained connected to the cockpit. The rest of the flooring had collapsed. How to extricate her wasn't clear. Warns joined Grubbs just as their section of the floor collapsed, and both of them went tumbling down into the first-class cabin. Trying to scramble to the edge of the wreckage, Grubbs fell again, this time into a hole in the first-class floor, which put him in the plane's cargo area. Now badly injured and bleeding, he struggled through a hole in the left side of the fuselage onto the grass. Warns, still inside the jet, fought his way to the edge of the wreckage through the now-burning plane interior before flinging himself out and apparently landing in the rubber raft that passenger Jack Ridout had inflated. Both cockpit crew members were burned, bruised, and in shock – but they were outside the plane.

Bragg, the first officer, had tried to shut down the engines after the collision, but the controls hadn't responded. Looking quickly out the right-side windows, he saw tremendous flames. Then he looked out the left side and saw fires starting on that side, as well. Next, he made an attempt to open the fire extinguisher handles, located on the cockpit ceiling, but he grabbed only air because the roof of the cockpit had been peeled off by the KLM jet. When he looked behind his seat, he could see all the way to the Pan Am plane's tail – the lounge, in back of the cockpit, was simply gone, along with the passengers who'd been sitting there.

Bragg got out of his seat, walked back a few steps, and saw that the floor had collapsed. He managed to swing down some cables into the first-class cabin area, and then jumped to the ground – breaking his ankle in the process. Despite his injury, Bragg did his best to direct rescue workers as they arrived, and he helped with the evacuation operations until airport personnel insisted that he leave for the hospital.

Juan Murillo, who'd been sitting in the seat just in back of Captain Grubbs, also managed to jump down to the first-floor level of the aircraft. He said later that he had a memory of being thrown out of the plane by an inflating safety chute. (It may also have been the inflating life raft.) Once on the ground, Murillo, who was relatively unhurt, ran to the C-3 taxiway, where he found Bragg and Cooper, and they returned to the airplane to help the injured.

Cooper had the most hair-raising time among all those in the cockpit. He was sitting in the second jump seat, behind Murillo. He'd paid no attention to the cockpit conversation before the crash, he later said. As a mechanic, he was mainly interested in watching the flight engineer, George Warns, monitor the various systems of the airplane.

Suddenly, Cooper would recall later, "Grubbs was shouting." Everyone ducked, and three seconds later "something flashed by the window."

Cooper was spun around and passed out. When he regained consciousness, he was hanging upside down in his special cockpit seat belt and harness (cockpit seat belts are more elaborate than passenger-cabin seat belts), halfway between the cockpit and the first-class cabin. Live electrical wires were all around him, and they were arcing, sending Jacob's ladders of electrical current into the air. A major explosion ripped through the plane, which lurched nearer the ground as the wheels collapsed and the landing gear sagged. Realizing that he had to move, Cooper demonstrated remarkable levelheadedness by grabbing some of the wires, holding them by their insulation in order to avoid getting a shock, and then testing their resistance to his weight by pulling hard on them. They felt as though they would hold, so he pulled himself up as hard as he could with one hand and arm, and unsnapped his harness attachment with the other, then swung on the wires like Tarzan, down to the passenger cabin level. From there he jumped down to the ground and began moving away.

Cooper found Murillo and Bragg, and all three returned to the plane, where they saw that the Number 1 engine – the outboard engine on the left wing – was still rotating at what Cooper estimated to be about 75 percent power. There was a fire underneath it, and sparks and pieces of metal were flying out of and off it.

Cooper later recalled seeing the emergency chute at the second exit on the plane's left side, known as 2-L, deploying and several people jumping into it before it collapsed. The 2-L exit was located in between the 17th and 20th rows of seats and was nowhere near the seats of any of the survivors of the crash, so it's possible that Cooper was seeing the rubber raft that Ridout had inflated at the 1-L exit. But one of the flight attendants also recalled one of the slides inflating.

The cries and screams of the still-living passengers were set against the dull crackle of the flames, the explosions, and the whining of the still-turning engines as Cooper and Murillo pulled some of the injured away from the fuselage. Cooper could see about 10 people on the wing itself, and he wondered if they all would live. One woman crawled toward him, both of her legs injured or broken. Cooper pulled her farther away from the plane. There were six more people near the Number 2, or left-side inboard engine, who were trying to work their way around a fire that had started under that engine. Cooper could not make his way to them, but he could see that many of the passengers were helping one another. And then, in one of the unforgettably wretched moments of the crash, as described later in Cooper's report: "A lady stood up beyond some wreckage on the left side, and was calling for help. I got near her – and she caught fire and fell into the flames."

The four surviving flight attendants were all assigned forward positions on the plane: Dorothy Kelly was stationed at the 1-L door, Carla Johnson at 1-R, Joan Jackson at 2-R, and Suzanne Donovan at 2-L. As the Pan Am plane taxied down the runway, it was a casual moment for the women. Carla Johnson had already strapped herself into the jump seat at 1-R, just behind seat 6-H and facing backward, as did all the flight attendants' jump seats. Dorothy Kelly was standing in front of her, and they were talking.

"Suddenly, without warning, there was a tremendous crunching sound, possibly an explosion," Johnson recalled later. "Things, debris, were flying all around me, falling on my head. I remember bracing myself with my hands over my head, trying to make myself as small as possible. I wasn't sure whether we were right-side up or not.

"But when the plane seemed to stop, I looked up and did not see Dorothy. I felt extremely calm, as if things were happening in slow motion. As soon as I realized I was in one piece, I looked at the door [her assigned door, 1-R] thinking to open it, but it was completely mangled.

"I unfastened my seat belt and had to climb out of a kind of webbing that was surrounding me, pieces of metal and debris. I began to move toward the other side of the plane. The entire top was gone, there was sky above me, and nothing looked familiar. At that point I began to point and shout at them [the surviving passengers] to get off the aircraft as fast as possible. My hair was blowing in the wind, and at this point I became very aware that there was a fire behind me, although I don't recall ever looking back. I began to push people in front of me, yelling at them to move faster. They all seemed in a state of shock. Several faces looked at me and seemed to follow instructions.

"I became increasingly aware of the fire creeping up behind me. Then there was an explosion. The floor seemed to give out below me, and there was jagged metal below me. Someone grabbed my hair, or perhaps it caught onto something. I landed on my hands and chin. The heat became more intense. I had to climb over some barrier and then fell onto the grass. There were pieces of metal everywhere. At that point I ran as fast as I could away from the airplane. Several explosions occurred almost immediately. When I looked behind, the entire aircraft was a mass of black billowing smoke. At that point I started back to see if I could help. But pieces of flaming debris were flying out of the engine, which was spinning. All the while

I was motioning and yelling at people to get away from the aircraft.... I also remember seeing two or three people on the very tip of the left wing. I couldn't imagine how to help them off. Every time I started back toward the plane, there was another explosion. I never saw what happened to the people on the wing."

In her statement, Joan Jackson commented on how fast the fog rolled in. "It was amazing how fast the mountains were obliterated," she said. After chatting with the other attendants about the possibility of being stuck on Tenerife, they were all relieved when the "No Smoking" sign was lit up and the plane began to taxi, she said.

"I sat down at door L-2 to talk for a moment to Suzanne Donovan, expecting to move over to R-2 whenever we received takeoff clearance. We commented on the deteriorating weather condition.

"Without any warning there was an incredible roar in the cabin. I felt no impact. It came from farther back in the cabin." Although the KLM jet's right landing gear had smashed through the cabin only a few feet forward from where Jackson and Donovan were sitting, the KLM's left landing gear had struck a much bigger blow farther back in the Pan Am economy section. "My first thought was the galley was sliding out of place. It also flashed through my mind, 'What kind of joke is this?'"

Unlike Johnson, Jackson at first smelled no fire or smoke. She hurried to her assigned door, R-2, but saw only flames outside and knew that she couldn't open it. "Fire!" she shouted, and ran back to the left side of the plane. "I remember it all seemed unreal, as if it were another exercise in our class. It seemed impossible to believe."

Many passengers sitting between the first-class section and where Donovan and Jackson were stationed – a distance of about seven rows of seats – had been killed immediately. The two flight attendants were just far enough away from the landing gear's impact to escape serious injury.

"I remember watching L-2 crumble into rubble.... As the door settled, I could see a small piece of sky about five and a half or six feet above my head," Jackson later reported. "I do not remember climbing out. The next thing I remember is holding my hand out to Suzanne, who was still inside the fuselage, and saying, 'Suzanne, take my hand!' She climbed out....

With Suzanne and I holding hands, we worked our way forward where the debris was slanting down and was closer to the ground.

"I could see the passengers from the FT section (their assigned section, just in back of first class) lying on their sides in their seats with their seat belts fastened. They were facing forward. I saw one or two move. Hand in hand, we tried to work our way forward. The debris shifted and Suzanne and I lost contact. I worked my way forward a few more feet to where the debris was about five or so feet off the ground. At this point a slide started to inflate. I believe it was the L-1 slide.... I looked at it to see if I could get to it, but the debris was shifting so much I had no firm foothold. There were about six people in front of me poised at the edge of the drop.

"I started to push them, yelling, 'Get off! Move!' One man turned around to me and said, 'Don't push!' I started yelling, '*Jump! Jump! Jump!*' in a cadence, hoping to get them to move out. At this point I believe the debris shifted again, and I think I tried to jump and get to clear ground. The next thing I knew, I was on the ground and scrambling up for fear the fuselage would roll on top of me. I jumped up and ran directly out from the aircraft. I tripped again and got up and ran. I saw Suzanne running towards me. We clutched each other and looked back. I believe by this time heavy black smoke was billowing from the left-side engines. The explosions started then...."

And what about Dorothy Kelly, the purser, who had been standing in front of Carla Johnson when the collision took place?

"There was a loud noise – things flying around, wind, and then something hit me on the head. My first reaction was to grab a blanket to cover my head, but there was nothing recognizable in sight – only twisted pieces of metal. The ceiling was gone – sky above, a high wall of metal behind me...the floor kept dropping lower under my feet. Then I saw an opening ahead [toward where the L-1 door might have been]. I started climbing towards the opening and saw a man ahead of me. I kept stumbling because the bottom kept falling lower. The man reached the top first and, after looking down, wouldn't jump. I screamed to jump, jump, and he did. I immediately followed. It seemed to be about 20 feet down, but bottom [at ground level] was full of jagged metal. There were explosions as I was

Flight attendant Dorothy Kelly can be seen bending over survivor Beth Moore on the left side of this photo. Survivors Grace and Byron Ellerbrock are on the right. The other two passengers are unknown. *This photo was taken by Manuel Fandiño, a freelance photographer who was at Los Rodeos Airport on the afternoon of the crash.*

getting out, and they continued, with fire visible as I looked behind me. I called and motioned to anyone who could see to follow, and pointed and waved to pavement forward of the aircraft."

At this point Dorothy Kelly was on her way to becoming one of the biggest heroes of the day because she then spotted Captain Grubbs lying near the fuselage. Badly burned and shaken by his jump from the plane, he could not move. "What have I done to these people?" he yelled, pounding the ground in anguish. Kelly grabbed him under his shoulders and urged, "Crawl, Captain, crawl!" After they had moved some distance away from the plane, Grubbs wanted to stop, but Kelly insisted that they move farther away. When she got Grubbs as far away as the C-3 turnoff, she left him and returned to help other passengers get away from the wreckage.

Suddenly, Kelly noticed Mrs. Moore, the woman on whom several people had landed when they were jumping off the wing, trying to crawl away from the wreckage. Kelly hurried over to the badly injured woman and leaned over her. "I won't leave you," she told Mrs. Moore gently. By then, Kelly's hair was sliding to one side and one of her own eyes was beginning to bruise from the impact of a blow to the face from flying debris. But Mrs. Moore remembers Kelly's face as angelic: round, attractive features, dark hair done up in back.

Kelly found another passenger – Mrs. Moore never found out his name – who, despite his own injuries, helped pull Mrs. Moore away from the wreckage. Kelly then stood watching over her until Bragg helped get the woman into one of the ambulances that were pulling up.

It was just about now that photographer Manuel Fandiño reached the site of the Pan Am plane. One of his more dramatic photographs was that of Dorothy Kelly leaning over Beth Moore, who lay on her back on the ground, one leg up. In the background, the Pan Am plane is burning wildly.

The crew continued the evacuations as well as they could. Ambulances, private cars, taxicabs, and airport vehicles were all pressed into service. As they filled up with the injured, they drove down the runway, then headed straight for one of the two area hospitals. One or two of the cars dropped their less-injured passengers at the airport terminal building.

It was all over for most of those on board Pan Am 1736 in a matter of about three minutes. Although some passengers later reported that they'd been trapped inside for at least five minutes, their own intensified senses may have stretched out their perception of the actual time interval.

The survivors had come from two sections in the aircraft: the first-class section, and an area several rows just in front and in back of the middle section of lavatories. In between those two sections was where the KLM jet's right landing gear had struck, and farther aft was where the left wing and landing gear had hit. The KLM jet's left wing had done the most damage – most of the passengers in the rear of the plane died immediately from the actual collision. For those just behind the first-class section, the fires killed many, as judged by pathology investigators. The corpses of those killed were studied to see if soot had gotten into their windpipes; if it had, that meant they had been alive but most surely unconscious from the fumes when the fires reached high intensity. If there was no soot in the trachea, this meant the person was dead before the fires began raging. Unfortunately, because of the severity of the collision and the resulting fires, many bodies were so badly damaged that it was not possible to determine their cause of death or even their identities.

CHAPTER 16

"I thought I'd lost you. I thought I'd lost you," Warren Hopkins repeated as he pulled Caroline away from the burning Pan Am jet. Both sobbed with relief as they struggled away from the flames. Still not even aware of the torn tendons in his foot, Warren helped his wife through the wet, high grass near the runway and headed for the fence that surrounded the airport, stopping once to turn around and look and listen. Black smoke billowed hundreds of feet into the air. The plane's engines were still whining. Pieces of metal zipped in every direction. Puddles of jet fuel were bursting into flames. Then he turned again and continued walking, still aiding Caroline because she was unable to rise fully to her feet. Mrs. Hopkins later would recall, incongruously, seeing beautiful blue and yellow wildflowers in the high grass.

When they'd crossed the taxi strip and gone several hundred yards away – past the perimeter of safety other survivors had reached – Warren stopped. Caroline was at that point able to regain her footing, and she stood alongside her husband, the sight of whom made her weep again: his head was bleeding severely, with blood running down his face and neck, soaking his shirt. He had only one shoe on. The other foot was protected merely by a sock, and that foot was injured.

Caroline thought for a moment, and then, with nothing else available, she stepped out of her half-slip and wrapped it around her husband's head like a turban. In the process, she dripped blood onto the slip from the gashes in her own fingers, an injury that had happened when she gripped the edge of the fuselage before jumping out. She now noticed her own cuts for the first time. For those, she reached into her left-hand jacket pocket and found a handkerchief that she wrapped around the cuts.

They stood briefly, looking back at the plane as the last surviving passengers jumped out and ran away – some, sickeningly, falling to the ground in flames. Then, with the single-mindedness of people in shock, they turned and kept walking through the high grass as best they could, trying to support each other. They walked to the perimeter of the airfield and headed for a hole in the wire fence. Looking through it, the Hopkinses could see a woman who looked to be in her fifties running toward them from a row of pink stucco homes lining the airport perimeter fence. The woman was calling to them in rapid Spanish, apparently urging them to come to her.

The woman rushed up to them and held Caroline Hopkins by the arm while an older man, apparently her husband, arrived just behind her to help Warren Hopkins. They guided the struggling pair through the fence opening and walked between them for about 25 feet past the fence. Then Warren Hopkins suddenly stopped because of a realization.

"Where are we going?" he thought. "There's bound to be emergency equipment arriving, and it's certainly not going to come over here."

Just then, the Spanish couple saw emergency vehicles driving onto the runway. As if by telepathy, they understood Warren's realization, and everyone swung around like an Ice Capades chorus line, heading through a triangular opening in the fence and back onto the airfield. The couple stayed with the Hopkinses until they had returned closer to the Pan Am plane, although safely away from the fires and explosions. Then they left, kissing Caroline, then Warren, and offering heartfelt but not-understood words of apparent deep sympathy.

Warren and Caroline stood for perhaps a minute, staring at what used to be Clipper 1736 – still uncertain of what had happened. The later explosions had almost completely obscured the plane's fuselage in deep black smoke and blazing orange flames, with several ferocious fires that awed and frightened the couple. Emergency workers were now helping people standing or lying closer to the plane. The Hopkinses could also see some prone figures on fire close to the plane, and they wept for them, and for those still inside.

Then they noticed three men standing a short distance away, between them and the plane's carcass. The men were all in uniforms: white, short-sleeved shirts with chevrons on the shoulders, and torn and burned black pants. It was Grubbs, Bragg, and Warns, standing silently and forlornly as if watching an ocean liner go down. Warren and Caroline limped over to them and stood for a few moments as they all studied the flames and destruction – a wretched, dismal ending for the humans and the machinery that had been alive and vibrant only minutes before. By that time the Pan Am plane had collapsed onto the runway. White-hot metal fragments were still shooting hundreds of feet into the air, standing out against the gray sky like a macabre Fourth of July display.

Then Warren Hopkins turned to Grubbs. With a rasping, exhausted voice, he asked, "What in the hell happened?"

Grubbs gestured wearily with his hand. "That crazy bastard did it. The KLM took off. He was supposed to be holding, and he took off."

Again, all were silent.

Warren and Caroline Hopkins took stock of each other. Caroline was soaking wet, head to toe, from being dragged through the grass. Her skirt had somehow ripped. Shoeless, her hosiery was in shreds and her suit jacket was soaked with blood, her own and her husband's. Warren was still wearing a French-cuffed white shirt that was deeply stained with blood. His head was wrapped like a swami in a green, flower-patterned petticoat. His left shoe was somewhere back by the plane; the exposed sock had been ripped through from the jump from the fuselage and the struggle to escape. Pain was breaking through: in Caroline's right shoulder from her plummet to the runway, and in Warren's left foot. Both felt as if they had just completed a marathon, and only the presence of each was preventing the other from having an emotional collapse.

And yet they were lucky, and they knew it. "All those people," Caroline would later recall, with an almost bottomless sadness. "A nightmare. Human hell."

They turned away, exhausted, and began making their way toward the airport terminal building.

Chapter 17

As Warren and Caroline Hopkins trudged away, ambulances and airline vans were pulling directly onto the field near the Pan American plane's carcass, and survivors were struggling into the vehicles. In some cases, passenger Jim Naik later remembered, a few people were thrown into the back "like sardines" by workers acting hastily. Some survivors were yelling with pain from their injuries and asking to die. Naik remembered an injured person with an eyeball loose in its socket. Others lay silently in bloody heaps on the bottom of the storage area of one of the rescue trucks.

Beth Moore was placed in the back of a van, and Dorothy Kelly got in with her. "Squeeze my hand as hard as you want," she said, offering it to Mrs. Moore, who did exactly that. With her broken bones, she was in pain such as she had never experienced. The gesture by Kelly was vastly appreciated.

Some of the survivors were driven directly to one of the two local hospitals – either the maternity hospital or the area's general hospital. Most of the rescue vehicles, however, stopped at the terminal building, where transportation to the hospitals was being organized. Cab drivers volunteered their services, some driving directly onto the airport taxiway. Private car owners showed up, doing the same.

While most of the survivors were driven to the terminal building from the wreckage, others, such as the Hopkinses, walked. Warren Hopkins was having increasing trouble walking because of his foot and had to lean on his wife. Two men hurried onto the taxiway to help them before they reached the entry door to the building.

As they approached the door, they realized this was indeed the building they had been unable to visit earlier because it was too crowded. Now, a section of the first floor had been roped off for the survivors, and the airport officials had pushed together about 20 chrome-trimmed black vinyl couches for the survivors to either sit or lie upon. Other survivors were stretched out on the floor.

Mrs. Hopkins once again noticed the beautiful flowers planted near the building's doorway. The couple climbed three steps, clutching a railing, and joined others already inside, among them, Joani Feathers and Jack Ridout, Edward Hess, Norman Williams, and Isobel Monda and her husband, Tony. They found an empty couch and flopped down next to each other.

Many of the passengers were weeping – a few were crying out from the agony of broken bones or burns. The parade of injured passengers continued into the terminal, some being carried in and others wandering in under their own power, zombie-like. To the right of the entrance door, across from where the Hopkinses were sitting, was a closed door leading into another room off the waiting area. The door had a Red Cross emblem on it. Whoever worked there was apparently out at the crash site because the door never opened.

The noise level in the terminal increased. Passengers who had been waiting for other planes were shunted off to a corner. But from that corner, they stared in horror and sympathy as more survivors were brought in. One man walked in, pants completely burned off, wearing only torn underwear, a belt and shoes. In deep shock, he wandered from person to person, mindlessly attempting to make small talk. Another man's hair was still smoldering. It was a living nightmare that was painting its way into Caroline Hopkins's permanent memory, along with everyone else in the room. She began shaking and could not stop.

One of the people in the terminal, perhaps a waiting passenger, circulated among the injured. He was about 60 years old, spoke perfect English, and was dressed in a light blue suit and white shirt and tie.

"Can I get you a Cognac?" he asked graciously, a startling contrast to the bedlam around him. Most passengers simply shook their heads no, but Caroline Hopkins asked for a glass of water. The man nodded pleasantly and then walked away, stopping in front of Joani Feathers and Jack Ridout, sitting nearby, to see if they, too, would like a beverage. He returned shortly with a tray of glasses of water, which he distributed among the passengers, starting with Joani Feathers and Caroline Hopkins, both of whom selected one and gulped it down. There were sarcastic jokes exchanged among the passengers about the dangers of drinking water in a foreign country and what would now happen to their digestive systems – as if they all hadn't just been through an experience far more shattering.

Mrs. Hopkins later saw the tray of glasses sitting on a nearby table but was simply unable to rise in order to get a refill.

Something later described as resembling axle grease was carried in a large jar among the survivors and spread on some of their injuries to help salve the burns and stop the bleeding.

Next, the exodus reversed: people began leaving the room as officials found cars to drive them to the hospitals. Joani Feathers and Jack Ridout got into the back seat of a cab with the same man who had held up his severely burned hands when the Reynoldses had asked him for help earlier on the runway. His silent shock had long worn off, however, and he simply sat in the back seat, rocking back and forth, moaning, "Oh my God, oh my God...."

They drove off. It was like being in a parade, Feathers later said, as people were lined up six and seven deep along the road. The news had already been flashed across the island by radio and television, with calls for all available doctors and blood donors to make their way to the Tenerife hospitals.

Their driver drove carefully but leaned on the horn all the way to the hospital, trying to keep onlookers from stepping into their path.

Others had different experiences with their drivers. Warren and Caroline Hopkins along with Edward Hess got into the back seat of a taxi. In the front was John Charles Amador, the man who had looked out his passenger window to see the KLM plane coming at theirs. He was one of the few survivors from the right side of the Pan Am jet.

Amador was sobbing deeply, having earlier been restrained by a member of the crew from going back into the wreckage to search for his traveling companion, Harry Harper. The back seat was quieter – until the moment the driver screeched away from the curb. "Slow down!" everyone in the back seat shouted together, as the driver weaved his way down the road and through the onlookers. "For Christ's sake, we just survived one wreck, we don't want to wind up in another one!" Hopkins yelled, banging on the back of the front seat. The driver, apparently under the impression that his passengers were urging him on, floored the accelerator.

"Doesn't anyone speak Spanish?" Hopkins and his wife asked, looking at Hess and Amador. Hess answered in the negative, but Amador, through his tears, managed to nod. "Please say something to him," they pleaded. Amador managed to struggle out a few words of caution in Spanish, and the driver obligingly slowed down for a few hundred meters – and then drove even faster.

"You're going to kill us all!" Caroline Hopkins screamed.

The Mondas had the same experience on their ride to the hospital, with a driver leaning on his horn. With the window open, a chilly breeze snapped through their cab. The driver drove as if his passengers had only minutes to live, despite Tony Monda's outraged yells to "Slow down! Slow down!"

In the middle of the ride, badly injured and in severe pain, Isobel Monda found herself starting to laugh wryly because she was suddenly reminded of driving around San Diego with her husband. She was the one always yelling, "Slow down! Slow down!" at him and his heavy-footed driving.

The Hopkins group arrived at the general hospital, where a worker rushed out and told them they could not be accommodated there – they would have to go to the maternity hospital several kilometers away. Off they went, with the driver again racing through the streets as if he were on the final lap of a Grand Prix race.

Caroline Hopkins vowed that she would never again complain about New York taxi drivers. Once again, Amador spoke to the driver, who slowed up a bit.

Arriving at the Residencia de Candalaria hospital, those in the cab were escorted inside the hospital emergency entrance to separate rooms. Warren and Caroline were taken to a room originally intended for one patient. They stepped inside to find Beth Moore lying on a stretcher on top of a table. The only other place to sit down – which Warren Hopkins needed very much to do because of his foot – was a small gray box in the corner. The Hopkinses managed to scrunch down and sit together on the box.

Mrs. Moore was conscious and visibly in pain. Trying to distract her, Warren and Caroline introduced themselves, and, through her discomfort, she politely responded. In the ensuing small talk, Mrs. Moore mentioned that her husband was a retired admiral. The Hopkinses told her they'd met Commander Whitehead, the former naval officer who had been the advertising spokesman for the Schweppes soft drink company.

"Oh, really? What class at the Academy was he in?" Mrs. Moore asked.

Warren Hopkins didn't know the answer but later remarked about how impressed he was with Mrs. Moore's self-control. Here they were, in the emergency room of a hospital in another country, her husband was lost, she was in pain from numerous injuries, and she was able to chit-chat about the U.S. Navy.

Mrs. Moore then asked Warren if he would help her find her husband. Perhaps he had gotten out of the plane after her and she had lost him in the confusion. Would he take a look for her in some of the other hospital rooms?

Hopkins did not relish the thought of doing that, given his foot injury, but was unable to say no. Before he left the room, Mrs. Moore signaled him close to her and said, "I'll tell you, Warren, if I can't be with him, I'd rather die right now."

Hopkins was not able to hobble very far with only one good foot but was able to make it across the hall to a room in which he saw doctors working feverishly on several patients lying on tables, the patients moaning or crying or unconscious. Mrs. Moore had described her husband as tall, with angular features and wearing a red sweater, and Warren remembered seeing Admiral Moore during the boarding process in New York the night before. But in the other hospital room, he saw no one resembling the admiral.

Figuring the doctors didn't want to be interrupted, and that only with luck would he find one who spoke English, Hopkins hopped back across the hall and gave Mrs. Moore the news that it was simply too confusing to be able to find her husband. The patients being worked on had some of their clothing removed, he explained, so the red sweater clue had done no good.

While her husband was out of the room, Mrs. Hopkins sat silently for a short spell. Still in shock from the experience, followed by lengthy exposure to the wet and cold air, she was unable to stop shaking. Spotting a pile of folded sheets on a wall shelf, she stood up and took one, wrapping it around her waist, then unhooked her skirt and pulled it off, dropping it into a wire basket along with her shredded nylons. The skirt, she felt, may have been adding to her chill. Several days later, facing the prospect of returning to the United States in a hospital robe, she thought of the skirt – too late. It had been thrown out, a nurse told her.

The three remained forlornly in the little room, continuing to wait for medical assistance. Out in the hallway and from different corners of the hospital, the cries and moans of the injured echoed off the tiled walls and floors.

CHAPTER 18

It's not surprising that members of the media become hardened to bad news. "Gloom is their game," author Gay Talese once wrote about reporters.[1] Death, destruction, disasters, crime, cheating – the less pleasant sides of life form much of what is presented in the electronic media and in newspapers. For seasoned reporters who've called dozens of grieving relatives over the years, or interviewed hardened police officers, the fact-checking will eventually become routine: "Anyone from around here involved in that crash?" "How old were they, and did they have any relatives?" "May we talk to the relatives?" "Can we get a picture of the local people who were in the accident?" "What did the husband and wife do for a living?"

After years of this, what a newsman or newswoman may find of heightened interest in covering bad events is the proportion – the size and impact of the catastrophe. In the world of news reporting, an event becomes bigger depending on the number of people affected by it. Some reporters would rather cover a plane crash than a two-car accident on an expressway. The adrenaline gets flowing when one is called on to gather information about a major event and then present it in an understandable manner. In more than one newsroom across the United States, reporters have joked about what would be the biggest disaster of them all: the collision of two fully loaded Boeing 747s, the world's largest airplanes.

---

[1] Gay Talese, *The Kingdom and the Power.*

Thus it was not surprising to hear the reaction of Nate Polewitzsky to the initial reports of the Tenerife disaster. In 1977, Polewitzsky was the international news editor for the Associated Press wire service. On the afternoon of Sunday, March 27, 1977, he was driving from Pennsylvania to his home in New York when he switched on his car radio to catch the latest headlines. Then came the announcement: worst crash in aviation history: more than 500 dead, apparent collision of two 747s on a foggy runway. And where? *In the Canary Islands?*

Polewitzsky, a gravel-voiced press veteran who responded to big events like a boxer to the opening bell, had one immediate and logical reaction.

"Oh Jesus, of all places to have that happen," he thought to himself. "Way off in hell somewhere."[2]

Although Sunday was his day off, Polewitzsky drove into midtown Manhattan and went to the Associated Press main office in Rockefeller Center. The desk man on duty, Robert Ohman, had the situation in hand, but Polewitzsky made a few suggestions for possible sidebar articles, the feature stories that would be sent to AP clients along with the main news story on the event itself.

"Why don't we try something on the Canaries in general," he suggested before heading for home. Later that evening, unable to stay away from the telephone, he called his office to suggest a story comparing the Tenerife crash to past transportation disasters. A reporter was duly dispatched to the AP library to do just that, coming out with the information that would later be sent around the world in articles to the television stations, radio stations, and newspapers that were subscribers to the AP news service. In those days, the AP transmitted its dispatches on 72-words-per-minute teletype machines. As the material came over the wire machines, copy clerks and news assistants ripped the articles off the machines and gave them to editors for their scrutiny. But the sources of information were few: the AP had only one stringer stationed on Tenerife, a reporter for a local newspaper. Other media had similar problems: what were the television stations to do with their need for video? A Tenerife television station had been permitted by

---

[2] This information is from Jon Ziomek's interview with Mr. Polewitzsky.

local officials to film the burning wrecks later Sunday evening on black and white film, but the major American networks wanted their own footage, not some borrowed from a local station.

Camera operators and reporters and photographers were dispatched from major cities in the United States and Europe, all trying to get to Tenerife. But the one runway at the island's only airport was closed because of the presence of hundreds of tons of wreckage littered across it. The route most media representatives took was by commercial flight to Madrid, then to Las Palmas. From there, some enterprising reporters rented airplanes that flew them over the wreckage so they could shoot footage from their plane windows. Others got on the ferry that ran between Grand Canary Island and Tenerife, its business having tripled since the crash, for a sea sickness-inducing three-hour ride between Las Palmas and Santa Cruz de Tenerife.

The Mencey Hotel on Tenerife filled up completely. But members of the media who were frustrated by the Spanish government's closing of the airport had only to wait in the Mencey's lobby in order to get part of the story because a dozen of the less-injured survivors of the Pan Am plane were put up there. For that reason, several names appeared regularly in the news dispatches that came from Tenerife: Jim Naik, Terrence Brusco, and Ed Hess, who were among the survivors staying at the Mencey.

Another survivor had also been put up at the hotel, a quiet man who did not feel as comfortable talking to the media as the others did. It was David Alexander of Palo Alto, California, who had been sitting in Seat 30-C next to his new friends, the Ronders.

On Monday afternoon, Alexander's camera was upstairs in his room as he walked through the lobby after having strolled the streets of Tenerife. He was tormented about the fate of the Ronders, who had been polite and friendly and with whom he had spent a nice time on the plane. *Why?* He kept asking.[3]

Still in shock, Alexander was stopped by a man who introduced himself as Hans Hofman, a Dutch freelance writer and journalist who was

---

[3] This information is from Jon Ziomek's interview with Mr. Alexander.

working, he said, for a newspaper called the Amsterdam *Telegraaf.* Could he have an interview?

Reluctantly, Alexander agreed. He had already talked by telephone to a reporter from the *Palo Alto Times*, his local newspaper. "I lost everything I had except me," he had quietly told the reporter.

Hofman and Alexander found a corner of the lobby, and Alexander related to him as well as he could his escape from the burning plane, occasionally stopping to check his injuries: a cut on his right cheek, a three-stitch wound on the top of his head that had been closed after taking a patch of hair from his scalp.

When he told Hofman that he had taken pictures of the burning Pan Am plane, Hofman interrupted his note-taking.

"Why don't you give me your photographs?" Hofman asked bluntly.

Alexander, still in a mental fog from his experience, could not understand the thrust of Hofman's question. "I don't want to do that," he answered slowly.

"Well, you want to get them developed, don't you?" Hofman asked.[4] "I can get them developed for you."

"Oh," Alexander said. Well, he did want to see what he had on the film. But he didn't know this man.

Hofman made a suggestion: take the roll of film to the hotel notions counter, which has a 24-hour developing service. Alexander would have his photos back the next day. "Are they black and white or color?" he asked.

"They're slides," Alexander answered.

Hofman urged Alexander repeatedly to get his roll of film, until Alexander finally consented and went to his room, returning shortly with the roll. "Come on," Hofman said, and they went to the small souvenir shop in the lobby. Hofman spoke in Spanish to the young woman behind the counter, and Alexander trustingly left the film with her as she slipped it into an envelope. Then they returned to their seats in the lobby to finish the interview, which took another 10 minutes or so. Alexander then returned to his room where he tried to rest, uneasily, for a while. Later in the afternoon, he

---

[4] In the 1970s, digital photography did not yet exist. All photographs required a laboratory in order to be printed on special paper.

returned to the notions counter to confirm what had been a growing suspicion: Hofman had gone to the counter and taken back the film.

"Where did he go?" Alexander asked, with near resignation. The woman answered in broken English that the man had said something about having to return to Amsterdam immediately.

And so he had. Hofman left on the inter-island ferry, made his way to the Las Palmas airport, flew back to Amsterdam, and had the slides developed. They were then sold to a news agency, which re-sold their use to major publications and media outlets all over Europe. The London *Sunday Times* ran one of the photos across the top of its front page the following weekend, politely giving Alexander a credit. *Paris Match* magazine used one of the photos on its cover the following week. *Der Stern,* a German publication, bought the use of several of the photos.

Alexander got none of the fees paid by those media outlets. And he never got his slides back, despite letters to both the *Telegraaf* and Hans Hofman. It wasn't until months later that he received a thousand dollars for the *Sunday Times'* use of his photo. No other money was ever forthcoming, although the use of the photos probably netted the photo agency many thousands of dollars.

The conflict was agonizing for Alexander; he had been deprived of his only record of the event, photographs that he had taken with a professional-quality camera. On that basis, he had a right to be furious and take whatever action he could against the thief.

On the other hand…he was alive, a survivor – with little more than scratches – of the worst disaster in aviation history. What right did he have to complain? A difficult question.

CHAPTER 19

Linda Hopkins slept late on Sunday morning, March 27. It was her last day of spring vacation before returning to school at the University of Oregon in Eugene, where the weather was still rainy and chilly in late March. However, in Palm Beach, Florida, it was warm and sunny. Linda, 19, spent a pleasant hour or so with her grandparents, Elmer and Mildred Kneip, eating brunch at a club near their villa. Then she went back to her room and slipped into a bathing suit to get some last hours of sun before flying back to Eugene.

The sun was warm, so she avoided getting sunburned by occasionally getting up from her blanket and returning to her room to do some packing. Her grandparents were in another part of the guesthouse that they'd rented, so she'd seen little of them since brunch. She emptied a drawer or two into her suitcase, and then went back to the beach for a few more minutes of sun before repeating the process. She thought of nothing in particular: the upcoming flight, a brief conversation with her parents the previous night as they were about to leave on a trip to the Mediterranean, the warm sun in Florida and how she would miss it in rainy Eugene, Oregon.

It was on her second or perhaps third trip back inside from the beach that she idly switched on a radio as she moved about the room. "…worst air crash in history…" the announcer was saying. "…two 747s colliding on a runway in the Canary Islands, the island of Tenerife…."

Linda froze. The announcer continued talking about the crash, saying something about the apparent lack of survivors and the possibility of more than 500 deaths. She began replaying in her head what she'd just heard. He had said the Canary Islands – where her parents were going! But he'd said Tenerife. They were going to Las Palmas, a different island. Two 747s...no survivors...her heart beat faster as she turned on a television set. She wasn't sure....

More news reports: some survivors on KLM, nothing about Pan Am. Her parents were on a Pan American flight, she remembered with rising fear. Somehow, she knew her parents were involved. But she decided not to say anything to her grandparents, Caroline Hopkins's mother and father, until there had been some official word.

A television announcer broke into the regular program with a news bulletin about the crash. "The planes had been diverted from a nearby island airport, Las Palmas, after a bomb had exploded there earlier this morning, closing the airport," he said, and Linda was now sure that her parents were involved – and very possibly were dead. Sick with worry, she dressed as quickly as she could. Again, not to worry her grandparents, she left the hotel and went down to the pool, where there was a telephone.

Calling a Pan American office, she was unable to get any fresh information. "My parents were on board, I think," she told the ticket agent.

"I'm sorry, but we don't have that information here," the agent told her.

"Well, can you at least tell me if that was the flight that was chartered for the *Golden Odyssey* cruise of the Mediterranean?"

"Just a moment," the agent said, then returned to the telephone shortly and said yes, that was the charter flight for the cruise.

It was the confirmation Linda didn't want: her parents were in a bad crash, the worst in history, according to the announcers. Linda paced back and forth by the pool for a few minutes, trying to hold back tears. Then she hurried back to her room and switched the television back on, only to find that the reports were getting worse: firefighting equipment was inadequate to handle the size of the fires at the crash site, and there weren't enough ambulances to get survivors to the hospitals.

It was time to tell her grandparents, Linda decided. The announcers had said there were survivors, she told herself. Perhaps her grandfather could find out more information. She hurried into a room of the villa that served as the study, to find that, after waiting more than an hour so she wouldn't disturb her grandparents, she had now picked the wrong time for her news – her grandfather was in the shower. Her grandmother, Mildred, was sitting in a chair reading, oblivious to the unfolding tragedy.

"There's been an accident in the Canary Islands, Grandma," Linda announced. "I just heard something about it on the news. Two planes crashed."

Mrs. Kneip was immediately beside herself with concern. "Oh God, oh God, get your grandfather out of the shower," she told Linda, who dutifully went to the bathroom door and shouted. But over the hiss of the water, Elmer Kneip was unable to hear Linda yelling. "Go in and get him," Mrs. Kneip insisted, so Linda opened the door and yelled, "Grandpa! There's been a plane crash in the Canary Islands! I think Mom and Dad were on it."

That time, Mr. Kneip heard every word, responding with "What? What? What?" Alarmed, incredulous, he quickly shut off the shower, wrapped a towel around himself, and hurried into the study, water dripping onto the carpet.

Mr. Kneip grabbed the phone and called Pan American while his wife switched on the television.

"Don't waste your time. They won't give you any information," Linda told him. "I already called them."

He tried anyway, hoping that some new information had just become available. But the call was unsuccessful. He then began making call after call: to the cruise ship itself, to see if his daughter and son-in-law had boarded; to a local newspaper; to his secretary, to have his passport and papers arranged for a possible quick trip to the Canary Islands. "I told them they should have gone to Switzerland or Germany," he said as he dialed.

* * * *

Adrienne Forst woke up shortly before 9:00 a.m. on Sunday morning in the bedroom of her home in the Bel Air section of Los Angeles. She was crying.[1]

---

[1] The remainder of the information in this chapter is from a combination of interviews and media reports.

Her cries woke her husband, Robert, who asked what was the matter. She'd had a bad dream, she told him. In the dream, she could see her name on a list, and it was being crossed off as if she were dead.

Mrs. Forst's parents – Meyer and Ethel Simon of Westwood – were not around to hear about that dream. They were thousands of miles away on a Pan American plane in the Canary Islands. It was then about 4 p.m., Tenerife time.

The Forsts spent a quiet morning and then, in the early afternoon, when they were driving their son to a Little League baseball game, the news came over the car radio – a plane crash. Mrs. Forst's parents were on that plane.

* * * *

Margaret Langhorn was alone with the family dogs when she heard the reports on television. With a deep fear, she was certain that was the flight her daughter, Nancy Langhorn, and a girlfriend, Rene Roberson, had taken. Mrs. Langhorn herself had originally intended to go on the trip, too, but had changed her mind as the departure day neared.

She repeatedly tried to call Pan American in Los Angeles but couldn't get through – the lines were tied up with frantic relatives. So Mrs. Langhorn waited until Monday morning, when a Pan Am representative called and said he was coming over to her home with bad news.

* * * *

Wanda Warns was driving along Interstate 80 from her home in Blairstown, New Jersey, to Dover, Delaware, for a visit with friends on Sunday afternoon, March 27. In the front seat next to her was her son, Kevin, 18. Elyse, 8, had stayed home. As far as Mrs. Warns knew, her husband, George, was flying back from the Canary Islands at that moment as a second officer or flight engineer on a Pan American 747 jet.

Mrs. Warns and her son chatted, then switched on the car radio. The announcement of the crash was the first item on the news. Badly frightened, Mrs. Warns pulled off the highway, turned around, and began driving back to Blairstown.

* * * *

Mrs. Jo White was driving with Mrs. A. H. Huckaby on Sunday afternoon near Griffin, Georgia, where the two sisters lived. They had planned to drive to High Falls State Park for the afternoon.

As had Mrs. Warns, the ladies happened to have the car radio on while they drove. The announcement of the crash sent them both into deep worry because Mrs. Huckaby's son was Victor Grubbs, the pilot of the Pan Am jet.

They tried to talk themselves out of their fear. "He must not be on it," she said to Mrs. White. "Yes," Mrs. White agreed. The plane, they both noted, had come from Los Angeles, and Victor lived in Centerport, New York, flying out of Kennedy Airport in New York. But there was increasing cause for worry as the reports continued – the plane had, indeed, stopped in New York to pick up passengers and to change flight crews.

Just as Mrs. Warns had done, the two elderly women canceled their day trip and returned home to wait by the telephone.

* * * *

On the West Coast, Roland Brusco Sr. also heard the news on the radio, about the time when Linda Hopkins in Florida had heard the first reports of no survivors.

Brusco went into shock. He was convinced that his wife and son and daughter-in-law were dead. "I have lost them forever," he told himself, and wept.

Brusco did not call his two daughters, nor did he call the parents of his daughter-in-law, Terri Brusco. He just didn't have the energy. He spent the afternoon thinking about his family: about how his son was to take over the family tugboat business someday, how his wife even had taken turns driving the boats during a 13-day strike of tugboat operators in 1969.

And he thought of one incident in particular: when he had turned down the opportunity to have breakfast with the three members of his family before they left Saturday morning because he didn't want to move his car. An opportunity to spend 45 minutes with his family – and it was gone forever because of concern about a parking space.

Still convinced that he'd lost three members of his family, Brusco spent the afternoon alone at his home in Lake Oswego, Oregon, near the border with Washington state.

* * * *

Karen Xavier, wife of Sam Xavier of Palos Verdes, California, who had been sitting directly in front of Norman Williams, in Seat 28-C on Pan Am 1736, had the opposite reaction to Roland Brusco.[2] Mr. Brusco was certain his family had been killed, but Mrs. Xavier was convinced that her husband had survived. He was tough, she believed, and only 33 years old. He'd have found a way out of the plane.

Mrs. Xavier and Roland Brusco Sr. were wrong: Xavier had died, and all of Brusco's family had survived.

* * * *

Some relatives had heard no news reports and were ignorant of the entire situation until they got transatlantic telephone calls – not easy to arrange in 1977 – from survivors, or from other relatives in the United States.

When Joani Feathers finally got to a telephone in the hospital at Tenerife, she called her mother, Berenice Batten, in San Diego. Mrs. Batten picked up the telephone in her home late Sunday afternoon to hear her daughter's voice from 5,700 miles away announcing, "Mama, I'm alive."

"Alive from what?" Mrs. Batten asked innocently.

"There's been an accident, but I got out of it," her daughter explained, not very clearly.

Still not realizing the scope of what had happened, Mrs. Batten asked her daughter if she would continue with the cruise. After all, she and her friend, Jack, had left only the day before.

"Oh no, Mama," Ms. Feathers said. "Most everybody on the plane died. Oh no."

* * * *

---

[2] "Xavier" is a pseudonym.

Diana Hopkins, 20, spent the afternoon in her dormitory room on the campus of Southern Methodist University in Dallas, Texas, studying for the final exam of her real estate class the next day. There were few distractions. Her roommate was out with her boyfriend, and Diana had kept the radio turned off. She pored over her textbooks as the afternoon lengthened. Back in Palm Beach, Florida, her grandparents had resisted an urge to call Diana after Linda suggested they wait for about another hour, in case Warren and Caroline Hopkins had been among the survivors.

Their wait was worth it. Shortly after 5 p.m. in Palm Beach, a call came through from a family friend in a Chicago suburb – Warren and Caroline were alive!

When they'd finally gotten access to a telephone at the Tenerife hospital, the Hopkinses were still in such shock that neither could remember any family phone numbers. Warren had called the friend because that was the only telephone number he'd had in his pocket just then, and he'd asked that the message be relayed to the family in Florida and around the country. Warren said only that he'd gotten a broken foot and that Caroline had a bad shoulder, but that neither had been burned.

After taking the call, Caroline's parents then called Diana to tell her, but decided to explain the situation as if she knew nothing about the day's event – which, it turned out, was correct.

It was about 4:30 p.m. in Dallas when the telephone rang in Diana's dormitory room, and she answered. It was her grandfather, with what at first almost sounded like the beginning of a joke.

"We have some good news for you and some bad news," he said, and then asked if she had seen any television news or had been listening to the radio. No, Diana answered, knowing immediately this was not going to be a joke.

"The good news is that your mother and father are alive – but they were in a plane crash," her grandfather told her. Somehow, Diana thought later, she knew he was going to say that it had been a plane crash. What else would have demanded that urgency?

They talked only briefly, Diana later not even remembering that her grandfather had told her that her parents were in good condition, considering what they had been through. She hung up, then called her boyfriend. She rushed over to his apartment to watch the Sunday evening news, which had the first film footage of the crash – the black-and-white film shot by the Tenerife television station – of the burning wreckage of the planes. Her parents got out of that alive? There had to be some burns. No one could get out of that inferno without suffering some burns, she thought. How painful! The scars...perhaps it would be better to be dead and not to have to suffer. Surely there would be much suffering.

It was not until nearly 8 p.m. in Palm Beach that Caroline's father was able to get a telephone connection through to the Santa Cruz Virgen de la Candelaria Hospital on Tenerife. "Hopkins? Hopkins?" the hospital switchboard operator repeated, struggling with the name. There was a brief silence, and then the operator said both were in surgery.

"I don't care how you do it, get one of them to the phone," Kneip insisted. "I'll make a very generous donation to your hospital. I'm going to stay on the line until you get one of them on."

"Hopkins? Hopkins?" the operator repeated.

His request was fulfilled. An orderly hurried down the hall from the central nurse's desk, where the telephone call had been transferred, to Caroline Hopkins' room. "Hopkins, telephone," he announced, waking her from a light sleep. It was now nearly one o'clock, very early on Monday morning in the Canary Islands. He pulled her bed away from the wall, and then, unlocking the wheels on which the bed rested, he rolled Mrs. Hopkins down the hallway at breakneck speed, like a college prankster gone mad.

They screeched to a stop at the nurse's station, and the telephone was handed to Caroline.

Her father did not waste words. "Are you burned, or do you have any broken bones?" he asked.

"Warren's foot might be broken," was his daughter's answer, "and I'm not sure about my arm. But no burns."

They were really among the luckiest, Caroline Hopkins explained to her father while her mother and daughter listened on extension phones.

"In fact, we were just about the first passengers to get off before the deep explosions," she added. The family's spirits began to lift.

"Hi, Mom," Linda then announced.

"Linda!" her mother said. Then, demonstrating that maternal instincts can overcome even the shock of the world's worst air disaster, she asked, "Are you having a nice time in Florida?"

The question sailed past Linda, not registering at all. Instead, she grilled her mother about how she was feeling and if they had lost all their possessions, including the jewelry that Mrs. Hopkins had taken with her. The answer was yes, and that her mother hadn't even gotten her purse out of the plane, let alone anything of value.

When the brief phone call ended, Linda's grandparents called Diana in Dallas to tell her what they'd learned. Then the telephoning began – aunts, uncles, family friends, cousins. Calls started coming in from the media and friends who didn't know the latest news. The phone rang all night and all the following day at their guest rooms in Palm Beach – a scene that was repeated in hundreds of homes in the United States and in the Netherlands.

In Amsterdam, KLM officials set up a special office for relatives of those who had been on Flight 4805, with a direct telephone line that was announced on radio and television. The phone line was in constant use for a week.

Although 394 people had been on board the Pan American plane and 248 on the KLM jet, the accident reached out to touch thousands more, causing grief and pain and worry and suffering to a greater degree than any accident in the history of aviation.

CHAPTER 20

What was going on? It was dinnertime on the *Golden Odyssey* and no one from the Pan Am flight had shown up yet. The 75 persons who hadn't taken that flight were getting acquainted with the ship: unpacking in their cabins, strolling about, waiting for the arrival of the plane so the ship could get underway and the first party of the cruise, the Captain's Welcome, could begin.

There had been some information about a bomb at the Las Palmas airport. Some kind of trouble there, a separatist movement or something. Still…where was the plane?

Most of those on board didn't find out the major news until they had sat down at their assigned dinner tables for the evening meal. Then came the announcement.

Marjorie Hanson's first reaction was a desire to rush off the ship and get to the crash. Unlike most of the other passengers, she knew some of those on board the plane because 21 of them had booked their cruise passage through her travel agency in Escondido, California. Then she realized there was nothing she could do for those on the plane. She stayed aboard.

Others were on the ship after not having taken the charter flight (Hanson had tried, too, but couldn't get a seat): Fred and Ingrid McCay of San Marcos, California; Hugh and Elaine Greer of San Diego; Jo Alice Gerhards, Janie Hahn, and Lucille Trigg, all of Escondido; Mr. And Mrs. Harry Keyzer of Mission Viejo, California, and Dr. and Mrs. Richard Stoughten of Rancho Santa Fe, California.

As had Hanson, the Stoughtens had flown on their own simply because the charter flight was full.

The mood of those on board the ship had been pleasantly anticipatory – until the news arrived. For Hugh Greer, the impact did not fully strike him until he walked below the main deck and down a hallway, seeing dozens and dozens of keys hanging in the door locks – waiting for guests who would never arrive.

The ship's crew members, too, had been affected. Among the fatalities was Tony DeLiyanes, a popular chef who had been sent to several restaurants in San Francisco for information about the food his American guests might request.

About 100 of those on board the plane were past customers of Royal Cruise Lines; thus, some of the crew members were familiar with them from past voyages.

Cruise line officials and the ship's officers decided to go ahead with the cruise. With 202 crew members and only 75 passengers, the ship pulled out of the Las Palmas harbor about two hours after its scheduled departure. It was clear that no one from the plane would be going on the cruise. Even those who had not been injured were in too much shock to think about continuing their vacations.

The ship left with one fewer passenger than earlier in the day, though. Gordon Brown had gotten off with his luggage. He was the Leisure World travel agent who had come over a few days early to look around Grand Canary Island. His wife, Jean, had been aboard the Pan Am flight, escorting 37 Leisure World residents who had bought their passage for the cruise through their agency, Good Time To Travel.

The first reports about the crash did not list his wife as a survivor. In fact, as Brown waited in the harbor area at the Royal Cruise Line office, it was not until 11 o'clock that night that he learned his wife had indeed survived.

Brown had already checked into a hotel in Las Palmas. He knew he would have to wait until Monday to get to Tenerife. Los Rodeos Airport remained closed, of course, because of the debris and the still-burning runway fires.

So, on Monday morning, Brown boarded an ocean-going ferry that got him to Santa Cruz de Tenerife around noon. He rushed to the hospital and quickly found his wife.

"There you are," she smiled weakly at him when he walked into her room. They could not speak, but simply touched.

By then, the *Golden Odyssey* had landed at Funchal in the Madeira Islands north of the Canaries, close to the mouth of the Mediterranean Sea. Those passengers remaining on board had been reassigned to better accommodations, and everyone had been moved so that they were closer together.

Many passengers and crew members were deeply depressed, but a decision was made to continue with the full cruise. After a few days, the "ghost ship" mood began to shake itself out. Assistant cruise director Fernando Oliveira, taking over for the late Beau Moss, noted that the passengers participated more in the games and sports and other shipboard activities than those on cruises with a full complement of passengers.

As Marjorie Hanson told a newspaper reporter after the cruise had concluded, "I think that being so close to death made us all appreciate life a little more."

CHAPTER 21

Beth Moore was sure she was dead. She was lying on a plain table in a dark room. There were gigantic blocks of blue ice stacked alongside and around her, up into the air as high as she could see.

"Well, I know I'm dead, but I didn't think it would be like this," she thought, not liking it at all.[1] Her discomfort grew as she lay there, looking up, and the discomfort turned into a chilly pain all over her body, and she couldn't stand it any longer. So she began screaming....

And then she was awake, in a hospital room, and not dead, but the pain was there. What had happened? The last thing Mrs. Moore remembered, she was being wheeled into a room for X-rays of her body. The doctors had studied the X-rays, seen that her femur had been severely broken, and decided to pull it back into the proper position. Several of them grabbed her leg on each side and, without giving her any painkillers, yanked her leg into the position to reset the broken bone. After that process, she received an anesthetic, which she was later told by a U.S. doctor is not normally given to adults. Nevertheless, it was strong enough to help her drift off into a hallucinatory state partway between her conscious pain and her mind's view of death.

Her image of cold was correct, however. It was a complaint made by many of the survivors in the hospital that night. Dressed and mentally

---

[1] This information is from an interview with Mrs. Moore several years after the accident. Other information and anecdotes in this chapter are mainly from other survivors, but also from media reports at the time.

prepared for Mediterranean holiday warmth, the survivors now found themselves in chilly and rainy weather on a tiny island in the Atlantic. Yes, they were cold.

And lonely. Many, in their beds, wept for lost loved ones. Husbands had lost wives; wives had lost husbands. Children had lost parents; friends had lost friends.

Few groups of airplane passengers ever develop what could be called a sense of community. But when everyone on a flight is going to the same destination for the same reason, the trip can become more than a typical airplane ride. At the start of the Pan Am flight, a group of 394 people had subtly moved toward one another, sharing the anticipation of a common good experience.

Now, that community had been shattered and another one had formed for the opposite reason: the common sharing of a nightmare. New friendships were created among the survivors that night in the hospital, and bonds between spouses who had survived were strengthened.

Perhaps what the Pan Am survivors needed most during their stay in the Tenerife hospitals, after their most immediate medical needs had been met, was compassion. The shock of the experience they had gone through could be met with the comfort of people who sympathized with their plight, and who could help cleanse the spiritual wounds that had opened with the loss of friends and relatives.

The compassion was certainly there – the doctors and nurses received praise for their concern from most of the Americans after the accident. The actual quality of the medical care was another issue. Warren Hopkins didn't get his head wound stitched up, for example, and it was the same with Caroline Hopkins's fingers. Beth Moore's broken back was not caught by the doctors on Tenerife, possibly because they were distracted by the shattered condition of her foot and leg. It wasn't until she was examined at Walson Army Hospital at Fort Dix in New Jersey that the extent of her injuries was determined.

The routine in Tenerife's hospitals also took some getting used to. The Hopkinses and about half of the other 60 survivors were put in the island's maternity hospital, which must have been disconcerting for the men, not to mention the many older women. The language barrier was a problem. When Caroline Hopkins was wheeled out of her room on the second day of her stay, she thought they had mistakenly gotten the wrong patient and were going to operate on her. "Does anybody here speak English?" she had called out as she sped down the hall, pushed by a determined orderly as if being wheeled on a giant skateboard. In response, she got smiles and nods from the staff members.

The cold tile floor in the hospital – which seemed to lack a heating system to fight the chilly March air – became a problem when getting from the bed to the bathroom, or to visit friends in one of the nearby rooms. Joan Jackson, one of the surviving flight attendants who had been put in the same hospital, spoke Spanish. At Caroline Hopkins's request, Ms. Jackson was able to obtain a pair of hospital slippers for Caroline late on the second day. The only problem with them was that they were far too large, with the toes extending so far out that the slippers made the slapping sound of clown shoes as Mrs. Hopkins moved about. The hospital accommodations were modern, although Mrs. Hopkins had to share a curtainless bathroom with some other patients. The bathroom mirror was set at an odd height that wasn't easy to use.

Both the Hopkinses were aware from the start of their hospital stay that they were among the lucky ones in the crash. Few survivors had been so unscathed – physically, at least – that they didn't even have to stay at a hospital. But it sank in to Warren and Caroline very quickly that most of those on board had died, including Beau Moss, the man with whom Warren had talked for hours; the unnamed couple who had been in their seats when they first boarded the plane in New York; Clara Johns and her friend, with whom they had chatted at JFK Airport prior to the flight's departure; and the two women sitting behind them and whose names they hadn't even learned. And that sea of faces in the plane, unfamiliar, but real people with families and friends.

Standing at the front of a 747 and looking back, one can be impressed with just how large the plane it is – the seat rows go on and on. And on Flight 1736, every one of those seats had been occupied. The magnitude of the event the Hopkinses had just experienced was sinking in steadily, and it was horrifying. All those people now dead. It wasn't even known yet how many. The horrifying memory remained: the plane burning like an oil well blowout, with raging flames sweeping the fuselage and human beings lying dead and dying on the ground, some alive or on fire.

It had to be like war, some suggested, but no, it was worse. Warren Hopkins had seen war, and he knew. In wartime, the young men of the country go to the battlefield, knowing full well that they face their own mortality. Here, on a runway on Tenerife, mothers, daughters, wives, and old men had to face that. That was not war. This was a cruelty of fate, a cruelty of the highest order – one that would create misery for many years. These people did not die for a cause; they were victims in a society that has placed a high value on time and speed and bigness, and then in turn asked too much of the monitors of that system.

Human error had done it – the mistakes of people just like anyone who has ever acted too hastily without thinking properly beforehand.

This reality was something that, over the succeeding years, had to be faced by survivors, just as their own injuries had to be overcome. That they were victims of a mistake, and not an act of God such as a hurricane or an earthquake or tornado, requires a special healing process. How does one grieve? What is there to grieve? Could they be angry at the pilots? The airlines?

The initial reaction of many of the survivors was to band together in the hospitals and in the hotel. Jack Ridout and Bo Brusco became friends during the time on Tenerife. Both were young and self-assured men who had just been through the worst experience of their lives, and they found some comfort in each other's similarities.

Tony Monda, unhurt except for a few cuts and bruises, took on the role of official greeter at the Residencia del Candelaria Hospital. He moved around to the different rooms and did his best to cheer up the people there, kidding with them when appropriate. He loaned his razor to those men who had lost their own on the plane. He encouraged couples who had been separated by the hospital's administrators to get beds in the same room. He became well known among the survivors as the man who had picked up his carry-on bag on the way out of the plane, an action that at the time seemed natural to him (although, to repeat the Association of Flight Attendants' position, this action is now strongly advised against). But to others, sitting farther away from the exits or more focused on just getting out of the plane, his act was almost lovably humorous, especially because Monda willingly shared the bag's contents, which included toothpaste and shaving cream.

Simple things became important. Grace Ellerbrock insisted on being put in the same room as her husband, with their beds so close together that they could reach out and touch each other.

"It was so important, under those dreadful circumstances, just to be able to touch and to know that we were together," she later said.

Because Mrs. Ellerbrock spoke Spanish, she could make herself understood when she asked for a bed in the same room as her husband. She also helped another survivor, Harold McGowan, locate his wife and requested – successfully – that the McGowans be moved into the same room. Caroline Hopkins spoke some French but was able to work it into only a few conversations.

As the tragedy's impact increased, the survivors reached deeper into their own wells of sympathy to help others. Warren and Caroline Hopkins sat up most of several nights with Penny Quade, whom they had not met until they were put in nearby rooms at the hospital. Penny's sister, June, would occasionally join them, but Penny did most of the talking. Her need to talk was met by the Hopkinses, who were sympathetic listeners and the same approximate age as Penny and June's parents. The young woman reviewed how she and her sister had begged their mother to get out of the plane after the collision, but the older woman had insisted that "the stewardesses are going to come" and tell them what to do.

When they finally had been able to convince Mrs. Ellingham to rise, they began pulling her toward the same exit area that Warren and Caroline Hopkins and others had used. There were very few people alive remaining in the first-class area, and the fires in the cabin had reached the galley area just behind them.

As they pulled their mother toward the exit, a section of the floor collapsed just where Mrs. Ellingham was walking between her daughters, possibly as the heat melted part of the fuselage frame. She disappeared completely into the bowels of the plane, lost among a tangle of miles of cables and wires and luggage and broken bits of airplane. With the fires now close enough that both young women were suffering burns, they had no choice but to leave the airplane. To see their mother disappear had embedded itself onto her consciousness, Penny told the Hopkinses. What more could she have done? What if their mother had burned to death? She had to find out for sure.

"Oh, Penny, you surely did all you could do, and more," Warren and Caroline Hopkins both told her. They urged her to continue her life knowing that she had done her very best to help her mother.

When we try to act like heroes, we must face the consequences of failure. Grace Ellerbrock had been in that place and succeeded, pulling her husband away from the burning fuselage. Now she was able to enjoy the touches from her husband, as well as the status of someone who has profoundly assisted another person. She had fulfilled society's highest expectations of us all in such a situation.

For Penny Quade, circumstances did not so allow, and now she bore the heavy feelings of not living up to that societal expectation. Had she done enough? The Hopkinses repeatedly attempted to convince her that she had. When another survivor told her that her mother had not burned to death but had succumbed to the fumes inside the plane, Penny got some relief from her agonized despair. If her mother was not meant to have survived, then at least her death had been painless.

Nevertheless, Penny said several times that she wished she could have taken her mother's place.

"No, no," the Hopkinses insisted. Her mother had lived a long and full life, and it was better that the young survive, they told her. Besides, Penny had two small children back in California who needed a mother. Little children need their moms, they told her. Penny heard the words, but her despair was deep. Eventually, as the night turned into early morning, she was able to settle down enough to sleep.

Other survivors helped one another the same way. Tony Monda listened to Ethel Simon, the woman who'd had a bad leg cramp during the flight from New York and had startled everyone when she yelled out because of it. Her husband had died of his injuries, and she wanted to share her deep grief. Monda sat in her hospital room as she wept.

Others had outside visitors: missionaries from the island and English-speaking citizens who had responded to a call through the local media for help in translating at the hospitals. Late on Monday, a young American woman appeared at the doorway of the hospital room that held Warren and Caroline Hopkins. She introduced herself as Catherine Germann, and she lived on the island, she explained. Could she get the Hopkinses anything? They chatted for a while and a friendship started, one which continued for years, with an annual exchange of Christmas cards and letters. Mrs. Germann, she explained, had been participating in a Vassar College study-abroad program when she met her future husband, a Spanish doctor. They eventually settled on Tenerife. Life was quiet on the island, except for the occasional political fights with the separatists, she said. When the announcement came about the plane crash, she hurried to offer her services as a translator and to assist the American victims as well as she could. The Hopkinses gratefully asked her if she could pick up a few personal items and toiletries for them.

A Catholic missionary visited Jean Brown's room and sat down near her bed. "Tell me about your experiences," he said. "It's important to get them sorted out."

"I don't want to talk about it," she said sadly. "I'm trying to put it all behind me. I just don't want to talk about it ever again."

"Oh yes, you do," the man insisted, surprising her, and he urged her to recall the details of the accident and how she had gotten out of the plane. She reluctantly gave in to his insistence, and they talked about her feelings of fear at seeing the flames and the wreckage, and of the loss of many of her friends from Leisure World. The talk, Mrs. Brown later realized, did her an enormous amount of good.

The value of talking about the experience would increase in the days and weeks that followed. It would be a counterreaction to the deepening impact of the experience on the survivors.

At the airport, the fires continued at both aircraft carcasses through Sunday night and until 3:30 a.m. Monday – despite the combined efforts of three separate fire departments and more than 100,000 gallons of water and fire-retardant chemicals. When the black smoke finally dissipated, the airport's lone runway was a scene of sickening carnage: hundreds of yards of ash, debris, broken metal, luggage, bodies, and parts of bodies. A vision of hell, all gray and black, all the color gone from this pretty island.

CHAPTER 22

For no particular reason, there was no breakfast served to patients in the Candelaria maternity hospital Wednesday morning, March 30. Warren and Caroline Hopkins and others simply went hungry.

They forgot their hunger, however, as they noticed a commotion among many people in the hallway: Spanish embassy officials from the United States and Madrid, U.S. aviation industry representatives, and several doctors. It had been decided to release all the passengers and send them back to the United States, where the most seriously injured would be placed in military hospitals as close to their hometowns as possible.

Nurses visited each room and gave the patients a plastic bag for personal items. All Caroline Hopkins had to put in her bag were her and her husband's toothbrushes (purchased by Catherine Germann), a small tube of Colgate toothpaste (with a label in Spanish), and two oranges and a tangerine from the nightstand. Everyone was told they'd be leaving at noon, but the transfer began before then – just when several people were trying to grab a quick nap.

Ms. Germann appeared at Warren and Caroline's room door just before noon and asked if they needed anything. Warren Hopkins still had nothing but bloody clothing, a shredded pair of pants and only one shoe, but how that would be remedied at this late date was unknown to the Hopkinses. Mrs. Hopkins thought a scarf for her head would be a good idea, remembering the chilly wind of three days earlier.

The flurry of last-minute visitors continued. Two missionaries stopped by and asked for names and addresses. They would send everyone a note, the women said. A female reporter from a Spanish media outlet interviewed Warren and Caroline Hopkins at length, using a translator for the questions and answers.

Orderlies arrived with two wheelchairs for the Hopkinses, who were pushed – this time, slowly – down the corridor to an elevator. As they waited, several of the nurses rushed up to them and hugged and kissed them goodbye. The gesture was sincere, heartfelt, and much appreciated. The incongruities were dizzying: badly injured Americans recuperating in a maternity hospital on a Spanish-controlled island after surviving the worst air crash in history while on their way to a vacation cruise in the Mediterranean Sea. The nurses were surely thinking that nothing like this would happen again – just as the survivors were hoping.

The Hopkinses were wheeled out of the hospital and down a ramp to a waiting ambulance. Others followed. Roy Tanemura was already in the ambulance, as was Florence Trumbull. News photographers snapped pictures as the Hopkinses gingerly got into the vehicle. They were in the first ambulance to pull away from the hospital; they would wind up sitting on the runway for more than 30 minutes before moving onto a U.S. military medical evacuation plane that had flown to Tenerife from Rhein-Main Air Force Base near Frankfurt, Germany. The plane had originated at an Air Force base in Florida and had volunteer reservists and a Delta Airlines pilot as part of its double-size crew. A medical team was on board, too. The turbo-prop plane had been specifically chosen for this task because it was small enough to be able to land on the taxiway that adjoined Los Rodeos Airport's still unusable main runway, everyone was told.

As the Hopkinses boarded the plane – Caroline walking, aided by two of the crew, and Warren being carried on a stretcher – Mrs. Hopkins threw a final glance over her shoulder at Los Rodeos Airport. Three days before, it had been crowded with tourists. Now, it was crowded with soldiers, government officials, and aviation industry representatives. Many members of the media were there, too, packed into a roped-off section of the runway.

Caroline recalled seeing one reporter sitting on the asphalt with his type-writer on his lap, tapping away, as the loading process continued.

The time on Tenerife ended, as it had begun, with cold, windy, and humid weather. However, there was no fog this day. The passengers moved into the plane, which was originally designed to carry soldiers or cargo. Everyone who was ambulatory had to sit sideways on "basket" seats. Those on stretchers were arranged in racks at the center of the plane.

When of the litter cases and the walking injured were aboard, the plane's doors were closed, and it moved down the taxiway, then lifted off from Los Rodeos. The loading process had taken about four hours, during which the door to the cockpit and the rear loading door of the airplane were open. This created a wind-tunnel effect that blew the chilly Tenerife air through the length of the airplane. With the passengers cold, in pain, unhappy, in some cases lonely, in nearly all cases without their possessions, in too many cases with lost loved ones, the exit from Tenerife was miserable.

The last stretcher carried Victor Grubbs, the Pan Am pilot, who was placed on the plane near Caroline Hopkins's seat. He had burns on more than 20 percent of his torso, arms, and back, and was confined to a stretcher for the entire trip. Before the plane took off from Tenerife, Caroline Hopkins watched as teams of U.S. and Dutch investigators squatted down by his stretcher to interview him. There was too much noise in the cabin to hear what they were saying, but the investigators kept nodding sympathetically as Grubbs spoke. They may have interviewed the other crew members, too, but Caroline didn't see that. First Officer Robert Bragg had a broken ankle, and Second Officer George Warns had burns on his hands and face. The last investigator finally left, patting Grubbs on the head in an odd gesture of friendliness.

After a short flight to Las Palmas, the entire loading process had to be reversed to move the passengers onto a C-141 transport plane – a jet this time, not propeller-driven. The C-141 Starlifter was large, with a pleasant blue interior, regular passenger seats, a galley in the center, bathrooms, and a section in the rear half of the plane for stretchers. Again, Warren Hopkins was carried in a stretcher but was told that after takeoff, he could join his wife in the regular seats.

As Caroline Hopkins walked onto the C-141, Jim Naik – the Royal Cruise Line official who had gotten drinks for the Hopkinses after the New York takeoff and chatted with them during the flight – suddenly appeared in front of her. "Caroline! I thought you were dead!" he said bluntly, but was obviously pleased to see her. They hugged. Naik insisted that Mrs. Hopkins sit with him and that they would save a seat for Warren. Elsie, his wife, was also on a stretcher but could not be moved. The plane had three seats on each side of a middle aisle, so there was plenty of room for about 75 passengers – the ambulatory passengers, plus military and medical personnel and some industry representatives. Only about 25 of the group on stretchers were even able to sit up.

They sat down and strapped themselves in, then waited for more than two hours until the loading process was completed and the plane taxied down the Las Palmas runway and lifted off, headed for the United States. As the plane took off, Caroline Hopkins later said, she had only one thought: "to get home as quickly as we could."

Shortly after takeoff, Naik, with a glance at the hospital robe Mrs. Hopkins was wearing, announced that he had a present for her. He pulled a paper bag from under his seat and handed it over, explaining that he had bought it for his wife to wear, but she was so badly burned that she was unable to change clothing. "I think it should fit you," he said. "You're about the same size."

It was a tan peignoir, into which Mrs. Hopkins changed with great difficulty in the airplane's washroom. Because of her right shoulder injury, she was unable to raise her right arm in order to slip it through the sleeve hole. However, she eventually worked it on and returned to her seat, grateful to Naik for giving her something that offered a bit of decency. She now had the peignoir, the hospital booties that flapped as she walked, and a scarf that Catherine Germann had brought her, which kept slipping off her head because of an absence of bobby pins.

The survivors' clothing situation added to the indignity of the entire experience. First, there were the crash and the injuries, followed by the psychological pain. Then, they were carried back into the United States on stretchers – or walked off a plane escorted by military police or Army personnel – wearing only pajamas or torn clothing, and under the examination of television lights and with news photographers firing strobe-lit cameras.

Beth Moore was also aware of the situation. Having been married to a former high-ranking Naval admiral, she was familiar with form and style. She was a controlled, intelligent woman, genuinely happy with the life she had created with her husband. The cruise was a metaphor for their smooth-sailing relationship, Moore being a former Navy man and both of them happy with each other. Then, "in one second," she would think later, "my life changed forever."

Now Mrs. Moore was returning to her home country on a stretcher, a widow, hurting so badly that she couldn't move.

As she was fastened into the stretcher holder on the plane, Mrs. Moore could see rows of other stretchers, each with a brown body bag hanging off it – just in case – and was swept with a wave of melancholy at not her own situation, but at the loss of dreams of everyone on the plane. Holding herself back from despair, she tried to smile. "What a picture this would make," she thought.[1]

Another stretcher patient was Jean Brown, who was placed on the top row of stretchers, with her head only inches from a speaker that was regularly blaring calls for one of the doctors or nurses to step to the back of the plane. Sleep was thus not possible. But Jean Brown kept one main thought: she was alive and going home.[2]

Unlike most of the other survivors, Mrs. Brown had been brought back from death in more ways than one. In addition to the fact that her injuries were severe but survivable, she had given herself up as lost in the first moments after the collision. As the plane was falling apart around her, she had decided she was ready to die. Then had come that reversal of her thinking. She had gone to the brink of death itself and looked over the edge, but had turned back, deciding to fight.

Others on the plane who initially gave up may well have made the same decision if given more time, but very few individual variations in the

[1] This information is from interviews with Beth Moore.
[2] This information is from an interview with Jean Brown.

human psyche are permitted in the middle of an evacuation from a burning jet. The thoughtful, the passive, the contemplative people are those who may not survive. Only one behavior will be successful: immediate action. There is even a difference in the inflection of the identical words used by Jack Ridout and Betsy Dickens, the former a self-made successful business-man sitting in first class with his girlfriend, the latter an elderly woman in economy class with her husband.

"This is it," Ridout announced, after he had regained consciousness from the knock on his head. It was a call to action, as in, "Now is the time to do something." When Betsy Dickens turned to her husband after the crash, her announcement was more of a final statement: "I think this is it," she had told him, with an implied acceptance of what was to follow.

Perhaps, as Jean Brown did, the Dickenses eventually would have decided that this was *not* the end – that their lives could go on if they acted quickly. But if there ever was a time that didn't permit studied reflection, the Tenerife crash was that time.

Many other survivors had to spend the long return flight on a stretcher, staring at the stretcher hanging above their own, among them, Albert and Florence Trumbull, Byron Ellerbrock, Mary Kay Hess, Isobel Monda, Elsie Naik, and others. One more was Agnes Compton of California.[3] Severely injured, with burns and broken bones, her condition deteriorated steadily until, about halfway through the flight over the Atlantic Ocean, died. Her last words were to ask for more pain-killing medication.

From Caroline Hopkins's seat (the seats in military passenger planes in those days faced backward as a safety precaution so that the seatback could act as a cushion in the event of a crash), she watched as a brown sheet was pulled over Mrs. Compton's body on the bottom tier, near the middle of the stretcher section. Another death. Numb, she turned her head away.

Warren Hopkins joined his wife shortly after takeoff, and they sat together for a while, others also sitting with those companions who had survived. Then, as the flight continued, the barriers gradually broke down. Although most remained strangers – their number had been so thinned

---

[3] This is a pseudonym, used to offer some privacy for this woman's surviving relatives.

out that few from the plane still knew one another – talking again became important, as it had in the hospital, and conversations became more intense. They created their own highly exclusive club of plane crash victims, and they helped one another. Bo Brusco continued his conversation with Jack Ridout. "We've been born again," he said, and Ridout readily agreed. Across the aisle from them was Joani Feathers, taking up three seats. A cut on the bottom of one foot had swollen her foot, so she had it elevated across the two adjoining seats. Behind her were Penny Quade and June Ellingham, the latter with both of her arms bandaged. Periodically, June Ellingham had to use the washroom on the plane and none of the nurses could take the time to help her. Because her head and both of her arms were bandaged, she needed assistance, so Joani or Penny or Terri Brusco would go along. It was yet another indignity for the survivors – returning in a hospital plane in pajamas or torn clothing, unable even to use the toilet without help.

The conversations continued among the survivors, at first rehashing the experience of the crash. Someone remembered a man yelling, "Let's not panic!" shortly after the collision, and he, the person remembered, had been doing exactly that – panicking. One of the men who'd lost his wife sat several rows away from the Hopkinses on the C-141, occasionally chatting with those around him. But he would periodically give in to his sorrow and put his head forward into his hands, rocking back and forth. Another husband who'd become a widower sat alone, forlornly. Caroline Hopkins thought his expression was so despairing that she was unable to approach him.

Warren Hopkins found George Warns, the flight engineer from the Pan Am plane, and they spent more than an hour talking about aviation. Warns had already been interviewed by Pan Am officials and was saying nothing about the crash, obviously under orders from the airline executives and safety investigators. But he and Hopkins, with Ed Hess and others sitting in, talked – with some irony – about how safe the Boeing 747 was. Warns had heard about one that had landed safely with three of its four engines shut down – a tremendous feat by the cockpit crew.

Warren Hopkins, a naturally friendly person, had introduced himself to several of the flight crew. To his astonishment, he found that he'd been a passenger on another of Captain Victor Grubbs's flights, a New York-to-London business trip several years earlier. As they discussed that previous flight, Hopkins recalled how friendly Grubbs had been – he remembered Grubbs coming out of the cockpit and chatting his way through the passenger compartment.

But for most of the passengers on this hospital flight, the conversations were a chance to continue working through what psychologists feel is the necessary process of finding the meaning of the calamity.

In the late 1970s, the term "post-traumatic stress" was not applied to situations like this – it was only used, with the label of "combat fatigue," for soldiers.

Florence Trumbull told fellow passengers about how she had gone off the back of the wing during the evacuation process, while her husband had gone off the front of the wing. Mrs. Moore told a nurse that she had just been bending over, adjusting her carry-on luggage under the seat when the plane suddenly began ripping apart. Caroline Hopkins again lent a sympathetic ear to Penny Quade. Those who could eat – and by now many on the plane were famished, having gotten no morning meal at the hospital – were treated to a military airline meal of thinly sliced roast beef and vegetables, their first meal since the previous night. They ate ravenously.

It would be hours longer before they got more food. As the plane neared the United States, the fruit juices that were being served freely began running low, and by the time the Hopkinses and eight others got off the plane at McGuire Air Force Base in New Jersey – headed for Fort Dix's Walson Army Hospital – they were again hungry. A Pan American representative drove the Hopkinses to Philadelphia to get them on the first plane to Chicago, and in the early morning hours of Thursday, March 31, while they waited in Pan Am's Philadelphia office, they were given packages of food that a representative had rounded up from various vending machines at the airport – a prefab cornucopia of packaged eggs, sausage, muffins, fruit juices, cereals, toast, jellies, bacon, ham, sweet rolls, milk, and coffee. American overkill, but an appreciated gesture.

Before they had gotten to Philadelphia, however, Warren and Caroline had to sit inside the plane at Fort Dix for more than an hour, along with the other passengers, while the red tape of their re-entry to the United States was removed. Because almost everyone had lost their passports, a State Department inspector finally stepped onto the plane to clear them. And here is where Caroline Hopkins became a lawbreaker after surviving the worst airplane crash in history. Desperate to return to their homes, all the survivors had to wait just a bit longer while they were asked the most mundane of questions:

"Is anyone bringing any fruit or flowers back into the United States?" the State Department representative asked the group, a question greeted with bemused laughter and shakes of the head.

And Caroline Hopkins forgot – she still had two oranges in her hospital bag.

CHAPTER 23

D r. William Reals was reading at home in Wichita, Kansas, on Sunday afternoon, March 27, 1977. Outside, the weather was rainy and chilly, much as it was nearly 5,000 miles away on the island of Tenerife.

The telephone rang. On the other end was Dick Rodriguez, a representative of the National Transportation Safety Board. Rodriguez was calling from the NTSB's office at Dulles Airport in Washington, D.C., and he wanted to know if Reals had heard about the Tenerife crash.

Reals hadn't. Rodriguez filled in the doctor on the basic information, then asked if he could put together a team of pathologists and leave for the Canary Islands as soon as possible.

"Yes, I can," Reals answered. "Can I take the Concorde?"

"We're not in that big of a hurry," Rodriguez answered dryly.

Dr. Reals hung up the phone and went into action – again. A nationally known forensic pathologist, he had been on medical teams investigating numerous plane crashes for the federal government. He'd done so by breaking away temporarily from his duties as a professor at the Kansas University School of Medicine. (At the time, he was also a vice president for medical affairs and director of laboratories at St. Joseph Hospital Medical Center in Wichita.)[1]

---

[1] Dr. Reals eventually became dean of the Kansas University-Wichita medical school and had a long and successful career in academics and as a practicing pathologist. He passed away in 2002. He was interviewed by Jon Ziomek about his Tenerife experience several years after the accident.

Reals had been on the federal government's medical investigating team for a dozen or so major crashes, dating back to shortly after the Korean War, when the Federal Aviation Administration was setting up the first such group in commercial aviation's early days of expansion. The FAA (known then as the Federal Aviation Agency) eventually eliminated its list of available civilian investigators, but Reals continued to be called because of his past experience in such cases. These included a 1961 United Airlines crash in Denver, a 1970 University of Wichita football team charter that crashed into the Colorado mountains, and a 1970 Southern Airlines charter crash in West Virginia.

The 1961 United crash in Denver was the same one later studied by Clyde Snow and his associates at the FAA's Office of Aviation Medicine (as it was known then) to determine evacuation patterns during an airplane emergency.

Reals's autopsies after that Denver crash had determined that 16 of the economy-class passengers had died from smoke fumes inside the aircraft while waiting to get out the rear emergency door. Before they had succumbed to the fumes, they could have turned around and gotten out of one of the exits in the first-class section. None did, however, partly because the aisle curtain between the two sections had stayed closed, and no one, in those moments of extreme haste, thought to open the curtain and look.

As a result of that crash, every commercial airliner now carries a sign in between the seating sections stating that the aisle curtain must be kept open during takeoff and landing.

Reals was now being asked to study the remains of the deceased Tenerife passengers and crew members to learn about their deaths and, thereby, contribute to learning the actual cause of the crash.

He was able, on this drizzly Sunday afternoon, to get only two local pathologists to accompany him. So he called Rodriguez back and told him to contact the Armed Forces Pathology Institute to get more help. He would meet the other doctors on the way, he said. Then he hung up and began packing. His efforts turned into an odyssey, traveling to the Canary Islands, then returning to the United States, fulfilling the responsibility he'd accepted – eventually taking weeks and involving international politics.

Reals and his two colleagues flew to New York early on the morning of Monday, March 28, meeting 22 military pathologists who had been rounded up by the Pathology Institute. All caught the first available flight to Madrid, arriving late Monday, Madrid time, as the survivors on Tenerife were settling into their second night at the island's hospitals. Because there were no flights to Tenerife – the airport there remained closed – they had to fly to Las Palmas. But there were no available flights to Las Palmas overnight on Monday, so the entire team had to stay in a Madrid hotel Monday night.

On Tuesday morning, they boarded an Iberia Airlines Boeing 727 for the flight to Las Palmas, sitting alongside more than 100 tourists who were not about to let a major plane crash two days earlier ruin their own planned vacations. There were others on the flight, too. In the seat next to Reals was an American lawyer representing a couple who had been on board the Pan American plane. So the lawsuits were being put into the works already, before the dead and injured had even left the island.

Reals and his team arrived at Las Palmas late Tuesday morning. Checking the schedules of the ocean-going ferries that regularly moved passengers between the islands of Tenerife and Grand Canary, they found that one ferry was scheduled to leave at noon. Rushing down to the dock, just as Gordon Brown had done only two days earlier, they boarded the small ship – and waited for an hour and a half until the vessel finally pulled away from the dock at 1:30 p.m.

The trip to Santa Cruz de Tenerife took three and a half hours on rough seas. By the time the ship had the destination port in view, many of the pathology team members were hanging over the gunwales or lying down on benches.

Their arrival was less than dramatic. No one met them or even knew they were coming. So Reals led his rubber-legged group of pathologists through the port of Santa Cruz de Tenerife to an office of Iberia Airlines. An efficient young agent called several hotels and successfully booked rooms for everyone. Despite the complexities of the journey, all were in their rooms by around 6 p.m. Tuesday, barely 48 hours after Reals had taken that phone call from the NTSB.

The next morning, it got complicated. The Spanish government initially refused to let Reals and his group see the bodies.

"The Spanish were not letting anyone down there," particularly people with cameras, Reals recalled later with amused consternation. Extremely tight security had been clamped on the entire airport. Even relatives of the dead and media representatives were having difficulty getting through.

After a lengthy conversation with government representatives, however, Reals and another pathologist and two U.S. Air Force photographers – just four members of the entire delegation – were told that they would be permitted to see the bodies.

The four took a taxi to the still-closed Tenerife airport, where they were met by Spanish government security officials. They were then escorted to a hangar that had been converted into a temporary morgue.

Before they entered the hangar, Reals paused to look at what remained of the two planes, both of which were visible on the runway but some distance away. Most of the acres of wreckage had already been swept to the side of the runway, making a massive pile of broken, twisted, burned aircraft metal, including several huge engines. Sticking up out of the mound of metal was the tail of the Pan American plane, rising more than 20 feet above the pile.

Reals studied the scene, then turned and went into the hangar.

Reals had spent much of his career viewing the results of airplane crashes. He was an amateur historian and had read about the mass killings during wartime. Compared to such events as World War II bombing raids, even the Tenerife crash represented a relatively low number of deaths.

But he was stunned when he walked into the hangar. In front of him, he saw row after row after row after row of caskets, separated into a Dutch section and an American section. The slick, varnished exteriors of the caskets were a stark incongruity to the wretched condition of the bodies they contained.

Human life cannot be sustained if an unprotected body is subjected to temperatures much greater than 150 degrees Fahrenheit. But the human body itself is remarkably tough.

As aviation fuel exploded and burned ferociously after the KLM-Pan Am collision, the temperature inside both jets eventually reached 4,000 degrees Fahrenheit. At that level, the planes themselves melted. The bodies of those inside became carbonized and blackened, shrinking in length and size into statue-like objects. The hands and arms stiffened and curled inward in a position called "the pugilistic pose" by those in the field because of the resemblance to a boxer's stance.

But at Tenerife, to Reals, the bodies almost seemed to be praying.

By the time Reals and his group arrived at Tenerife, all but about one dozen of the bodies had been embalmed. This followed Spanish law, which calls for embalming within 48 hours of death.

The process was so difficult for personnel on the island that the Spanish government had to send a warship to the port of Santa Cruz de Tenerife with the proper materials: 4,000 pounds of cotton, 8,000 pounds of zinc chloride, 8,000 pounds of zinc sulfate, 4,000 pounds of sawdust, and 600 caskets. The grisly cargo had arrived Monday, and undertakers had been working nonstop ever since.

The process was to cut open the bodies and remove the viscera and brains, then clean them with zinc sulfate. Cotton swabbed in zinc chloride was placed inside the body cavities, and then the bodies were closed. Then they were wrapped in gauze, sprinkled with sawdust, and placed in tin inner caskets. Thirty tinsmiths were working around the clock to make the inner caskets, which were placed inside the outer boxes made of highly varnished wood.

A Spanish newspaper reporter wrote at the time – how he learned this wasn't clear – that the less-burned bodies from KLM 4805 still had looks of horror on their faces. And every watch on board the KLM plane had stopped at the same time – about seven minutes past five o'clock.

The Dutch bodies were easier to identify than the American bodies even though some of the American bodies were not burned badly. This was because of the Dutch system of nationalized health care, by which most Dutch have a dental examination every year. The national dental records are an excellent source of identification because teeth don't burn. Four dentists were flown from the Netherlands to Tenerife to help with this process.

For identification of the American bodies, Reals was needed. But the work wasn't to be done on Tenerife; the relatives were already asking for return of their loved ones. Reals had been asked to investigate the possible causes of the accident from the perspective of a pathologist, but the Spanish government's reluctance made that extremely difficult.

There was little more to do except identify the American bodies, but the Americans wanted to quickly return the bodies to the United States. That required clearing the Spanish governmental red tape in order to move the bodies, which wasn't Reals's responsibility.

Late Wednesday, barely a day after he had arrived, Reals could see that his work was done. So, on Thursday, he flew back to the United States on a plane sent over for Pan Am and government representatives. He arrived in New York late Thursday and was back at his own home in Kansas by Friday afternoon.

Again at home, he received another telephone call, this one from the Pentagon. A military spokesman asked him if he would move to active duty as brigadier general in the Air Force, a position he held in the Air Force Reserve. Pan American, faced with the staggeringly difficult task of identifying 322 bodies from in and alongside their plane, had turned to the government for help. Would Reals head up the team that would do the work at Dover Air Force Base? Yes, he would, he answered, and soon was on his way.

The bodies – in their coffins – arrived on Sunday, April 3, borne by two Pan American Boeing 707 cargo jets. The jets landed at Dover Air Force Base in Delaware, the mortuary for which has been the arrival point for the bodies of most of the soldiers who died in the Vietnam War and the two Gulf Wars. The Dover mortuary is still used for military personnel and dependents who die overseas. It's one of the only mortuaries in the world that can accommodate so many bodies at once.

(A bizarre note: about 18 months after the Tenerife crash, the Dover mortuary received even more bodies at one time when a religious cult of Americans in the South American country of Guyana committed mass suicide. The Dover center received and stored more than 900 bodies during that tragic event.)

This time, Reals and the base personnel had a rough job because the fires after the KLM-Pan Am collision had burned many bodies beyond recognition.

The planes arrived in the late afternoon with their grim cargo, landing in weather that had been the same for the vacationers one week earlier: overcast, with dark skies.

Two priests and a rabbi said prayers over the caskets as they rolled down ramps out of the planes.

Each casket, covered with a spray of flowers, was rolled to a waiting hearse. Seven hearses, borrowed from nearby mortuaries, made continuous round trips for nearly five hours to move all the bodies to the base mortuary.

There were no relatives to meet the bodies because almost none had been identified. The accompanying death certificates had been left blank.

The identification process began on Monday morning, April 4, with Reals supervising Armed Forces Institute of Pathology technicians, military forensic dentists, 22 FBI fingerprint experts, anthropologists, and a team of 18- and 19-year-old recruits from Fort Bragg, North Carolina, who had been assigned to a graves registration unit but instead were sent on loan to Dover for some nightmarish on-the-job training.

The green recruits, some of whom may have stayed green during this work, had one macabre task: to unwrap the bodies and prepare them for the identification process. Pan American workers had contacted relatives of those who were listed as missing and asked for information such as dental records, identifying birthmarks, or body characteristics. The first identification was made quickly – one man had worn a pacemaker, which hadn't been destroyed or lost in the fire. Most weren't so easy.

Numerous challenges hampered the identification team in its work. One of the first issues was that five of the bodies were Dutch, mistakenly shipped with the American bodies to Dover. At the end of the work, an exchange was made with Dutch pathologists, who had received four American bodies. In those cases, fortunately, the bodies had been readily identifiable.

The burned condition of many of the bodies made internal medical histories the only way to identify some of them. But because many of the dead were elderly, a disproportionate number of them had worn dentures – thus making dental charts useless. X-rays were taken of entire bodies, from head to toe. The FBI team members took as many fingerprints as they could and compared them with those at the California Department of Motor Vehicles. Old injuries and physical characteristics were matched against those sent in by relatives. The particular style of a tooth filling would be studied and X-rayed from several different angles to see if identification could be made from that.

The teams kept a large chart for each victim, adding clues as they discovered new facts about the bodies: blood type, dental work, scars, unusual jewelry.

One man was identified by a surgical clip in his leg that turned up in an X-ray, another by a heart bypass valve, and still another by a relative's description of an unusual ring.

Reals found that about 20 to 25 of the bodies were immediately identifiable because they were not as severely burned as were some of the others and the facial features had remained recognizable. In a few cases, a wallet even remained in a pocket or purse.

At the end of the first week of work, they had identified more than 150 bodies. Another 75 were identified by the end of the second week. At that point, Reals returned to civilian life in Wichita and went back on Air Force Reserve duty. He left Armed Forces Pathology Institute Deputy Director Col. William R. Cowan in charge of the remaining ID work. Only one more week was put in on the effort, and the experts finally acknowledged that there were 114 bodies they were not going to be able to identify.

It was not a pleasant situation. For 24 couples and families, one of the dead had been identified while the spouse or other family member had not – thus ratcheting up the grieving process.

The 114 unidentified victims were flown by Pan Am to El Toro Marine Corps Air Station in California and carried, again by a stream of hearses from neighboring mortuaries, to Westminster Memorial Park, where a

This memorial marker is in Westminster Memorial Cemetery north of San Diego. A mass burial was held here for many of the unidentified victims of the disaster.

special 10,000-square foot section had been set aside and donated by the park for the crash victims.

The bodies were buried in Southern California because so many of the passengers aboard the plane had been from that state and region.

On April 27, each of the unidentified victims was buried in a separate, numbered concrete vault. Media reports of the time conveyed this chronology for the process:

At 2 p.m., a Catholic priest, a Protestant minister, and a rabbi conducted the rites of the dead, standing over the 114 coffins lined up neatly in rows. A funeral director called the roll, from Wilma Achatz to Charles Ziebell. As each name was called, an assistant placed a long-stemmed rose in a large vase in front of the three clergymen until the vase contained 114 roses.

As with all the other expenses associated with the crash, Pan American paid for the funeral services and for transportation of relatives and friends to the services. The day was handled as tastefully as possible. A choir sang and Eagle Scouts carried the roses to the white caskets, according to media reports.

Some members of the group of mourners walked among the rows of vaults, touching and wondering which one contained their son or daughter, mother or father, aunt or uncle, or good friend.

Photo courtesy of Inez de Goede

This memorial marker is in Westgaarde Cemetery in Amsterdam. The names of the dead are inscribed on plaques surrounding the central sculpture.

Those who had arrived early for the ceremony heard the cemetery's general manager say that burials would not begin until the services were over. The process would continue through the night and, he cautioned, might take as long as 24 hours.

At the news that the burials would not take place immediately, one young man broke down into sobs.

"I want to be here to see at least one of the vaults put into the ground," he wept. He was assured that indeed he could stay for that. The man dried his eyes and turned away, passing among the vaults, no doubt wondering which one contained his lost mother. Suddenly, he angrily kicked at one of the coffins, a futile gesture against the gods who were preventing him from knowing exactly where she was. He, along with so many others, was robbed of the completion of the grieving process that would have come if they had known which casket was their relative's, and then have been able to watch it lowered into the ground for its final rest.

CHAPTER 24

D r. John Duffy is a tall, soft-spoken, articulate man who, in 1976, was teaching psychiatry at the Uniformed Services University of the Health Sciences in Bethesda, Maryland. A former Air Force flight surgeon, he also spent time as a consulting psychiatrist for the Federal Aviation Administration, and eventually served as an assistant U.S. surgeon general. His interest in aviation – and also in the workings of the human spirit – spanned decades.[1]

It was not surprising, then, to hear of the idea that occurred to Duffy one day near the end of 1976:

How come no one had ever studied the effect of airplane crashes on the survivors?

The idea came to Duffy after he'd had conversations with officials of the Emergency Mental Health and Disaster Assistance section of the National Institute of Mental Health. They had done follow-up work with survivors of a flood and a tornado. Their orientation was to natural disasters – it had apparently not occurred to them to study aircraft disasters.

"Boy, I think I have something here," Duffy told himself after the meeting.[2] He set up a meeting with Calvin Frederick, who was then the EMHDA section chief, and explained his idea. The NIMH should have

---

[1] Now living in Florida, Dr. Duffy remains on the faculty at the Uniformed Services University of the Health Sciences and the University of Central Florida Medical School.

[2] Dr. Duffy was interviewed in the 1980s and again via several email exchanges in 2015.

a national conference on this subject, Duffy suggested – invite airline and behavioral experts and crisis intervention workers.

Frederick liked the idea, too, and passed it along to his superiors – but then it got lost in the bureaucracy of the government. Duffy heard no more about the idea until the winter of 1977, when a formal rejection came back to him. Duffy recalled that the official rejection note said the idea was ridiculous.

Duffy, a mild-mannered man, got irritated. He pushed the application into the bureaucratic machinery a second time, and then waited again. And waited. By mid-March he still hadn't heard anything, so he went directly to Dr. Bertram Brown, then-director of the National Institute of Mental Health.

"Listen, Bert, I don't like to go over people's heads, but I think you've got some dumb people in your shop down there," Duffy told Brown. "I had an excellent idea that got turned down, and I'd like you to take a look at it." Brown agreed to do so.

It was the third week of March 1977.

On March 27, the crash at Tenerife took place. Barely a week later, Duffy received a message from Brown's office: "Conference approved. $30,000 allocated for expenses."

Years later, Duffy talked about his motivation for this first-ever conference. He had been convinced that the psychological trauma of any event, natural or caused by humans, produces a psychological response.

"In the case of aircraft accidents, the individuals are far more vulnerable," he said. The reason is because there is no sense of community among the passengers that is lasting and supportive. In a flood or tornado or earthquake – disasters that have received much attention in Duffy's field – survivors can join with one another and pledge to rebuild their street or neighborhood or community, and there is a shared strength in that. In fact, according to a study by the Ohio State University Disaster Research Center, a major percentage of those who survived a 1974 Xenia, Ohio, tornado – which killed 33 and injured 1,200 – stated later that their survival was a positive event because it boosted their confidence in themselves.

That confidence, said Duffy, is "a process, a shared idea: 'We have survived, and we will build our home again, and we will ignore the fact that this might happen again and go about our ways in a very positive fashion.' I think that kind of process does in fact occur in some of the natural disasters.

"I find it rather interesting that the natural disaster is an act of God, if you will. When a tornado strikes a community, there is not the sense of blame that one finds in a man-made disaster.[3] In other words, there's no need to point a finger or even to raise the question of who is to blame. Because if anyone sent the tornado, it was God.

"But in an aircraft accident" – for example, Tenerife – "obviously something went wrong, and it had nothing to do with God. There were clear sequences of events that occurred."

An extension of that thought is that there might be some anger directed at the airlines. Most survivors would, in fact, deny that they are angry – but the survivors and the relatives of those killed in the Tenerife crash did sue.

One survivor, however, made no bones about doing so. He said the accident was a stupid occurrence and blamed both KLM and Pan American.

"If they'd had any judgment, they wouldn't have been on that [expletive] runway, and all those people wouldn't have died," he said several years after the accident. "That's what I said in my deposition, and that's what I'll say in court, and I don't care whether I get one penny or one dime. That's the way I feel about it.

"They were stupid. Our pilot was stupid and their pilot was stupid. And they cost not only the people who died in the plane, and not only the people who were injured in the plane, but they caused typhonic repercussions: the kids, the families, unbelievable sorrow. You murder 600 people and you're going to cause pain that will go on for generations. And that's exactly what they did. Their bad judgment, their lack of *whatever*, cost a lot of people a lot of pain and suffering."

Most survivors don't express themselves with such anger. Many survivors, when approached to discuss the Tenerife accident, were reluctant to

---

[3] For example, one might recall the unresolved frustration, sadness, and anger expressed by relatives of those on board Malaysia Airlines Flight 370, which disappeared in the southern Indian Ocean in March 2014 after taking off from Kuala Lumpur, Malaysia. Bits of the plane's wreckage have been found near Madagascar, but neither the jet nor any of its passengers have been located.

talk about it – they want to put it behind them, as Jean Brown had told the missionary who visited her in the hospital.

"Denial is our most important and most powerful psychological mechanism," Duffy said. "It's the one we bring into bear the quickest. And of all of them, it's most successful. Compared with repression, sublimation, reaction formation, denial is clearly the best in terms of just helping people get by."

That's not to say it's always the healthiest reaction. Indeed, Duffy and others such as psychiatric social worker Margaret Barbeau have said that denial "robs one of a conscious awareness," as Duffy put it. "We might go about with the belief that we've solved the matter."

Duffy told the story of a sailor aboard a U.S. destroyer during World War II. He was asleep in his bunk deep below deck when, during the middle of the night, his ship was torpedoed.

"You can imagine what kind of an experience that would have been," Duffy said. "He was blown out of his hammock, deep in the bowels of that metal ship, and he somehow made it out and got into the water. And he was picked up by a rescue ship and was assigned to another ship and completed the war.

"He went into civilian life as a welder. One day he had a job of going down into an empty gas storage tank to repair a crack. And he went down and was working on it. It was dark and he lit his torch, and there was a residual of gas, resulting in a mild explosion." The man immediately had a complete psychological breakdown.

"He had successfully integrated that first experience, by anyone's standard. The next event that psychologically was so close to the original reopened the whole process, and in fact he became very much a psychological cripple.

"It's sort of the old 'fickle finger of fate' – if he had not approximated that experience again, he might have gone through life well-adjusted, as far as anyone could tell.

"I think it's true for all of us that we have our emotional break point. And perhaps, for healthy people, that break point would require an awful lot of stress; whereas, there are other people who are very vulnerable, and just a small degree of stress can precipitate an emotional decompensation."

So an individual's emotional reaction to a stressful event can be as important as the event itself. And because of the intensity of the experience of a plane crash – "the violence and dismemberment and distortion and everything else" – even for the healthiest person, "it might breach his vulnerability level." Thus, previously calm and controlled people may weep uncontrollably, while others might go into a sort of catatonic shock.

"I think there are very few similar events in the society that can approximate it in terms of horror and stress."

In his work, Duffy established four stages that survivors of disasters often pass through in their journey toward finding a meaning of the event. These were originally devised for survivors of natural disasters, but he said these would also apply generally to aircraft crashes. The phases are:

1. Heroic phase
2. Honeymoon phase
3. Disillusionment
4. Reconstruction

In the Heroic phase, taking place at the time of the event and shortly afterward, survivors have strong and direct emotional reactions to what they've just experienced.

That gives way to the Honeymoon phase, which Duffy said runs from about a week to about six months after the event, depending on the individual. For those who've lived through the calamity, there's a sense of having shared in something very dangerous and conquered it. After a tornado or flood or other natural calamity, various governmental bodies rush in with money and assistance, and agencies are helping the community reestablish itself. That usually doesn't happen with air crash survivors, so this phase does not easily apply to them.

The absence of this kind of assistance for airline crash survivors is important. They have no sense of community because after the accident and hospitalization, they return to their own cities and states, where most people haven't gone through the same experience.

Although a major portion of the passengers on the Pan American plane at Tenerife were from Southern California, another large segment was from

Northern California, plus there were passengers from throughout the continental United States, Alaska, Canada, and Hawaii. (Warren and Caroline Hopkins were the only two passengers from Illinois.) Aircraft accident survivors move quickly into the third phase, Disillusionment, which can last anywhere from several months to several years.

"Then we really see what has been hidden," Duffy said. "The disappointment and anger and resentment for the entire experience begin coming out. In the case of a natural disaster, during this time the federal and state agencies pull out, and the community is on its own again, possibly worse off. The shared sense of community fades. For the air disaster victim, the lawsuits are now underway, and competitiveness comes in about who is getting what kind of settlement, and why was that one couple able to get more money than them?"

But that blends into the final phase, Reconstruction, during which all the victims realize that they have to solve their own problems, rebuild their homes, and go ahead with life itself.

"I think for plane crash victims," Duffy continued, "what makes them so much more vulnerable for emotional problems is that the kind of supportive network or structures which encourage them is within the person of the underwriter, who says, 'We're going to pay for your hospital bills, and we're going to do something for you.' But there is no shared community, no group community response to kind of shore people up and carry them through.

"So it may very well be that we see the Disillusionment phase coming in much quicker and probably much more devastating in that it comes almost on the heels of the Honeymoon, and there's no period of Reconstruction. Almost within a week or so of an aircraft accident, an individual is probably already beginning the Disillusionment phase, because they now find themselves back in Peoria or Oshkosh, or wherever he is, with no other emotional supports or anyone really caring about them at that point." The media representatives have stopped calling, and the neighbors have all come over with casseroles and wished the victims well, but after that, the survivors are on their own.

They now face the final question of the entire experience: what did it mean? "An individual has to be able, eventually, to explain the event some way or another in a way that makes sense," Duffy said.

"I think that religious people will explain it one way: the hand of God."

Sure enough, some Tenerife survivors did react that way, deciding they'd been saved because God had a plan for them. One surviving couple, devout Christians before the crash, believed that firmly. The husband told reporters he'd heard part of the 23rd Psalm as he was climbing out onto the wing of the plane. His wife told a reporter that after the collision, when she became aware of the devastation around her, "I said, 'Jesus, help me, help me,' and he did." As soon as they got back to their home in California after the crash, they went to their bedroom to pray.

Others, notably Mario Tyzbir, also of Leisure World, and Joani Feathers of San Diego, eventually also decided on a religious meaning for the crash. They had been saved for a reason, they decided. For Tyzbir, it was a particularly difficult time. His wife had been killed after he had been unable to pull her out of the plane, and he faced the agonizing question of why he had made it out but she had not. He finally decided to accept that "Someone Else" had answered that question for him. Roy Tanemura of Kelowna, in British Columbia, had to face the same question. Tanemura was already a devout Buddhist – a religion that calls for the acceptance of life's struggles in a calm way. As Tanemura's wife had told him in the past, "Someday we must part, and when that time comes, you must be brave and carry on."

Tyzbir strengthened his religious commitment after the crash. But the image of being unable to save his wife – her hand had slipped out of his – caused deep evaluative thinking about the value of life. He finally decided what he told Norman Williams in *Terror at Tenerife*, a book about the crash and its religious components: that his wife had been taken for a reason, and he was willing to submit to the Lord's will.

Joani Feathers said later that she had not been very religious until after the crash, when she found comfort in praying – possibly, she thought, this was God's way of communicating to her, and that it was time for her to do something.[4] But first, she went into a downward spiral. She lost sleep. She had crying fits on Sunday afternoons. (The crash was on a Sunday afternoon.) She lost her appetite, daydreamed constantly, and began losing her ability to concentrate. She began stuttering. As she later described it, she had memory lapses at her interior designer job so strong that she would forget the first part of a sentence she herself had just spoken. She became snappy and irritable if someone called to complain. "I've just been through the worst aviation crash in history, and this person is complaining about the color of their draperies," she would think to herself.

A reporter from a Phoenix newspaper called her for an interview six weeks after the crash. "How has this changed you?" the reporter asked. "I remember you when you were a policewoman in Phoenix. Are you now going to turn your life over to God? Become a Jesus freak?"

"No, of course not," Feathers answered. But the question started her thinking. I guess I should be thankful, she thought to herself. She began dating a former minister and peppered him with questions about the Bible and evolution. He finally suggested that she attend a Bible class, which she did, and began finding comforting answers to her plague of unsettled thoughts and nightmares. Someone else was watching over her and protecting her.

Then Joani's friend suggested that she test the Lord one night and ask Him, through prayer, to take away the nightmares she'd been having. She did, and the dreams stopped that very night. She decided to test the Lord again, praying to Him to stop another problem that had developed after the crash – stuttering. And that worked, too.

Joani Feathers married her friend and spent the next several years teaching Sunday school. "I've dedicated my life to God. Wherever He wants me to go, I'll go," she later said.

Although the marriage was not successful, her spiritual strength remained. From policewoman to Sunday school teacher. And the catalyst for that change was the Tenerife plane crash.

---

[4] The information about Mr. Tyzbir is from several media reports of the time. Ms. Feathers talked later to Warren and Caroline Hopkins, and also was interviewed by Jon Ziomek.

Joani's companion on the trip did not have the revelations she did. Jack Ridout, a man of total self-confidence, did find himself becoming more contemplative, however. "I think anybody who was on that plane, and lived, is going to have some kind of a problem — mental, physical, or whatever," he later said.[5] "I don't begrudge anyone or downgrade anyone who has a pain because they think about that incident. Because if you ever wanted to see six hundred dead people burning, that'd be the place to go and see it. That's not a very nice description, but I'm sorry, that's exactly the way it was. There wasn't anything very nice about it."

In the winter of 1978, Ridout also remarried to a Pacific Southwest Airlines flight attendant. The next summer, about 15 months after the Tenerife crash, they went on a cruise from California to Vancouver and then to Juneau, Alaska.

"To tell the truth, I wanted to see how I was going to react on a cruise," Ridout recalled. "I had to have a suite near an exit" on the ship. "I wasn't going on it unless that's the way it was.

"I was paranoid, just paranoid. Every person I looked at on that ship was a person who I looked at on that [Tenerife] plane, and I thought to myself, 'Hey, those people should have been able to afford the luxury of going on a ship.' It's tough, you know?"

Grace Ellerbrock, who pulled her husband away from the burning Pan American plane, made an interesting choice when she and her husband returned home to Laguna Hills. Although a devout member of the Congregationalist faith, she could feel no special religious calling then. While other survivors were deciding that God had saved them, she, who already had that devotion, decided that the reason for her and her husband's survival was more pragmatic. She was able to jump off the wing of the burning plane without breaking any bones, she noted, which enabled her to help pull her husband to safety. And because they were alert passengers, they were able to respond to the emergency.

"If there is an answer that God has, it has not been revealed" to her, she said in an interview two years after the crash. "I am quite religious. And I'm

---

[5] Mr. Ridout was interviewed several years after the crash.

very grateful, and I have great faith. But I can't say that I have been saved for some particular crusade." Regarding the claims of exactly that by other survivors, Mrs. Ellerbrock noted, "I think that's marvelous. I haven't had that revelation."

On the return flight from Tenerife, Warren and Caroline Hopkins spoke to many of their fellow survivors. One man whose wife they'd chatted with became seriously ill after returning to the United States – he could not understand how or why he had been spared death. He went into a severe depression thinking about the numbers of dead around him on that horrible afternoon, and as a possible result of his weakened mental state, he suffered a heart attack. Although his own physical injuries had not been severe, his ability to cope with the shock of the crash and its aftermath was weak. He spent months in the hospital after his heart attack before finally, with the daily encouragement of his wife, achieving a level of mental and physical strength that enabled him to leave the hospital.

It was true for many survivors, including Caroline and Warren Hopkins, that their perceptions of life tended to change. One of the women with whom they'd become friendly returned home to an eventual divorce from her husband – life for her changed too much for her to go on in the same way that it had been before the crash.

Eighteen months after the crash, Joani Feathers, Warren and Caroline Hopkins, Dr. John Duffy, and Don Foster (the Southern Airways crash survivor discussed earlier in this book) were all on an NBC talk show, *America Alive*, with Jack Linkletter. On that program, and at a later lunch, Foster told everyone how he'd just been divorced from his wife shortly before he took that fateful flight on Southern. After the crash, when he was resting in a local hospital, his ex-wife was extremely solicitous and worried, calling and visiting regularly. As with others, Foster's perception of his daily life had changed. His appreciation rose for his former wife's gestures. Everything looked different to him. After several months, they remarried. But after more months, they again divorced.

Many of these changes demonstrate an interest in starting fresh, as a way of putting the horror of the crash behind them. Jim Naik became friends with Warren and Caroline Hopkins, and for decades, he and Warren would talk on the telephone every year on the crash anniversary. He told the Hopkinses he considers himself "very lucky, and I take things as they come. Probably the rest of my life course will be changed because I want to take more trips, I want to do more traveling, but I don't take things that drastically, that seriously. Today *may* be my last day. I say, today is a good day, let's enjoy it."

To get to that point, though, Naik said he had to overcome the nightmares that plagued him for more than a year after the crash. At first, he got them regularly and often. Sometimes his dreams would be of the plane, other times they would be of the bedroom being on fire. And sometimes the dreams would be so intense and horrible – dreams of being trapped and not being able to get out – that he would wake up screaming.

Jean Brown never had a nightmare. Not a single one, after she had talked to the missionary in the hospital at Tenerife. However, she said later she sometimes would find herself pausing in the middle of her day's activities to recall what happened.

Unlike others who recovered from their physical injuries in weeks, Mrs. Brown had to spend two months at the Brooke Army Medical Center burn unit, and for years after the crash she bore an additional burden of being a survivor: she wore, around the clock, a pair of special support stockings to prevent scars from forming on her legs. Thus she had a constant reminder.

"Sometimes I wake up in the middle of the night and think about it," she said. "It isn't a nightmare kind of thing, but it's on my mind a great deal, and I keep wondering how long it's going to be, whether it's always going to be this way."

Although Mrs. Brown was a cheerful person, she was not able to resume a normal life or help her husband at their travel agency as much as she would have liked. The sadness at losing so many friends had created an empty spot inside her.

"Jean is a cheerful person with a positive approach to overcome problems," her husband wrote more than a year after the crash. "In her doing this she often understates her personal experiences.

"She is probably right in saying she has not had a nightmare – she does not dream, as such. However, she continues (and possibly more frequently) wakes up with a start and is mentally rehashing the accident and can't return to sleep. She has a haunting feeling regarding so many of her 'flock' having perished.

"I have been retired but have had to re-enter the management [of the travel agency] since Jean's accident. At 73, this has been a strain on my health. Jean finds it difficult to work at the office as her mind is brought back to her continuing healing discomfort, [and] by well-meaning friends asking about it. Since the pain, the discomfort and the sleepless nights are going on into the third year, she has increasing difficulty in maintaining an optimistic frame of mind.

"This we have learned is not unique with Jean. Dr. [Dan] Johnson, one of the country's top experts specializing in crash victims' after-effects, has found these and other of Jean's current problems among many who survived crashes. The late development of trauma apparently is not too uncommon."[6]

David Alexander had gone through the same mental process as Jean Brown in the accident. First, he had relaxed and accepted that he would die, and then he changed his mind and decided to fight his way out of the airplane.

After the accident, Alexander returned to his home in Palo Alto, near San Francisco. He was depressed about the accident, about the loss of the people he'd met on the plane, and about his photographs. One of the first things that his attorney did was take him to a psychiatrist, whom Alexander saw for several sessions.

"That was extremely helpful," he later commented. "I managed to rid myself of a lot of emotional pain, which, believe it or not, did cause a certain amount of physical pain." [7]

Alexander was one of the lucky ones whose sleep had not been not disturbed much, he said, but he found it difficult to concentrate on others around him. A sensitive man, he reacted severely when, in the autumn of

---

[6] These remarks were made in a letter to Jon Ziomek. Dan Johnson is cited in several parts of this book.

[7] These quotes and the accompanying information are from an interview and correspondence with Mr. Alexander.

1978, a Pacific Southwest Airlines plane crashed in San Diego. He mourned for those who lost their lives. Yet the other side of him – the side that had rejected his initial willingness to die in the Pan Am plane and urged him up and out – has spoken up, too. He forced himself to go on the very same cruise in 1978 that he'd intended to take in 1977: same cruise line, same ship, same plane ride over from the United States.

"I decided that living in a state of fear is not living at all," he told reporters before he left. "I've decided that to really be a whole person again, I want to fly. I've rehabilitated myself."

The following year, he took a further step by tracking down Hans Hofman in Amsterdam and confronting him about his photos. Eventually, many years later, he published his own first-person account of his Canary Island experiences in a book called *Never Wait For The Fire Truck*. The book included his photos.

Others took longer to recover. Bo Brusco and his wife, Teri, told *Us* magazine in May 1978 that they couldn't face returning to work. (It was the opposite for Warren and Caroline Hopkins, who wanted to keep busy.) Cleo Brusco, Bo's mother, had fought off thinking about the crash until she went to a basketball game. "I started to go in [the arena], and then stopped," she told the magazine. "There was going to be a fire in there. People were going to be stampeded. The whole atmosphere was claustrophobic. I couldn't go in.

"The next night, watching the TV news, there was a film on an apartment fire; the building was in flames. I had to turn it off. I couldn't bear it."

Some survivors maintained a fatalism about the accident. Tony and Isobel Monda were that way. Despite his long-standing religious devotion, Tony felt simply that their number wasn't up, a view his wife shared.

"I was in the [military] service for almost thirty years," he said. "My life was on the line lots of times. No, good Lord, let's face it: we're all fatalists at heart. When we've got to go, we've got to go. That's where it is. And in fact, I told my wife, she'd better get the idea of staying home out of her head because we're going to fly again. And we did. And we're going again."

The Mondas went on a Mediterranean cruise – although on a different cruise line – in June of 1978.

Isobel Monda acknowledged that she wouldn't have gone if her husband hadn't insisted.

"Well, for a long time, you couldn't think of anything else, and you'd wake up and you'd have to do something to keep your mind of it, because the first thing you do is think back on things like that," she said two years after the accident. At that, she began remembering the crash and what has troubled her ever since she was lying on the runway looking back at the burning Pan Am plane.

"Why didn't they get out? Every time I would think about it, I would think, 'Why didn't they get out?' To this day, I still think, 'Why didn't more people get out of the plane?' I can't figure it. The people at the back…they must have all been alive at the end of the crash."

In fairness, anyone sitting in the Pan Am plane just where the KLM jet struck would have been killed instantly. But Mrs. Monda was correct that many more people survived the initial collision than eventually made it out of the plane, for reasons discussed earlier.

"Time is always a healer," Mrs. Monda summarized. "When I wake up and think about it, I get a book and try to read something, and just not think about it.

"Well, it just wasn't our time to go. I maintain that."

"You've got to remember," added her husband – who did his own cooking for a month before his wife came home from the hospital, and he readily acknowledged that he didn't like doing so – "humans have controls. And humans are going to make errors. I've made a lot of errors. Sheesh, if I got mad at myself for making errors, I'd probably be in the nuthouse right now. But as long as humans are going to control things, regardless of how complex, computers or whatever, someone is going to push the wrong button."

Everyone found a resolve to go on, but in his or her own way. Roy Tanemura's Buddhist faith was a source of support.

"As time goes on, I realize how fortunate I am, to be back with no burns," he reflected long after the crash. "My injuries are not fully recovered. I can't do that much. But anyway, considering the kind of accident that I went through, I suppose I am a very fortunate man to be back. It is a miracle to be back.

"The bright side is that I have a wonderful family. My two kids support me in everything that I do. I could look on the gloomy side, but time doesn't wait for you. You've just got to carry on." And so he did, continuing with his surveying business.

Perhaps the survivor who had to call on the most inner strength was Beth Moore, who had lost so much.

"In one second," she would later recall with sad resignation, "my life changed forever."

She spoke of her late husband. "We had the most perfect relationship and the most perfect marriage that two people ever had. And I guess this is why it has been so difficult. I had him for eighteen months, and now it's eighteen months since I lost him. It's really a rugged one and I just can't..." her voice broke.

"It's the psychological thing, because I will never forget. There isn't anything a psychiatrist can do for me because they can't take away the picture that's there. I lay on the ground watching those two burning planes and knowing that my husband was in one of them."

Mrs. Moore spent months in and out of a San Francisco hospital when she returned to the United States. She required a prescription painkiller and needed a walker to get around her home. As she walked, she could see pictures of her late husband that had been previously placed around the house. She did see a psychiatrist for about six sessions while she was recuperating in a hospital.

A doctor's report said Mrs. Moore was handling her situation "normally and as well as it could be done," she said. "But he didn't do anything for me. He listened to me when I cried and cried and cried my heart out, telling him about my husband and what had happened to him. What could a psychiatrist do to me that would be helpful in that?"

On one of her releases from the hospital a few months after the crash, she had been at home for three weeks when she fell in her walker, tripping on the hem of her bathrobe. As she fell, Mrs. Moore reached out for the nearest object to steady herself but accidentally pulled a television set on top of herself, re-breaking her leg. That sent her back into the hospital for another dreary recuperation. A year later, Mrs. Moore met an intelligent man whom she described as somewhat psychic, who told her to talk to one of her late husband's photographs. Perhaps her question of why he had been unable to get out of the plane would be answered, the man suggested, and this could bring her some mental ease.

Her life had suddenly become very, very hard at the age of 67. Prior to the trip, she had loved to cook for her husband, but now, not only was she alone, but she wasn't allowed to cook or drive. Everything had to be done for her, a situation that her tough spirit found repulsive.

"I hurt all the time. I'm not without pain at any time. But I'm not a complainer. That would be stupid and vapid.

"Well, I have accepted the fact that he's gone, certainly. Certainly I have. That's not because I want to!

"And I know that if I don't put forth a great deal of effort to make the rest of my life as meaningful as I can, then no one else is going to do it for me. No, this is up to me now."

Mrs. Moore was one of many who decided, in time, to try and travel again. She did the same thing David Alexander did, flying from San Francisco to Los Angeles to see if she could take the strain of flying.

It was difficult. On Mrs. Moore's flight, as the plane approached Los Angeles International Airport, the noise of the landing gear being lowered into place sent her into deep, weeping fear. On the flight back, a friend accompanied her, holding her hand and comforting her.

Jim Naik and his wife also traveled again, taking a Mediterranean cruise six months after the crash. "It was uncomfortable in the beginning, but it's like you have to make it or you won't travel again the rest of your life," he reflected.

The Ellerbrocks took a trip to Denver after Byron spent six months in bed recuperating from his broken pelvis. And the Trumbulls traveled again. Life went on, everyone trying to live their lives as normally as they could. As Charles Catanese, the psychologist who studied some of the Tenerife survivors, wrote, "Psychological trauma can be a permanent and devastating experience," which can create special sensitivity to activities such as renewed traveling. "But a new equilibrium is eventually reached."

Warren and Caroline Hopkins both flew again – Warren sooner than Caroline because of his business requirements. "I work harder than the crew," he later said wryly, describing his mental gyrations to keep the plane on course. On one of his first plane trips after the accident, he was returning to Chicago from Tampa, Florida, when the plane flew through an electrical storm – an experience that shook him badly. When he did have to fly, he said, he would sit in his seat, locate the nearest emergency exit, study it for a while, and then order a drink. Nevertheless, his alertness during the Tenerife experience – which had served him and others so well – stayed with him.

Caroline reported that, for months after the crash, she was intimidated by the tall stairway in her own home.

Six months after Tenerife, the Hopkins family decided to have its Thanksgiving dinner at the Drake Hotel in downtown Chicago with Caroline's parents and one of their daughters, Linda. Diana was away at college, preparing for final exams.

The day before Thanksgiving, a producer at the local CBS television station called and asked if the family could be filmed at dinner, apparently thinking they would be at home. Caroline explained that the family would be dining out, and the station could do the filming if permission was obtained from her parents and the hotel. The permission was obtained, and as a result, the Hopkins family dinner was broadcast on local news as an example of a family with a strong reason for giving thanks that year. It did turn into something of a media event. The Hopkinses had to change their table choice in order to accommodate the electronic equipment, and there were camera wires running through the hotel's kitchen. The other patrons must have wondered who the celebrities were. A few tables away from the Hopkins group was the then-mayor of the city of Chicago, Michael Bilandic, who was ignored by reporters.

Caroline didn't fly after the accident for nearly a year. She was in the middle of preparing a dinner for herself when her husband called from New York, asking her to join him. She agreed on the spur of the moment – possibly the only way she would have agreed to get on an airplane. She had to rush to get a bag packed and arrange for a ride to the airport, thus giving her no time to contemplate what she was about to do. But once on

247

the phone with the airline, she asked specifically for a seat close to an emergency exit. The reservations clerk was amazed when Caroline told her who she was and why she needed that particular seat. One of the hardest parts of the flight was walking down the jetway onto the plane, Caroline recalled. Once on board, she "shook like a leaf," as she put it, during the entire flight and "chattered like a madwoman" with one of the flight attendants. The attendant was incredulous that Caroline had survived the crash – but also kind and supportive. By an odd coincidence, the flight attendant's husband worked for an aviation insurer and was researching the Tenerife crash.

In what would become a pattern for Caroline, she took no good jewelry with her on that trip – or ever did again. On all subsequent trips, "prior to departure, she'd send us a note listing her traveler's check numbers, the location of any valuables, and an explanation of any unfinished business," daughter Linda recalled in 2016. "My parents traveled extensively in the years following the crash. They were very selective choosing airlines and cities they flew in and out of, with regard to safety."

The successful trip to New York didn't cure Caroline of her travel jitters. On one of her next flights, this time returning from a Florida visit to her parents, she "had an emotional crisis." After landing at O'Hare Airport, and while still in the plane, Caroline happened to glance out the window at what looked to be more than a dozen pieces of firefighting equipment nearby, with lights flashing.

She panicked. No announcement had been made about any trouble with their plane, so Caroline assumed that the equipment was for another plane that was just landing. In her fear, she became convinced that the other plane was going to collide with theirs. "Let's go!" she said to Warren, and jumped into the aisle just as their plane began moving toward a gate. Caroline was overwhelmed by emotion and compassion for the passengers in the other plane, still convinced the other plane was going to crash (it didn't). "Oh, those poor people," she sobbed, as much for past victims as for future victims. "Those poor people up there!" Warren and a flight attendant were able to calm Caroline.

Flying eventually returned as a part of regular life for Warren and Caroline Hopkins. But every time she flew, Caroline reported, she felt as though she was working as hard as the cockpit crew – it was a draining and frightening experience.

The extra attention to flying safety carried forward a generation for the Hopkins family (and surely others). "My family prepares for flights differently than we used to," Linda Hopkins said recently. "We no longer travel with any valuables. Each member of our family is given a detailed itinerary prior to departure, and I always wear flat shoes. (That's in case of a need to evacuate. The FAA strongly recommends good shoes for all travelers – no high heels, no flip-flops, etc.)

"I always put particular emphasis on safety when booking flights," Linda continued. "We plan each trip with considerable thought to all aspects of air safety, and hope for the best.

"Personally, I refuse to travel on such dates as 9/11, Memorial Day, the Fourth of July, or New Year's Eve, as those dates strike me as potential terrorist threat dates. When the terrorist threat level is at 'high alert,' we do not fly."

Dr. Duffy noted that for many survivors, especially those who've lost a loved one, "their greatest emotional upset is around the question of 'Why did I survive?' The 'Why me?' reaction.

"And that has to be answered. 'Why was I saved? Why did my wife die? Why did my girlfriend who sat next to me die, and why am I walking around? What does it all mean?'

Those in "this kind of struggle must find answers to that."

Everyone's response to these questions will be different in certain ways, Duffy continued. "People's responses are individualized. It's a constant dilemma. On the one hand, we talk of what we know of the generalities of the emotions and the response. But in fact, there is enough individuality in every instance so that you have to look at where people were at that point in their life, and what they have come from, and where they hope to be going, and where they eventually find themselves."

For those who answer the final "What does it all mean?" question of the crash with a religious response, by explaining it was God's will – that is just as valid as saying it was due to the seat the person was in, or "luck," "chance," or any non-religious answer. The bottom line is that the answer satisfied the person enough so that they could get their life going again.

Most importantly, Duffy emphasized, the question must be faced. "Too often after such an experience, there is a profound pressure to shut all the doors, close everything up, and go on with life."

But, he warned, that response – "the stiff upper lip approach" – is punitive. "I think it's a macho kind of ethic. It was primarily directed toward males, in that they should not show any kind of emotional response or reaction to what happened.

"The message given to survivors should simply be, 'You have undergone one of the most profound experiences in any one person's lifetime, and it would be perfectly healthy and normal to have some degree of emotional upset as a consequence. And *there's nothing wrong with that!* It doesn't show weakness. It's not a sign of being crazy, but just a sign of being human.

"And when those signs of emotional upset appear, these people should feel very comfortable about getting help wherever they can find it."

Psychiatric social worker Margaret Barbeau said that there is another danger to those who deny themselves the grief and confusion that come with the disaster. If one limits emotional expression by excessively suppressing the painful feelings and thoughts, one may simultaneously restrict the capacity to feel warmth and joy, she suggested.

"The more we express something, whether by speaking, writing, art work or some other outlet, the less terrifying it is each time we share it. These are ways of gradually, over time, reducing the terror of the experience."

It's like a bell-shaped curve, she said. If you cut off one side of the bell – say, the unhappy part – you might be cutting off the other side. For example, rescue workers who shut their minds and hearts to the destruction and unhappiness around them may later have trouble going home and relating to their children in a spontaneous way.

A problem with this approach is that in this society and culture, many of us have not been encouraged to learn how to deal directly with distressing feelings. For example, how many of us can confidently and comfortably offer condolences to someone who has lost a relative or friend? Many of us become completely tongue-tied and shy in such moments, and we wind up doing nothing.

"Actually, the most helpful thing in that situation is to 'be there,'" Barbeau said. Keep in mind the following points, she suggested:

"An initial phase of 'psychic numbing' is helpful and natural for many people, and this helps them cope with the immediate situation."

However, she added, "It is important for short- and long-term physical and emotional healing that the victim be encouraged to fully express whatever thoughts and feelings he is experiencing.[8]

"A victim's own timing and emotional rhythm must be recognized and honored, and he must not be pushed to express unless he wishes to do so.

"If someone manifests 'psychic numbing' and/or physical symptoms of distress for a period of weeks or months and appears to be avoiding working through the realities of the event, he may benefit from professional help to facilitate the natural healing process.

"The original symptoms of physical distress, emotional pain, preoccupation, nightmares, etc., may be reactivated at a later time – for example, the anniversary of the event, a similar experience, or hearing about a crash, or another type of trauma. The appropriate response is to reassure the victim and to help secure professional help if symptoms persist."

Indeed, after the 1978 San Diego Pacific Southwest Airlines crash, police officers who had participated in the rescue work later reported that exact problem: sleepless nights and a numbing sense of the entire experience and their own feelings.

"But the antidote for that, and prevention for that, is to encourage people to go ahead and feel whatever they feel, and not force the feeling but do not shut it down," Barbeau said. "And to allow whatever comes up [to the surface] to be okay as a feeling: rage, or anger, or sadness, or tears, or needing to be alone or with other people. Inside people there is a natural healing force, emotionally, like our bodies. And what we have to do is stay with that rhythm.

---

[8] Ms. Barbeau was interviewed by Jon Ziomek.

"I use the example of somebody cutting their leg. Our body wants us to get well, and what we do is create a condition when it can spontaneously do its own thing. So the force of all our bodies all the time is to create antibodies that heal it.

"And so it is with psychological and emotional trauma. The natural forces within us have their own way of working out our feelings."

Barbeau said it's important to have the support of others with this. The "Don't think about it; it'll go away" message is unhealthy, she said, as it would be if someone expresses discomfort with the tears or grief of those who are suffering. "The inhibiting of the naturalness of people is what causes the problem. If people are left to do their thing with a lot of love and support, they will get better."

Those people who have indeed been able to go through that process successfully, Barbeau continued, will arrive at the ultimate question that Duffy mentioned: the search for meaning in what happened.

"We call it a construction of meaning," Barbeau said. "Some people find it in religion, or they find it through a new sense of purpose in their lives because they've survived. They find it in looking at the birds and smelling the flowers.

"They try really hard to pull something that has some positive aspect to it out of that experience so that it isn't all lost. They want a sense of mastery over the powerlessness of the crash. And at that point, people make a kind of a peace with themselves, and they have a stage of what we call adaptation or acceptance.

"But what I always tell people is that they will never forget it. Don't set the goal of forgetting. What we want to do is take the sting out of it, or the hurt. Because the memory will always be there."

A few survivors of tragedy are able to turn their grief in a constructive direction – by helping other victims, for example. *Jolt: Stories of Trauma and Transformation*, by Chicago writer Mark Miller, cites many examples of individuals of trauma who've found the strength to channel their own internal pain – by giving speeches, for example, or creating a foundation.[9]

---

[9] Post Hill Press, 2018.

But Barbeau noted that there are groups who have special problems assimilating the experience of a disaster into their lives. Children and elderly people have the most trouble, she said.

Children are included because "so many times their own processes don't get acknowledged, and people try so hard to shield them instead of including them in the grieving."

She said she spoke with a woman who witnessed the crash of a passenger jet while driving in her car. Her 19-month-old daughter was sitting in her car seat at the time and also saw the crash. "The mother thought, 'She's only nineteen months; she won't know anything is going on,'" Barbeau recalled. "And I said, 'Don't be so sure.' The little girl would pick up her mother's response, if nothing else, and she would need some help.

"So the kind of thing we would suggest for that child is to give her some airplanes to play with, and let the child re-enact the accident if she wants to. And get the mastery of being in control of the toys. They can't talk it out like an adult. They have to play it out, or draw it out, with pencil and paper or crayons."

The elderly – of whom there were so many at Tenerife – had special issues, too. "As all of us age, we have increasing losses all the way along," Barbeau continued. "Retirement is loss of income, loss of sense of purpose sometimes. Loss of physical health. So aging has so much loss in it already.

"Another loss sometimes makes it so much harder to pick up and start over, at what we perceive as almost the end of our life, anyway. None of these things are universally true, but generally we have found that there are some groups that are special risks and that need special kinds of attention."

Perhaps the most vulnerable group is composed of those individuals who, before the calamity, were themselves sensitive and uncertain about their feelings. After an experience such as a plane crash, the things around a person in his or her life tend to look different – one example being Bob Foster, the Southern Airways crash survivor, who remarried his ex-wife two months after the crash he survived. One of the women on the Tenerife Pan Am plane returned home with a fresh look at her own life and was divorced within a year. Jean Brown later said that life gained a sparkle it didn't have before. She never knew death could come so quickly, she said, and as a result lost her fear of it. Warren Hopkins said he developed a looser attitude toward his life, a more spontaneous kind of existence, similar to Jean Brown's reaction. Told of Mrs. Brown's approach, Hopkins agreed. "I feel the same," he said.

Similarly, those with more at stake, emotionally, before the crash could plunge into deeper despair after the crash. Beth Moore was one such person. After her first husband had died, she had not expected to marry again. But she had, and made the commitment to the retired admiral – thus his loss was a greater blow to her because of this special commitment she had made later in her own life.

Several years after Tenerife, Caroline Hopkins would still occasionally reflect on the experience. She knew, she told others, that she had an incredibly sharp husband. No one else had demonstrated such quick presence of mind on the plane. For that she was very grateful.

But there were other times when she couldn't shake the memory of the burning plane, the tremendous flames and black smoke, the explosions that shook the earth, the horrifying sight of people limping and crawling on the ground, with skin and clothing blood-soaked. And worst of all, those in flames…the terror of having to jump, the insecurity of flying, the trust passengers put in flying, and how that trust was violated.

Warren became very thoughtful about what happened. He said once that so many comments from friends about the religious significance of their survival had put a lot of pressure on him.

"I got comments from friends: 'Well, you were saved, you've got a mission now,'" he said.

"You have to sort it all out and figure maybe you were just lucky. And if we were saved for a reason…" his voice trailed off. "We're not religious people. Someone's going to have to point the way. If they point the way, we'd probably go, but we haven't had it happen.

"I don't know how else to relate to the religion issue. I'm not putting it down. I'm just saying that a lot of people get religion from something like this. Where do you affix the responsibility for the outcome? When you feel you've got to have an explanation for this, a lot of people might be prone to turn to religion.

"It could be luck, the fact that you were able to move and get out. Or the fact that you feel maybe God helped you. Or you were located close to where you could get out. There's many ways of looking at it."

Warren decided, finally, "I think it was predestined. You feel, really, that you were given the opportunity for some reason, but you don't really know what that is."

Life became more pronounced for him, as it did for Caroline – experiences became more intense. Warren noticed in succeeding years that even his dreams became more vivid. He said he felt more relaxed about getting through each day. Caroline did, too, but was more subject to periods of tension and sadness and bad memories.

Years after the crash, both acknowledged that they were not the same people they were before the crash. Yes, they had unhappy memories, but their lives continued, albeit with new challenges.

"I see now how people spent too much time on complaints," Caroline said. "We should all remind ourselves often just how lucky we are – we've only got one life, and we should live it and laugh, have fun, and enjoy it. We are looking forward to a happy, healthy life with our dear family, although it is small, and our many special friends.

"I give my most heartfelt thanks for every morsel. We are most fortunate in many ways, and it's great to be alive."

CHAPTER 25

Caroline and Warren Hopkins arrived at O'Hare Airport in the late morning of Thursday, March 31, 1977. Pan Am had ordered a limousine to take them to their home, but several friends were also there, offering rides. Caroline and Warren went with their friends, not in the limousine. By then, they'd barely slept at all in nearly 36 hours. Television news footage of their arrival showed two people near exhaustion and suffering from a lingering shock.

But both brightened up when they arrived at their home in the northern Chicago suburb of Northbrook. Their homecoming was noisy and cathartic, emotional for all. The house, Caroline would later remember, was "like a flower shop." Neighbors waited at the door and on the street, with smiling and relieved faces. Television news trucks lined the street. The Northbrook police had sent a squad car. Mrs. Hopkins was even able to temporarily forget that she was still wearing those giant Tenerife hospital booties.

Warren Hopkins opened the front door using the keys he'd accidentally left in his pants pocket at JFK Airport in New York, and the house quickly filled with friends and family.

A neighbor hurried into the kitchen and made coffee. Another neighbor brought over a carton of half-and-half for the coffee, figuring that perishable items like dairy products wouldn't have been kept in the refrigerator while Caroline and Warren were away. The coffee and cream accompanied a giant "Welcome Home" sheet cake, baked by yet another neighbor.

Caroline reveled in the greetings, although at some point she snuck up to the bedroom to replace those hospital booties so that she would stop tripping in her own home.

One television news truck stayed in front of the home for more than an hour, capturing footage for use on later newscasts.

The Hopkinses had barely gotten home when another car from O'Hare arrived. It was Caroline's parents and one daughter, Linda, just arrived from Florida. The reunion resulted in tears of happiness.

The telephone rang so often during the first few days – calls mainly from friends and well-wishers but also from media representatives around the country – that two family members were assigned to answer the phone all day long. Diana, their older daughter, called from Texas to say that she was on her way.

In the middle of the hullaballoo on that first afternoon, one of those many calls came from a Hopkins neighbor, Pat Buehler, who started the conversation by asking, "What time do you want dinner?" She'd made an entire roast beef supper for the household. Four other neighbors showed up with Pat, bearing a bottle of wine.

They all wanted to deliver the meal and wine and then leave Warren and Caroline alone (an impulse that was explained in the previous chapter by mental health professionals). But Caroline and Warren wanted company and wisely insisted that everyone stay. One friend at the dinner later confessed that, on her way over, she had thought, "What can I possibly say to these people?" But everyone was just willing to let the Hopkinses talk, which they readily acknowledged that they needed to do. They valued the companionship – it helped them stay focused on being home.

The morning after their return, Caroline and Warren woke up to a phone call from Caroline's mother. She'd be right over with a few groceries, she announced. She arrived with bag after bag, most of which wound up sitting in the pantry for weeks because Caroline and Warren ate out almost every night for the next three months. Both were so restless that they had to get out of the house – often.

Good things kept happening to Caroline and Warren Hopkins after they returned: a party thrown by neighbors – the first potluck meal their neighborhood had ever had. A giant "Welcome home, Warren and Caroline" banner hung over the hosts' home. Another friend had climbed a precariously high ladder to hang it.

The Hopkinses learned that reporters had called many of their friends. Using what are known as cross-check telephone directories, which list phone numbers by address, not name, reporters had gotten the numbers of people nearby. One neighbor couple, themselves away on vacation during this period, returned to find their answering machine full of messages from various news agencies asking about Warren and Caroline Hopkins.

The front door rang often with visitors and telegrams and flowers. They even got one note from "Teller window number 72" at their local bank. One of their earliest visitors was Dr. Osmond Akre, a family friend who'd survived a plane crash during World War II.

Among the cards they received was a batch from the St. Norbert's Catholic School second-grade classes, where two of their neighbors' children attended. Caroline and Warren spent hours with the cards, moved to tears at the simple sweetness of the thoughts:

- "I am verey glad you diden't get serisly hreat! I was verey scard when I hard that you were in the plane crash. P.S. I missed you! Love, Lisa H."
- "We're very glad you did not get killed. Patrick."
- "I am very sorry what happened the airplane, but I am glad you are safe and I hope it does not happen again. And it is very sad to hear what happened, and again, I am very sorry what happened. Coleman."
- "I hope you get well soon, because I hate it when people get hurt. Matt."
- "I am very glad you survived in the crash. I hope you didn't get hurt. Your neighbor, Bobby."
- "I am so glad you are safe. God is with you. I love you. Have a nice Easter! Love, Theresa."
- "I don't know you very well but I'm glad your home. Senserely yours, Krista."

- "I hope your not hurt that bad. I have three pets a cat and dog and fish. I hope you like my card I worked very hard on this card. We pray for you. We're finessed with our second book. Mary."
- "I like you and I hope you are a bit of O.K. I hop you get beter because I want you to and if I can repay you I will do good. I will try to do good. I mene I cant do it all. I have other tings to do. But I will be O.K. O.K. That's fin. O.K. I hope you get beter. Laurie."
- "Roses are red violets are blue do not worry God is with you! Dana."
- "God watch over you for ever and ever. Julia."

Because the children's letters were from a Catholic school, it wasn't surprising that some of them had a religious message. But many messages the Hopkinses received from friends had a similar spirituality:

"Ask Jesus to come into your hearts and make your lives new," one card said. "Ask Him to take away the pain of your memories. He will. He loves you very much."

"There was no question but what you were God-directed and God-protected..." said another card.

"...sincerely grateful that the Lord watched over you and cared for you...."

"Doesn't it make you feel that God has something special in mind for you in this life?"

Caroline and Warren Hopkins were not particularly religious people. Nevertheless, the intensity of these messages was indisputable and gave them much food for thought. There were other letters, too, with more existential messages.

"...Remove the total picture from thought as quickly as possible," one card writer suggested. Easier said than done, was Caroline Hopkins's reaction to that one.

Over the next few days and weeks, with the Hopkinses and surely with the other survivors, the phone calls slowed down. Telegrams and letters tapered off. Diana and Linda returned to college, and Caroline and Warren were in a house that was empty of people. Many of the Hopkinses' friends didn't call, believing that they wanted to be alone in order to regain some emotional strength. A number of their friends later acknowledged that they hesitated because of uncertainty about how much, or what, to say about Caroline and Warren's terrible experience.

"You no doubt will want privacy when you return home, and we certainly would not intrude," one of their friends wrote.

In fact, company was exactly what Caroline and Warren wanted. They found it difficult to face day after day – and especially evenings – alone in their home. So they went out nightly to avoid dwelling on the memories. They went through what many other survivors suffered: nightmares, daymares, lapsing into silence when others would be talking, mentally carried back to that foggy runway, the quiet in the aircraft cabin as the Pan Am jet taxied slowly…then the sudden collision and the flames.

Caroline kept as busy as she could, but that wasn't very busy. Her gardening, long a special joy, was curtailed severely because of her shoulder injury, which required treatment three times a week by a physical therapist. Even hair combing was a chore, and she couldn't put on a coat without help. She drove only with great caution and developed a fear of falling out of the car, especially on overpasses.

But she tried. She answered every single one of the several hundred cards and letters. She sent a scarf to Catherine Germann on Santa Cruz de Tenerife as a thank-you for her help before Caroline and Warren returned to the United States.

But the pain and discomfort were with them around the clock. Peculiarly, Warren lost his senses of taste and smell for several months. Caroline's pre-existing fear of heights had intensified to the point that she could not face the stairway in their home without apprehension, or go up a store escalator without company. One or both of them lay awake most of each night because their minds would not stay at rest. The meaning of the experience hung over them. Weeks and months went by as they struggled, emotionally and physically.

One of their friends sent a poem:

"It's today that I am livin', not a month ago,
Havin', losin', takin, givin', as time wills it, so.

Yesterday a cloud of sorrow fell across the way.
It may rain again tomorrow, it may rain, but say —
Ain't it fine today?"

Perhaps that one, with its admittedly corny verse, offered the best advice: just take things one day at a time, try not to dwell excessively on either the past or the future, and enjoy the moment.

CHAPTER 26

Notes from Caroline Hopkins's journal and clipping files:

Immediately after the accident, representatives of the three involved nations began proclaiming the innocence of their respective participants. The Spanish said the control tower personnel had behaved properly. An early statement from KLM Royal Dutch Airlines blamed the Pan Am pilots. The U.S. government denied all responsibility.

By the time the sequence of events was revealed, so much rhetorical fog had been generated that the average person may have had no idea what really happened. Much of the evidence, though, gradually pointed toward the decision by the KLM captain, Jacob van Zanten, to begin his takeoff without specifically getting takeoff clearance from the control tower.

* * * *

In that era of international aviation, the process of getting "clearances" from air traffic controllers at international airports was not as clear as now, in the 21st century, because of different rules in different countries. A senior pilot interviewed long after the crash said he would always double-check his clearances at international airports in those days, just to avoid what happened at Tenerife. He did this before the Tenerife disaster, and continued this policy afterward, but with a renewed discipline.

"Are we cleared for takeoff?" he recalled once asking a controller at the Rome, Italy, airport. "Oh sure," was the casual reply. The pilot then repeated his question. "Are we cleared for takeoff?" he demanded sternly, irked at the controller's tone. "Roger, cleared for takeoff," the chastened controller replied carefully and precisely.

"I don't move," the pilot said. "I confirm."

* * * *

Many of the major airlines pulled their advertising from newspapers and television while major coverage of the crash lasted. They apparently didn't want the news to be interfering with their message to consumers about how much fun flying (usually) is.

* * * *

Several dozen residents of Santa Cruz, California, died in the crash – a horrible irony. Santa Cruz is the sister city of Santa Cruz de Tenerife, where the accident took place.

* * * *

Several Chicago media outlets were able to reach Walter and Caroline Hopkins when they were still in the hospital on Tenerife. Mrs. Hopkins was quite touched by a reporter for the Chicago *Tribune,* who asked if he could do anything for her. (That reporter was a young David Axelrod, who later left journalism and entered the world of political consulting.) She asked him to call her parents in Florida, and he did so. The *Tribune* later printed a letter from Caroline's father, Elmer Kneip, thanking the newspaper for its courtesy.

* * * *

After getting the news about his daughter and son-in-law, Mr. Kneip – whom Caroline had never seen take an alcoholic drink in his life – asked his wife to pour him a glass of bourbon. Then he started calling around to fly a team of doctors to Tenerife and announced that he would accompany them. Only his daughter's insistence that they weren't badly hurt got him to cancel the plan. Meanwhile, a neighbor of Caroline and Warren, a reconstructive surgeon named Randall McNally, who'd worked in military hospitals during World War II, started to make arrangements to fly to the Canary Islands. Dr. McNally and his wife were all too familiar with this kind of tragedy: Mrs. McNally's brother, his wife, and their four children had all died in a commercial plane crash in Asia several years earlier.

* * * *

The Canary Islands media expressed fury at Antonio Cubillo and his organization, the Movement for the Independence and Self-determination of the Canaries Archipelago – members of which had planted the bomb at the Las Palmas airport that had begun the horrendous chain of events. *El Pais* [*The Nation*] newspaper wrote in an editorial that the collision was "one of the most absurd accidents in recent memory," and sarcastically suggested that the MPAIAC group "can certainly feel proud of its feat: 560 dead.[1] They can go to sleep tranquil. Will tourism leave the island chain? [Tourism was, and still is, an integral part of the Canaries economy.] Tremendous! Citizens sleep badly? Great!"

In the days following the crash, the local political parties in the Canaries – the Democratic Popular Party, the Spanish Socialist Workers, the Democratic Spanish Union, Canary Democratic Party, Canary Union, Independent Canary Democrats, and Communist Party of the Canaries – called for somehow silencing the nightly shortwave radio broadcasts Cubillo was then making from Algeria, possibly by extraditing him. Cubillo remained in Algeria, though, and continued his broadcasts. To the charge that his group caused the accident, he said it was the fault of the air traffic controllers, who shouldn't have been allowing the planes to move around in bad weather.[2]

* * * *

Prince Charles of Great Britain, who had been on an official tour of Western Africa at the time of the crash, stopped in the Canary Islands on March 29 to offer condolences. Messages of sympathy and concern traveled back and forth between the various capitals. King Carlos of Spain sent them to President Jimmy Carter in the United States, as did Queen Juliana of the Netherlands. Pope Paul VI sent a note of regret to the bishop of Santa Cruz

---

[1] The final body count was 583, not counting those who died later of their injuries.

[2] His group even set off another bomb the next year, killing one person. But in 1978, Cubillo's organization stopped its armed terrorism. Cubillo eventually returned to the Canary Islands and started another political party. He died in 2012.

de Tenerife, and even the Soviet Union government expressed sympathy to the presidents of KLM and Pan American.

* * * *

KLM received $40 million from its insurers for the loss of its Boeing 747. Pan Am received $23 million, a lower amount because its 747 was older than KLM's plane. The London insurance market – with Lloyd's of London the main carrier – was liable for about 40 percent of those amounts, with the rest divided among insurance company pools in Scandinavia, Switzerland, and the Netherlands, according to media reports.

By the time all the personal lawsuits were added up, survivors and relatives of those killed asked for $2 billion in damages. The actual payouts totaled around $110 million, averaging nearly $180,000 per fatality, an amount limited by an international aviation agreement that has since been upgraded. The amounts for those injured averaged a bit higher. From the insurers' perspective, it's considered more of a liability for someone to have to go on living with an injury and bad memories than to have the insured person die, especially if the deceased was elderly and had lived most of his or her life.

* * * *

Shortly after Caroline and Warren Hopkins returned to their Illinois home, a Pan American representative called to ask if Mrs. Hopkins had lost a five-carat diamond ring in the wreckage – a piece of jewelry that was easily worth tens of thousands of dollars. No, she told them. She'd lost her jewelry, but nothing on that scale.

* * * *

Not the U.S. government's finest moment: the State Department and the U.S. Air Force got into a squabble over who would transport the injured and dead back to the United States. The Hopkinses were told this by a friend, John Stetson, who became secretary of the Air Force in 1978. Stetson told Warren and Caroline that the Air Force was ready to send a plane for the survivors but that the transportation of the dead would be the responsibility of the State Department. In fact, Pan American freighter jets brought back the corpses.

Dutch victims were transported by ferry to Las Palmas and then flown from there to Amsterdam, where a mass memorial service was held.

* * * *

On the evening of March 30, 1977, an interdenominational memorial service was held in a Catholic church near the Los Rodeos Airport. More than 2,000 people attended, including relatives of some of those who had been killed, and who had traveled there from the United States or the Netherlands.

* * * *

Life went on. The day after the crash, the motion picture industry's Academy Awards ceremony was held. Editors had to decide what to give more prominent coverage in their Tuesday morning newspapers, the awards winners or second-day reports on the crash. For the record, two actors from the film *Network* received the best actor and best actress awards, Peter Finch, who received the award posthumously, and Faye Dunaway. *Rocky* beat *Network* for the best picture award. The Academy Awards results were placed on Page One near the follow-up articles about the crash, even in Canary Island newspapers.

* * * *

The week after the crash, hundreds of people betting in the state of Massachusetts lottery played the number series 7-4-7-0, apparently following the prominence of the 747 airplanes. Incredibly, that number sequence was drawn. But so many more people than usual had bet on the numbers that the pari-mutuel payout for a $1 bet was reduced from the usual $6,000 to $2,044.

* * * *

Warren Hopkins told a friend about the men's room attendant at the 21 Club restaurant in New York, who had offered words of faith and goodwill just before he and Caroline left for the airport. Warren had pondered those words later, as he lay in the Tenerife hospital. The friend was struck by the entire episode – and made a point for several years of visiting the 21 Club bar, just to stop into the men's room to say hello to that same attendant and get more of those kind words.

266

EPILOGUE

The Spanish government, which had jurisdiction over the investigation of the accident, did not release its report on the crash until 18 months had passed. In fact, by the time the report was released, Tenerife's Sud (South) Airport had finally opened – a process that had been spurred on by the 1977 crash. Also, Los Rodeos Airport (now known as Tenerife North) received a ground radar system, which would almost certainly have prevented the collision.

(Technology has advanced to the point that ground radar is being superseded by a satellite-based system known as Automatic Dependent Surveillance-Broadcast. The ADS-B system is to be completely phased in to U.S. aviation by 2020. It also works for planes in the air by using Global Positioning Satellite (GPS) technology and is more precise than radar. If it had been in place in 2014, when Malaysia Airlines Flight 370 was lost in the south Indian Ocean, the plane may have been located.)

During the 18 months after the Tenerife crash, the transcripts of the cockpit tapes from both airplanes were kept locked away, and every facet of the investigation remained confidential. The Hopkinses hired John Kennelly, a nationally known aviation law attorney, who even tried to get the U.S. Supreme Court to pressure the Spanish government to release the tapes. His effort was unsuccessful. The delay was never explained. When the United States is the governing body for an aircraft accident investigation, the transcripts are usually released in a few weeks.

The Spanish may have been self-conscious about the accident happening on their soil and were trying to be as cautious as possible with every step of the investigation because of its magnitude. (More than 40 years later, it remains the worst aviation disaster ever, by number of fatalities.) There may have been hesitation because the transcripts contained points of embarrassment for all three parties.

In the eventually released cockpit voice recorder transcripts, Pan Am pilot Victor Grubbs expressed his willingness to hold his Pan Am 747 at the entrance to the live runway at Tenerife because he knew the KLM jet was already on it.[1] But the air traffic controllers did not consider that possibility. The Spanish left the Grubbs comment, "We could hold here, if he'd let us," out of some of the summaries.

Additionally, Dutch officials noted that some static on the radio exchanges indicated that controllers might have been listening to a soccer game on a separate radio in the control tower. The implication was that the controllers weren't giving their work as much concentration as desired.

Also, the raucous joking in the Pan Am cockpit less than a minute before the collision can't be looked upon very well by the Americans, as well as the fact that the crew missed its turnoff on the runway. In the days immediately after the crash, Pan Am officials heatedly denied that Grubbs had missed the turnoff, claiming that the pilot and his crew were justified in assuming the C-4 turnoff from the runway was the same as the C-3 turnoff referred to by the air traffic controller because the angle of the C-3 turnoff was steep and in the wrong direction.

And the Dutch, of course, could only be unhappy about what the transcripts contained: evidence that Captain van Zanten was apparently distracted during the crucial moments before and during the takeoff attempt. So well thought of was this pilot that the first reaction by some KLM officials to the news of the crash was that they should send an experienced senior pilot – Jacob van Zanten, for example – to investigate.

Nevertheless, the Dutch government remained bitter at the result of the final Spanish report's conclusion because of the degree of blame that

---

[1] The author has a copy of the transcripts, and portions are available online.

was placed on their pilot. To the Dutch, the failure of the Pan Am pilots to see, and turn onto, the C-3 taxiway was a key factor.

This is what the final, carefully worded Spanish report said:

> *The fundamental cause of this accident was the fact that the KLM captain:*
>   *1. Took off without clearance.*
>   *2. Did not obey the 'stand by for takeoff' from the tower.*
>   *3. Did not interrupt takeoff on learning that the Pan Am was still on the runway.*[2]
>   *4. In reply to the Flight Engineer's query as to whether the Pan Am had already left the runway, replied emphatically in the affirmative."*

Factors contributing to the crash, the report continued, were:

1. Van Zanten's tension regarding his overtime restrictions.
2. The weather conditions at Tenerife that afternoon.
3. The squeal that disrupted radio communications temporarily in the KLM cockpit.

The report said that further contributing factors included:

▶ Inadequate use of language between the controller and the KLM crew when the KLM first officer told the tower, "We are now at takeoff," and the controller replied, "Okay. Stand by for takeoff clearance," a confusing exchange;

▶ The fact that Pan Am missed the assigned runway turnoff; and

▶ Heavy traffic congestion, which caused the controllers to direct unusual taxiing maneuvers.

Finally, the report noted other unusual factors, including the Las Palmas bombing, van Zanten's refueling decision (which made his jet heavier and slower), and an otherwise unexplained reference in the report to KLM's takeoff at less than full power.

The report contained several recommendations. One was that the word "takeoff" not be used in international air traffic control clearance – a change in procedure that did happen in succeeding years, but which had already

---

[2] This point was awkwardly worded. Obviously, van Zanten didn't understand that the Pan Am jet was on the runway.

taken place in the United States, as was explained earlier in this book. Another recommendation called for greater standardization of aeronautical language used in international aviation. This, too, has happened in the years since the crash. A third recommendation was "the placing of great emphasis on the importance of exact compliance with instructions and clearances," which is a fancy way of saying that controllers should ensure pilots are doing what they're told.

Although the international aviation industry had never considered such changes in language before, it did change its procedures to follow the standardized language that had been in existence in U.S. aviation procedures prior to this crash. No pilot or air traffic controller in the United States, before or after 1977, would have acknowledged communications by merely saying, "Okay" or "Roger." Instructions are repeated back. The word "takeoff" is spoken only when actual takeoff clearance is given, or when canceling that clearance. "Departure" is the correct word up until that point.

Eventually, the Federal Aviation Administration tried out some devices that would help prevent similar accidents in the future.

At an FAA experimental facilities center in New Jersey, a simple idea was developed for use on runways: a traffic light.

The light would be placed at the end of runways, and planes would not take off – even if the pilot thought he or she had heard the tower controller give takeoff clearance – unless the traffic light turned to green. The purpose of such a device was to override any possible mental lapse such as the one that apparently happened to Captain van Zanten.

The traffic light system was tested in autumn of 1978 and then installed at Hartford International Airport in Connecticut. It seemed a positive step, but technological advances took that idea and moved it forward a notch. In the early 2000s, Dallas-Fort Worth Airport installed a series of red lights that flash at runway entry points and crossing points whenever a runway becomes active, warning aircraft crews to not enter. The FAA announced in 2009 that tests of this system, known as RWSL (runway status lights), had been successful. It installed the lights at dozens of airports over the next few years.

The FAA's Civil Aerospace Medical Institute has produced many reports over the decades, all with recommendations for improved flying safety.

In recent years, the agency has struggled with the increase in mobile phone usage, which can be distracting for passengers when flight attendants and crew are trying to emphasize safety tips to passengers. Some people may remember the December 2011 incident involving a famous actor who would not stop playing the "Words With Friends" app when his American Airlines flight was getting ready to take off.

Technology continues to make it ever easier for people to stay connected during a flight, but CAMI officials have resisted this, along with other interested groups such as the Association of Flight Attendants. More than half of all air crashes happen during takeoff or landing, according to a study by The Boeing Company that is cited by CAMI as justifying limiting passenger access to their electronic devices during these parts of the flight.

"Combined, the research and accident statistics indicate that usage of PEDs [personal electronic devices] during critical phases of flight would unnecessarily increase risk, discount passenger safety, and disregard the many efforts to identify and rectify the shortcomings related to passenger safety awareness," the previously cited September 2013 FAA memo stated. "In particular, use of PEDs should continue to respect the clean cabin environment during the pre-flight briefing and critical phases of flight, since the focused attention of passengers to PEDs creates the type of competition for passenger mental capacity now widely known to cause many highway accidents.[3]

"At a time when many states have or are looking to outlaw cell phone usage while driving, it would seem inexplicable to promote such usage during the times when passengers should instead be paying attention to their immediate surroundings and becoming better engaged in their situation. The minor delay in accessing their PEDs can be made more tolerable by providing passengers better awareness of the safety issues that they face

---

[3] The Boeing study showed that 41 percent of all accidents with fatalities from 2003 to 2012 took place during an aircraft's final approach or landing, with another 16 percent during takeoff and initial climb. This study was among many cited in the previously mentioned 2013 FAA memo. See footnote 20.

and by provisions for quick and easily accessed (e.g., seatback pocket) stowage of PEDs during these periods of restricted use, which would establish their immediate availability for inflight usage and mitigate evacuation delays caused by loose equipment and/or exposed power cables."

The FAA memo included a retrospective look at the January 2009 crash-landing of a U.S. Airways Airbus in New York's Hudson River. Half of the passengers who were later surveyed about the accident admitted to not paying any attention during the safety briefing, and 89 percent didn't even look at the safety card, according to a CAMI study cited in the memo.[4] "It should not be surprising, then, that the passengers did not know what 'brace for impact' meant,[5] nor did they retrieve their flotation seat cushions or life preservers, nor could they properly don a life preserver they were given," the FAA memo continued. "In effect, these passengers were clueless and lucky that the plane went down in a river with many rescue resources available." This 2009 crash and its successful mid-river evacuation by the flight's remarkably skilled crew were the center of the 2015 motion picture *Sully*.[6]

The strongly worded CAMI report – which called increased passenger PED usage "inexplicable" – was barely a month old when it was rejected by its parent agency, the FAA, which announced it would permit expanded use of cell phones and tablets, even including during takeoffs and landings. The airlines were in favor of this expansion because of its perceived greater convenience for passengers, but safety officials at the Association of Flight Attendants union were distressed. "Using these devices is going to distract people, and especially when they're packing things away," said Chris Witkowski, director of the union's air safety, health and security.[7]

The FAA report, released on October 31, 2013, did state, "Make safety your first priority," and an accompanying poster told passengers to "listen to the safety briefing" and obey the flight crew.

---

[4] Ibid.

[5] The pilot, Captain C.B. "Sully" Sullenberger, had given this warning to the passengers shortly before the plane's water landing.

[6] The official NTSB final report on this crash is available online. The NTSB Accident ID is DCA09MA026. The crash happened on Jan. 15, 2009, and is listed as taking place in/near Weehawken, New Jersey. The report was released March 19, 2009. Here's the link: http://dms.ntsb.gov/pubdms/search/hitlist.cfm?docketID=47230&CFID=818288&CFTOKEN=71811991

[7] Interview with Jon Ziomek.

But this wasn't the first argument about safety that the flight attendants union lost with the airlines. During the 1990s, the AFA asked permission for its flight attendants to have more intense exit-row discussions between flight attendants and passengers who sit in overwing exit rows – the union wanted stronger verbal confirmation from passengers that they understood their responsibilities – but some airlines pushed back on this, stating it wasn't necessary.

The AFA was successful in a lobbying effort with the FAA to keep passenger cabin exits no more than 60 feet apart. A waiver of that rule had been requested by the Airbus manufacturer (to 74 feet), but strong resistance by the AFA – because of concerns about increased evacuation times – resulted in a rejection of the waiver request. The AFA was also a part of the 2017 and 2018 debate about economy-section seat size – again, because of a concern that smaller seats could be more difficult to evacuate in an emergency. This followed announcements by several airlines that they would begin using smaller economy-section seats beginning in 2018.

The point about overwing exits is valid, though, because a Rutgers University study of emergency aircraft evacuations, discussed in Chapter 14, suggested that those exits are underused during emergency evacuations.

But who has time to study safety methods for airlines, or other modes of transportation? Crew members do, but who else? The answer is simple: *do it yourself.* Training can consist of spending one minute before your plane takes off simply reading the safety card and paying attention to the safety briefing. Take these simple mental steps, as recommended by the AFA:

1. Look directly at the two exits that are closest to your seat, and also at the spot in the main aisle where you'd turn to get to those exits. In an emergency, it's possible that smoke may obscure your view of the exit, but you'll know where to turn if you've already seen the correct spot on the aisle floor.

2. Look directly at the compartment holding the oxygen mask and say, "Me, first." If there's smoke in the cabin, or a decline in pressure, you may have less than 20 seconds to put on your mask.

So…no, you can't get yourself trained as well as a member of an airline flight crew. But the act of paying attention is a form of training. As many have suggested in this book and elsewhere, our brains work better when we're familiar with a problem. Ignorance and fear can increase our uncertainty and can even paralyze us.

"The best way to negotiate stress is through repeated, realistic training," Amanda Ripley summarized.[8]

This is even true in automobile safety. An autumn 2015 statement from the National Safety Council said that many Americans, confused by the "torrent" of safety technology available on new automobiles (blind spot monitors, adaptive cruise controls, collision warning systems, automatic emergency braking, lane drift warnings, etc.), are choosing not to use the safety equipment at all. The owner's manuals are not explaining the safety equipment properly, the NSC suggested. It and the University of Iowa, with the U.S. Department of Transportation, held a national campaign to inform drivers about their automobile's safety equipment. The campaign included a website, MyCarDoesWhat.org. An August 2016 *Wall Street Journal* article noted that automobile manufacturers should consider the example of aviation safety officials as new technology is introduced. Aviation officials have moved toward simplifying cockpit displays and improving crew training because of a concern that new technology is confusing.[9]

But just as some drivers will turn their attention away from safety because of their uncertainty or confusion, it also remains a challenge to get the attention of many airline passengers. The primary reason many passengers gave for not paying better attention, according to one FAA study, was that they'd already seen the presentation and read the briefing card on previous flights. But that's been shown to be inadequate. "It is a challenge to get the passengers, who are often harried by the time they get on the airplane, and *teach* them about safety," CAMI official Cynthia McLean said in an email to the author of this book. Passengers "may say they are listening or looking…but they aren't *learning.*"

---

[8] *The Unthinkable*, page 75.
[9] "Aviation's Lessons for Self-Driving Cars," B-1, *Wall Street Journal*, Aug. 1, 2016.

In a 2003 memo explaining why safety briefings and safety cards are required, the FAA has noted that "an alert, knowledgeable person has a much better chance of suriviving any life- or injury-threatening situation that could occur during passenger-carrying operations." In that same memo, the FAA called on the airlines to "make the safety briefings and cards as interesting and attractive as possible," and has encouraged the airlines "to be innovative in their approach in imparting such information."[10] In recent years, airlines have tried videos with humor, with cartoon or animated figures, or with an assortment of airline employees giving separate pieces of safety information in order to hold passengers' attention.

The FAA has also spoken directly to passengers, telling them to pay attention to the flight crew. "We all need to think about safety – even just for a minute," states an FAA Passenger Safety Tips website. [11]

Mrs. McLean, a senior human factors research specialist with the FAA's Civil Aerospace Medical Institute, is among the safety officials who urge passengers to take a moment to orient themselves to the aircraft cabin. She also recommends that shoes not be taken off until after takeoff and the flight crew has turned off the seatbelt sign, and get those shoes – lace-up shoes, nothing with high heels – back on your feet before the plane begins its landing. And she also recommends long-sleeved shirts and pants because of the protection they'd offer in a fire.

"Survivors of the Tenerife accident have provided aviation cabin safety researchers with a wonderful insight into how people behave in airplane emergencies," Mrs. McLean noted. "The passenger successes and failures from this one event remain relevant and are illustrative of the potential benefits of continuing the efforts to improve passenger safety awareness in the face of marked public apathy."

* * * *

---

[10] These quotes are from a July 23, 2003, U.S. Department of Transportation Advisory Circular titled "Passenger Safety Information – Briefing and Briefing Cards." AC No: 121-24C. The author is listed as John M. Allen, for James J. Ballough, director, Flight Standards Service. Here's the link: https://www.faa.gov/documentLibrary/media/Advisory_Circular/AC121-24C.pdf.

[11] "Passenger Safety Tips," Federal Aviation Administration website. No author is listed. Here's the link: https://www.faa.gov/travelers/fly_safe/safety_tips/

In the years after Tenerife, the airline industry began encouraging the members of a cockpit crew to speak up and work better as a team.[12] This process is known as Crew Resource Management. It became a requirement after the Tenerife collision, and has been gradually phased throughout the aviation industry.

A 2013 Japan Airlines crash was an example of a cockpit crew not following this guideline. Some members of the cockpit crew failed to question the captain's decision about the proper approach speed for landing at San Francisco International Airport. The jet then dropped too quickly and skidded off a seawall. One person was killed during the evacuation that followed.

Mark Rosenker, NTSB chairman in 2007, said in the 2000s there were 325 "runway incursions," as they are called (any unauthorized vehicle on a runway) every year, 25 of which were "extremely serious," according to NTSB labels. "That's too many," he said on a PBS *Nova* documentary.

Serious runway incursions happened at O'Hare Airport in Chicago and Boston's Logan Airport in 2005, but accidents were avoided because cockpit crew members spoke up. "Had the copilot [in these incursion cases] not felt free to speak up, hundreds of people could have died," the *Nova* documentary observed.

In January 2016, United Airlines announced it was giving its pilots retraining in the Crew Resource Management program. "The extra training is designed, among others things, to teach captains how to solicit and respond to input from junior pilots," a United spokesman said in an explanatory *Wall Street Journal* article.[13]

Such steps are positive and welcome. The success of Crew Resource Management – which is essentially team-based management – has moved into other professional fields, too, such as the TeamSTEPPS program in healthcare.[14]

---

[12] There are many references in professional and popular media explaining the increasing importance of Crew Resource Management. Captain Sullenberger was even asked about it during his interviews following the January 2009 U.S. Airways emergency landing in the Hudson River. Additionally, the FAA recognizes its importance. For example, here's an FAA cover memo on the subject from March 19, 2013, titled "Advanced Crew Resource Management (ACRM) Training": https://www.faa.gov/training_testing/training/aqp/training/crm/

[13] "United Calls In Pilots For Training," *Wall Street Journal*, Jan. 30, 2016.

[14] "Safer Air Travel Through Crew Resource Management: crew resource management has prevented accicdents and saved lives in the aviation industry, and may save lives in hospital operating and emergency rooms." No author. February 2014. American Psychological Association, "Psychology: Science in Action." Here's the link: http://www.apa.org/action/resources/research-in-action/crew.aspx

After Tenerife, though, the airline industry was slow to respond in other ways. In March 1977, the same month as the Tenerife accident, the National Research Council division of the National Academy of Sciences released a study of airplane cabin fires, with a list of suggested remedies to this problem. Among the suggestions was to improve the fire resistance of seat cushions, wall and ceiling materials, and overhead insulation. Also, the NRC suggested that decorative carpeting on the walls of cabin interiors be eliminated because of flammability.

Further, it was suggested that all smoking be eliminated on board every airplane. (Fires in airplane bathrooms are the fourth most frequent reason for in-flight fires.) Failing that, airlines should install smoke detectors in every lavatory on every plane. Finally, the report recommended that flight crew members – the people most responsible for passenger safety during an emergency – wear flame-retardant clothing.

Again, that was in 1977. The FAA didn't ban smoking on domestic U.S. air routes until 1990, and smoking wasn't banned on international flights for *another decade.* Some smokers still try to sneak an onboard smoke, though, which is why current air travelers get a warning before takeoff about "not tampering with lavatory smoke detectors." Onboard smoke detectors weren't installed until 1997, after years of resistance by the industry. Airline executives agreed to the change after a 1996 crash in Florida following a fire in the cargo section of a ValuJet DC-9 that killed 110 people.

Slow – but steady – improvements were made in the flame-retardant capabilities of airplane interior materials in the decades since the Tenerife crash. The fumes that had been released as fires started in the Pan Am plane had been a factor in the reduced number of survivors.

On the other major theme of this book – disaster psychology and helping passengers who have been in crashes – many airlines resisted this even more deeply than the safety devices. Flying is very safe, they correctly point out – why bother dealing with such a morbid subject, which affects relatively few people?

When Dr. John Duffy was putting together his 1978 symposium on air disaster psychology, he invited every single U.S. air carrier to send representatives. Only one, United Airlines, actually did.

"I got a rather – I would interpret as – almost violent hostility from the airline medical directors on this topic," he said years later. "They were angry, and they are ultra-sensitive about this topic. They don't want to talk about air crashes.

"Which really upset me because it isn't as if I want to emphasize that aspect. But I do want to explain that there are things you can do, responses you can contribute that can significantly reduce some of the trauma.

"Each airline has a response team when one of their aircraft crashes. Not a single person in that team is taught anything about principles of crisis mental health. They're taught to interact with the survivors and relatives and friends.

"Emergency response plans at airports are highly sophisticated. If your only problem is that you've lost an arm or a leg, they do beautifully. But if you're suffering any kind of emotional trauma, they don't have the faintest idea of what to do with you, or what might be the cause of it."

After Duffy's 1978 conference, held at Hilton Head Island in South Carolina, there was a noticeable spark of interest in the subject among behavior professionals. Psychiatric social worker Margaret Ann Barbeau attended that conference and went on to a counseling career that included treating plane crash victims on the West Coast. The Association of Flight Attendants, the nation's largest flight attendants union, had a representative at that conference, and it now sends counselors to talk to its members who have been involved in accidents.

Duffy said he believes all airline personnel should receive training in how to handle people traumatized by an air disaster. For starters, he would like to see an academic center and clearinghouse that would be staffed by mental health professionals. Help for this project could come if the aviation insurance companies would pressure the airlines to support it.

It seems safe to say that the turning point for professional attention on this subject was the crash at Tenerife. That crash was directly responsible for getting Duffy the government funding for his seminar.

When a Pacific Southwest Airlines jet crashed in September 1978 (only several miles from the homes of some of the Tenerife survivors), the media gave more attention to the topic of crisis psychology.

Alan Davidson, president of the Academy of San Diego Psychologists, started by saying that the PSA San Diego crash "had an impact on the human psyche beyond what we humanly know."

"We can expect an increased number of neuropsychiatric hospitalizations in San Diego in the next *decade*" (author's emphasis), added psychologist Ed Schneidmann, a UCLA psychologist, including "higher-than-normal divorce, suicides, and other psychological disruptions."

In *Time* magazine's January 8, 1979, issue, a Behavior section article detailed how rescue workers in that San Diego PSA crash were complaining to behavioral professionals of the same problems experienced by the Tenerife survivors: sleeplessness alternating with bad dreams, and a numbing reaction to the entire experience and to their own feelings later. More than a dozen police officers who assisted in the rescue and cleanup operations in San Diego wanted to talk to professionals about their experiences, the article stated. Similar help was sought for rescue workers after a 1979 DC-10 crash in Chicago.

"The response required for immediate intervention and reduction of long-term problems," Margaret Ann Barbeau said in an interview, "is to encourage people to go ahead and feel whatever they feel: rage or confusion, or sadness, or tears, or needing to be alone, or with other people.

"In addition, victims need to know that they are not 'abnormal' or 'crazy' if in later months or years, the original symptoms re-appear and require some more working through.

"Within people there are natural healing forces: physical, psychological and emotional. The natural forces within us have their own way of working through the trauma, providing that the environment and circumstances are supportive of natural processes. Often the recovery process can be hastened and more thoroughly accomplished with professional counseling."

And perhaps that is the essence of helping people who have suffered through an air crash, a philosophy that rises above the specifics of aviation disasters and is applicable to anyone in the world who is troubled: we must respect our feelings and those of others, not try to hide them or deny them or force them into something they're not.

Photo courtesy of Jesús M. Pérez Triana

This memorial sculpture was placed on Tenerife on the 30th anniversary of the crash. Designed by Dutch artist Ruud van de Wint, it depicts a spiral staircase connecting the earth and sky.

As safe as modern transportation is, we know there will always be accidents – some of them severe. What we must do is become proactive passengers who know how to help ourselves and others, during the accident and afterward, when the emotional pieces are being put back together. And that gets done not by hiding the fact that accidents really do happen, but by dealing with the possibility in a mature and sensible way; by helping passengers to understand their safety options beforehand; and, if a tragedy should happen, by giving them the emotional support they need. After all, how can we *not* help one another? The people around us are, ultimately, all we've got in life.

"The salvation of man is through love and in love," psychiatrist Victor Frankl once wrote.[15] "In utter desolation, when one has only suffering to endure, loving contemplation can bring fulfillment."

---

[15] Viktor Frankl, *Man's Search for Meaning*, (Boston, MA: Beacon Press).

For further information, and to see photographs and videos about the Canary Islands crash...

▶ **www.project-tenerife.com**
This website, originally prepared in Dutch, is a thorough review of many aspects of the disaster, including cockpit voice transcripts and links to videos such as from the BBC (see below). Originally prepared in Dutch but based on the official Spanish government report, the site translates into English.

▶ **http://www.pbs.org/wgbh/nova/space/deadliest-plane-crash.html**
This is the website for a PBS Nova program documentary about the Tenerife crash, called "The Deadliest Plane Crash," that aired Oct. 17, 2006. The program can be watched online. It includes a short interview with Warren Hopkins, among other survivors.

▶ **https://www.youtube.com/watch?v=HuvND-1pwNU**
This is a BBC news report for a program called "Witness." The report centers on an interview with the copilot of the Pan Am jet, Robert Bragg. Although a short report (it runs just more than four minutes), it contains video footage of the immediate aftermath of the collision.

▶ **https://www.youtube.com/watch?v=mQrndLai0lw**
This is an eight-minute explanation of the crash, including printed transcripts of parts of the cockpit conversations. Almost all of it is re-created, but the end of this report includes some still photos of the crash aftermath and a bit of video. The report is called Crash of the Century, by Cineflix.

▶ **http://www.planecrashinfo.com/cvr770327.htm**
This is the printed transcript of the last six minutes of the cockpit voice recorders in both jets and the control tower.

▶ **https://www.youtube.com/watch?annotation_id=annotation _930670&feature=iv&src_vid=B0YGeUzBaYE&v=mB8Yho3NhsI**
This YouTube site has still photographs of the Pan Am jet and the KLM jet, and other jets, on the Tenerife taxiway shortly before the

crash. The photographs give a sense of how crowded the small airport was on that afternoon.

▶ **http://www.businessinsider.com/deadliest-plane-crash-in-history -2014-3**
"How A Tiny Island Runway Became The Site of the Deadliest Plane Crash Ever," an excerpt from Cockpit Confidential, by Patrick Smith, posted March 27, 2014. This report includes a diagram of the runway, the taxiway turnoffs, and the collision point.

ACKNOWLEDGMENTS

The work on this book started many years ago. Delays resulted from a variety of personal and professional matters, and some of the people cited here are now deceased. Regardless, their contributions remain appreciated.

A number of survivors from Pan American Flight 1736 were kind enough to share with Caroline and Warren Hopkins and Jon Ziomek their experiences at Tenerife in the months and years after the crash. We thank Jean and Gordon Brown, Grace Ellerbrock, Kim Fox, Floy Heck, Tony and Isobel Monda, Jim Naik, Pam Rich, Jack Ridout, Roy Tanemura, and Florence Trumbull, with special thanks to Joani Holt Feathers, Beth Moore, and David Alexander. Don Foster, survivor of a Southern Airways crash that took place one week after the Tenerife accident, generously gave us time to discuss and compare his experiences.

Catherine Germann, a former resident of Santa Cruz de Tenerife, provided useful information about the island of Tenerife.

Behavioral experts whom we interviewed contributed important information. Dr. John Duffy, former professor of psychiatry at the Uniformed Services University of the Health Sciences, was invaluable with his contributions. Margaret Ann Barbeau, a psychiatric social worker in the Los Angeles area who has treated plane crash victims, was also exceptionally helpful. Special thanks also go to psychologist Dan Johnson of The Interaction Company, who shared much fascinating information about crisis behavior. And psychologist Charles Catanese generously let us pluck useful information from his doctoral thesis on the psychological damage of the Tenerife plane crash on some of the survivors.

Danelle Pollard of the Civil Aeromedical Institute of the Federal Aviation Administration, located in Oklahoma, provided us with an important study about airplane disasters and passenger evacuations. Cynthia MacLean of CAMI graciously answered detailed questions via email about the current state of airline passenger safety. Roland Herwig of the FAA's public affairs office directed our contact with Mrs. MacLean. The CAMI files of reports and PowerPoint presentations (available on the internet) were integral to this book's theme.

Various flight personnel lent generous assistance and offered good information: Association of Flight Attendants officials Dinkar Mokadam, OSHA specialist; Chris Witkowski, director of air safety, health and security; Heather Healy, director of the employee assistance program; and Candace Kolander, former coordinator of air safety, health and security. Ms. Kolander is now with the Air Line Pilots Association. Also, B.V. "Vic" Hewes, former chair of the rescue and fire committee of the Air Line Pilots Association; Del Mott, former air safety director for the Association of Flight Attendants; Carmen Azzopardi, former director of health and safety for the Pan American World Airways flight attendants union; Kathy Russo, Ms. Mott's counterpart for the American Airlines flight attendants, and Dick Patterson, Pan American World Airways captain.

Two members of the National Transportation Safety Board were generous with their time and suggestions: Gerit Walhout of the human factors division; and investigator Douglas Dreifus, both of whom were involved in the Tenerife crash investigation.

Dr. Barton Pakull of the FAA's behavioral sciences division also had a helpful perspective for us. And the International Civil Aviation Organization and the National Academy of Sciences both contributed information during the research portion of the work for this book, as did the public inquiries section of the NTSB.

Other helpful experts in related fields were Dr. William Reals, pathologist; Pat Mieszala, psychiatric nurse and clinician at the Cook County, Chicago, hospital burn center (now known as Stroger Hospital); Dr. William Sugiyama of Walson Army Hospital at Fort Dix, New Jersey; and Daniel Pesut, psychiatric nurse, formerly of the Brooke Army Medical Center in San Antonio, Texas, and later an instructor at the University of Michigan School of Nursing.

Chaplain John Bailey of the Brooke Army Medical Center also gave us information about the victims who were treated there after the crash. Vanderlyn Pine, sociology professor and chair of the department at State University of New York, contributed to our work.

Two people who steered us initially in the right direction were Dr. Jan Fawcett, then-chair of the psychiatry department at Rush-Presbyterian-St. Luke's Medical Center in Chicago (now Rush Medical Center), and Dr. Roy Grinker, chair of the psychiatry department at Michael Reese Hospital in Chicago (now closed).

Warren Shore, a mutual acquaintance, brought the Hopkinses together with Jon Ziomek.

Professor David Rand of Yale University talked with one of the authors about the nature of heroism. John Leach, a research fellow at the University of Portsmouth in Britain, provided copies of his extensive research on the biochemistry of stress and survival. New York University's John LeDoux steered us to his useful book *Anxious – Using the Brain to Treat Fear and Anxiety*. Laurence Gonzales's *Deep Survival* book is a fine review of survival behavior.

Two members of the media were of special assistance: Nate Polewitzsky, former international news editor of the Associated Press in New York at the time of the Tenerife crash, and Marjorie Brinkhuis, a reporter for *Panorama*, a Dutch magazine. Special thanks to Carroll Stoner; Laura Kwerel, Washington, D.C., journalist; author Craig LaMay of Northwestern University; Chicago writer Jack Hafferkamp; and Mike Cygan, all of whom were ready with an encouraging word and relevant questions during various stages of this work. Patricia Wood Winn, press and public relations manager of the Tourist Office of Spain in Chicago, was wonderfully helpful with her contacts.

Attorneys: Matt Jacobs of Gray, Krauss, Sandler, Des Rochers in Los Angeles could not have been more supportive. M. J. Harris, formerly with Gardner, Carton and Douglas in Chicago, worked on early legal issues for us. Thanks also to John Kennelly of Chicago; Gerald Sterns of San Francisco; John Trumbull of Novato, California; Sheldon Zenner of Chicago; and Louis Lang of Chicago.

Debra Englander walked us through the intricate process of pre-publication, along with the supportive Maddie Sturgeon of Post Hill Press.

Four translators helped with international newspaper clippings. Martha Marks of Northwestern University was an enormous help with Spanish; Elizabeth Martinson with her flawless Dutch was a real find; and Dana Hutchinson and Esther Levin Kogan were our French experts.

Additional research assistance was provided by Kate Loewy, who did an unbelievable amount of work organizing hundreds of newspaper clippings, as did the remarkable Rosalie Loewy Ziomek.